MORE PRAISE FOR *ASTROLOGICAL TRANSITS*:

"Hands down, this is the best book I've read about planetary cycles. In *Astrological Transits*, April Elliott Kent explains in an engaging, insightful, and user-friendly manner how the movements of the planets through the heavens stimulate changes in our lives. Furthermore, she shows you how to predict the types of changes you might experience, when to expect them, and how to make the most of them. If you've ever wondered why your life goes through ups and downs, or you want to peek into the future to see what it holds for you, read this book."

—**Skye Alexander**, author of *Planets in Signs* and *Magickal Astrology*

"Kent makes the intricacies of reading transits accessible and fun. Laced with reassuring common sense, it's also thorough enough to teach you everything you need to know about interpreting past, current, and future skies. Yet the real delight is the author's witty and insightful take on the factors. Even after twenty years of being an astrologer, I know there will be many future moments when I'll look at a chart, my mind will go blank, and I'll genuinely wonder, "What does Saturn transiting the 4th house mean?" That's when I'll jump for my copy of *Astrological Transits*."

—**Dana Gerhardt**, astrologer

"April Elliott Kent is one of only a few authors who can make the ancient art of astrology fun and easy to understand. Her most recent book, *Astrological Transits*, will tremendously help the new astrologer make sense of the often-complicated study of planetary cycles. Ms. Kent's writing is concise with a heavy dose of humor, which makes it an easy read. Well done!"

—**Susie Cox**, astrologer and author

"Life can be stormy, unpredictable, and even the most self-aware can miss a golden opportunity while admiring the scenery on deck. If you've longed for a reliable rudder, a capable guide to gracefully steer you in the most advantageous direction, look no further than this book. With wit, wisdom and ease of storytelling, April Elliott Kent generously reveals the secret we all want to know: how to best flow with the celestial tides of change. *Astrological Transits* will change how you navigate your life."

—**Jessica Shepherd**, author of *Venus Signs*

"For many, astrology is mysterious and baffling, especially when it is used to predict the future. In part this may be because many of those who write about it either obfuscate with unnecessary spiritual bafflegab, or at heart don't really know how it actually works themselves. April Elliott Kent not only clearly knows her stuff, but also writes in a straightforward and engaging manner. This book is both a pleasure to read and is genuinely informative."

—**Matthew Currie**, columnist, Beliefnet.com

astrological TRANSITS

THE BEGINNER'S
GUIDE TO USING
PLANETARY CYCLES
TO **PLAN**
AND PREDICT
YOUR DAY,
WEEK, YEAR
(OR DESTINY)

APRIL ELLIOTT KENT

SAGITTARIUS

SCORPIO

LIBRA

VIRGO

FAIR WINDS

Brimming with creative inspiration, how-to projects, and useful information to enrich your everyday life, Quarto Knows is a favorite destination for those pursuing their interests and passions. Visit our site and dig deeper with our books into your area of interest: Quarto Creates, Quarto Cooks, Quarto Homes, Quarto Lives, Quarto Drives, Quarto Explores, Quarto Gifts, or Quarto Kids.

© 2015 Fair Winds Press

First published in 2015 by Fair Winds Press,
an imprint of The Quarto Group,
100 Cummings Center, Suite 265-D,
Beverly, MA 01915, USA.
T (978) 282-9590 F (978) 283-2742
QuartoKnows.com

Fair Winds Press titles are also available at discount for retail, wholesale, promotional, and bulk purchase. For details, contact the Special Sales Manager by email at specialsales@quarto.com or by mail at The Quarto Group, Attn: Special Sales Manager, 100 Cummings Center, Suite 265-D, Beverly, MA 01915, USA.

ISBN: 978-1-59233-683-8

Digital edition published in 2015
eISBN: 978-1-62788-279-8

Library of Congress Cataloging-in-Publication Data available

Cover and book design by Megan Jones Design

For chart calculation and personalized reports, visit Astrodienst at www.astro.com.

The charts and tables in this book were generated using Win*Star professional software from Matrix Software, www.astrologysoftware.com. Reprinted with permission.

To Mom and Dad,
from your littlest Saturn transit.

CONTENTS

part I:
TRANSITS AND HOW TO USE THEM

chapter 1
AN OVERVIEW OF TRANSITS

In 1993, Jo was experiencing one of the most challenging periods of her life. She had lost her mother, given birth to her first child, and left her abusive husband; she was struggling with depression, raising her child as a single mother on state assistance.

Somehow, she found the strength and determination to complete the manuscript for a book she had started writing a few years earlier. "Had I really succeeded at anything else," she later wrote, "I might never have found the determination to succeed in the one area where I truly belonged. . . . Rock bottom became a solid foundation on which I rebuilt my life."

Within five years, Jo—writing as J. K. Rowling—was a multimillionaire. Her Harry Potter stories became the best-selling book series in history and spawned one of the highest-grossing film series of all time.

Destiny is what happens when circumstances meet character. Writing was part of Rowling's character; she began writing when she was six years old. But her spectacular journey from poverty to phenomenal success all took place during an important transit of Saturn to her birth chart. Saturn transits push us to the limits of our endurance and force us to cultivate inner strength and resourcefulness. Another person might simply have given up, and few of us would have blamed her if she had. But J. K. Rowling's experience is an inspiring example of meeting a challenging transit head-on and doing everything possible to turn failure into success.

TRANSITS: WHEN THE UNCHANGING SELF ENCOUNTERS THE WORLD

There is a part of you that doesn't change much, really, from the time you're born until the day you leave the planet. In astrology, we look to your birth chart to find insights into this true, unchanging self. Take a snapshot of the sky at the moment of your birth, from the place where you were born. It's as though a nuclear blast happened at that moment and imprinted the heavens on you. That is your indelible, astrological schema. That's the person you are inside.

But then you learn to walk, you go to school, you fall in love and get your heart broken, you have a child or lose a parent, and each of those experiences leaves a mark. So you're not precisely the same person you were on the day you were born.

Astrology acknowledges both realities: that there is an unchanging core deep within each one of us, and that a shy, vulnerable infant can grow into a poised, strong adult. The birth chart is what we set out with, the knapsack full of traits and native weaponry that we carry into the world for sustenance and protection. But along the way, we encounter the world, it encounters us, and things change.

Astrologers call these encounters *transits*.

WHAT ARE TRANSITS?

In astrology, the term *transits* refers to the ongoing movement of the planets, in contrast to their positions at your birth or when some other notable event occurred. Because they are connected to current reality, transits reflect our *collective* reality, the world we're all living in together. Transits are like cards that the world deals us, and what we do with them—how we play the hand—is what changes us and determines the course of our destiny.

Your birth chart is a snapshot of the sky at the moment you were born. But what happened in the next moment? The planets continued to move, that's what happened. Some of them move quickly, and others at the pace of drying paint. Take a snapshot of that same sky from the same place just twenty-four hours later, and you'd see some changes, but not many.

Some slightly different stars would be rising on the horizon and culminating overhead. Most noticeably, the Moon would be in another part of the sky. The Moon is our fastest-moving celestial companion: In just twenty-eight days, it makes a complete lap of the ecliptic, covering 360 degrees and every zodiac sign.

But everything else on that next day will most likely be just about where you left it. You'd have to come back in a month to see much movement from Mercury, the Sun, Venus, or Mars. Jupiter occupies the same, narrow 30-degree span of sky for an entire year, and Saturn for about two and a half years. As for Uranus, Neptune, and Pluto . . . well, you wouldn't see them at all, but rest assured, they'll have hardly budged.

We live in an orderly universe, and nowhere is this more evident than in our solar system. The planets move in predictable cycles, revisiting the same points in the zodiac at regular intervals. For instance, each year, within a day on either side of your birthday, the Sun returns to the same point in the sky that it occupied at your birth. "Many happy returns" indeed!

INNER AND OUTER PLANETS

Mercury, Venus, and Mars, our transiting neighbors closest to the Sun, are often referred to as the *inner planets*; in astrology, we include the Sun and Moon in this group. An aspect—or geometric angle—to your birth chart from the fast-moving planets—the Sun, Moon, Mercury, Venus, or Mars—happens so quickly and so often that these transits tend to have few long-term consequences. They may, however, act as triggers for slower-moving transits happening at the same time.

PLANET	CYCLE THROUGH THE ZODIAC	AREAS OF LIFE AFFECTED
Sun	365 days	vitality, creativity, confidence
Moon	28 days	emotion, daily routine, maintenance of one's body and home
Mercury	88 days	learning, communication
Venus	a little under 1 year	relationship, finances
Mars	2.5 years	work, conflict, sexuality

The transits of the *outer planets*, Jupiter, Saturn, Uranus, Neptune, and Pluto, on the other hand, are rare and take a long time to complete their work. They symbolize processes in your life that unfold slowly and usually have far-reaching consequences. Some of them leave you profoundly changed.

PLANET	CYCLE THROUGH THE ZODIAC	AREAS OF LIFE AFFECTED
Jupiter	12 years	education, travel, adventure
Saturn	29.5 years	career, responsibility, maturity
Uranus	84 years	change, disruption, rebellion
Neptune	165 years	spirituality, illusion, disillusion
Pluto	250 years	transformation, inner strength

TRANSITING PLANETS IN THE SIGNS OF THE ZODIAC

When a transiting planet changes signs, it adopts the costume of that sign. As I write this, Mercury is in Aries; the tone of this moment in time is to "perform" Mercury (communication, commuting, reading, thinking) in the style of Aries—which is to say, *fast*, direct, and to the point. The expression "too long, didn't read" (TL;DR) was probably coined by someone with Mercury in Aries!

In a few days, though, Mercury will enter Taurus, which is a very different costume indeed. The tone for communication will shift to this sign's more deliberate, slow, and considered style.

This doesn't mean that the whole world as one will be hypnotized to speak, think, and drive slowly. By nature, people who were born with Mercury in Aries, for example, always process the world at lightning speed, and Mercury moving into Taurus won't change that. What it will do is present situations that encourage these people to slow down and practice a little more patience. Chances of the Mercury in Aries person enjoying this are slim. But that's okay. As my teacher was fond of saying, "It's a transit—it will pass."

PLANETS TRANSITING THE HOUSES OF YOUR BIRTH CHART

Planets transiting the houses of your chart bring action and awareness to particular areas of your life. In the first house, it's brought to your front door. In the sixth house, it's taking place where you work or in something related to your health regimen. In your tenth house, your career, reputation, or calling provide the avenue for responding to the transit. (Part III of this book explores transits in each house of the birth chart.)

Depending on where you were born, some houses of your chart may be larger than others. Because transits will always spend more time moving through these houses, they take on a particular importance in your life. And because some transiting planets move much more slowly than others, it's like the difference between having the postman drop by (Mercury) and having an invalid relative move in to be cared for the rest of his days (Neptune).

TRANSITING PLANETS IN ASPECT

An aspect refers to a particular geometric relationship between two planets. If you don't know how to find and read aspects, you will likely feel it is a bit of a struggle to work with transits. You can get a list of current transiting aspects to your chart at Astrodienst, a free online resource (www.astro.com), but it's much easier to work with transits when you are able to compare them to the planets in your chart and find the aspects yourself.

Astrologers use a variety of aspects to examine transiting connections to the birth chart. Most commonly, we use these:

ASPECT	DEGREES	KEYWORD	DIFFICULTY
Conjunction	0 degrees	intensity; subjectivity	neutral; may be harmonious or challenging, depending on the planets involved
Sextile	60 degrees	opportunity	harmonious
Square	90 degrees	conflict	challenging
Trine	120 degrees	ease	harmonious
Quincunx	150–180 degrees	adjustment	challenging
Opposition	180 degrees	balance	challenging

If you find it difficult to identify aspects, you're not alone. It gets easier with practice, though. Begin by understanding that, generally, particular aspects can be found between planets that are in specific signs. Here is a quick guide to help get you in the neighborhood. (Note: A conjunction is usually found between planets in the same sign.)

PLANET IN THIS SIGN	LOOK FOR SEXTILES IN . . .	LOOK FOR SQUARES IN . . .	LOOK FOR TRINES IN . . .	LOOK FOR QUINCUNXES IN . . .	LOOK FOR OPPOSITIONS IN . . .
Aries	Gemini, Aquarius	Cancer, Capricorn	Leo, Sagittarius	Virgo, Scorpio	Libra
Taurus	Cancer, Pisces	Leo, Aquarius	Virgo, Capricorn	Libra, Sagittarius	Scorpio
Gemini	Leo, Aries	Virgo, Pisces	Libra, Aquarius	Scorpio, Capricorn	Sagittarius
Cancer	Virgo, Taurus	Aries, Libra	Scorpio, Pisces	Sagittarius, Aquarius	Capricorn
Leo	Gemini, Libra	Taurus, Scorpio	Aries, Sagittarius	Capricorn, Pisces	Aquarius
Virgo	Cancer, Scorpio	Gemini, Sagittarius	Taurus, Capricorn	Aries, Aquarius	Pisces
Libra	Leo, Sagittarius	Cancer, Capricorn	Gemini, Aquarius	Taurus, Pisces	Aries
Scorpio	Virgo, Capricorn	Leo, Aquarius	Cancer, Pisces	Aries, Gemini	Taurus
Sagittarius	Libra, Aquarius	Virgo, Pisces	Aries, Leo	Taurus, Cancer	Gemini
Capricorn	Scorpio, Pisces	Aries, Libra	Taurus, Virgo	Gemini, Leo	Cancer
Aquarius	Aries, Sagittarius	Taurus, Scorpio	Gemini, Libra	Cancer, Virgo	Leo
Pisces	Taurus, Capricorn	Gemini, Sagittarius	Cancer, Scorpio	Leo, Libra	Virgo

If transiting Mars, for instance, is currently at 8 degrees of Sagittarius, then it is sextile any planets at 8 degrees of Libra or Aquarius, square planets at 8 degrees of Virgo and Pisces, trine planets at 8 degrees of Aries or Leo, quincunx planets at 8 degrees Taurus or Cancer, and opposed planets at 8 degrees of Gemini.

However, this is not a hard-and-fast rule. Occasionally, a planet in one sign can make aspects to planets in signs other than the ones listed here due to aspect orbs.

ORBS

Two planets can be considered in aspect to one another even if the aspect is not exact. An exact square aspect, for instance, refers to two planets separated by exactly 90 degrees. But most astrologers observe that the influence of an aspect is experienced for a certain number of degrees, or *orb*, on either side of that exact angle. What astrologers don't necessarily agree about is how many degrees of orb should be allowed!

For transits, I tend to allow larger orbs (more degrees on either side of exact) for slower-moving planets and smaller orbs (fewer degrees on either side of exact) for faster planets, and I give more weight to aspects that are approaching (or opening) the exact angle than those that have already completed that angle (separating, or closing).

My orbs for transiting planets:

Moon: 1 degree on either side of exact

Sun, Mercury, Venus: 3 degrees on either side of exact

Mars, Jupiter, and Saturn: 5 degrees on either side of exact

Uranus, Neptune, and Pluto: 7 degrees on either side of exact

For example, if transiting Pluto, planet of power and transformation, is at 13.33 degrees of Capricorn, and your natal Midheaven (tenth house cusp) is at 15.45 degrees, then Pluto is about 2 degrees away from making a trine (120 degrees) aspect to the Midheaven (representing career matters). That's definitely close enough that you should be experiencing some intense developments related to your career. Since it's a harmonious aspect, you might safely assume that the possibility exists for career empowerment at this time.

Here's where it gets tricky. Let's say transiting Jupiter is at 1 degree of Virgo, and you have natal Mars at 28 degrees of Aries. Virtually any astrologer would call this a trine aspect. "But how?" you might cry, glancing at that handy table and finding that Virgo's trines most often occur in Taurus and Capricorn. It's because 28 degrees of Aries is only 2 degrees from flipping into Taurus, and therefore only 3 degrees from transiting Jupiter. So keep an eye out for what astrologers call "out-of-sign" aspects.

FOLLOWING TRANSITING CYCLES

Each transiting planet's cycle can be broken into phases similar to lunar phases. The first half of a planet's overall cycle through the zodiac is the waxing, or growing and initiating period; the last half is the harvesting and concluding part of the cycle. The greatest tension in the cycle occurs at the first and last quarters and the opposition point.

Using Saturn as an example: Saturn takes roughly 29.5 years to complete one cycle. The halfway point is at 14.75 years (29 ÷ 2), and the quarters come at about 7½ and 22 years.

The ages of 7, 14, 22, and 29 then become very important ages for each of us, because they are the ages when transiting Saturn is at points of greatest tension to its position in our birth charts. These are ages when we are called by Saturn to develop greater maturity, self-mastery, and authority.

PLANETARY RETURNS

A planetary "return" refers to the moment a planet comes back to the same point in the zodiac that it occupied at your birth. Each year you have a solar return within a day of your birthday, each month a lunar return, and every twenty-nine years a Saturn return. Astrologers cast a chart for the precise time of the return and read it for the highlights of the planet's new cycle.

RETROGRADES

All planets (other than the Sun and Moon) have periods of retrograde motion, when they appear to be moving backward. They're not, of course; it's an optical illusion based on their position relative to the Sun and to Earth.

Retrograde planets are indicated in a chart or ephemeris by the symbol R_x.

A planet in retrograde motion seems to work differently than usual: Matters associated with the planet are unstable and unpredictable. These are considered poor times to initiate matters related to the planet (e.g., getting married when Venus is retrograde, filing a lawsuit when Jupiter is retrograde), usually because you don't have all the information you need to make an informed decision.

The rule of thumb with retrograde cycles is that they're fine for doing anything that begins with re-, such as reviewing your work, revisiting old projects or relationships, renovating your house, or revising plans.

Mercury is retrograde for about three weeks at a time, three times each year. Mercury rules communication, technology, transportation, siblings and neighbors, and learning. Its retrograde periods are good for catching up with old friends, visiting places you've been before, reviewing contracts, and finishing old projects. But it's best to avoid purchasing cars, computers, or phones; signing agreements; or traveling either to new places or on a tight schedule.

Venus is retrograde approximately forty to forty-three days every eighteen months. These are good times for recovering money owed to you, reviewing your finances, redecorating, or reuniting with people from your past. But it's a good idea to avoid getting married, forming other legal partnerships, making major purchases, or undergoing cosmetic surgery and making other radical changes to your appearance.

Mars is retrograde approximately fifty-eight to eighty-one days every two years. During these times, examine how you deal with anger, assertiveness, conflict, competition, and sexuality. If possible, avoid starting a new job or business, entering a competition, or picking a fight. It might not be the best time for elective surgery, either. It's fine to return to a former workplace or profession, catch up on your rest, and resolve old conflicts.

The outer planets, Jupiter through Pluto, are retrograde for half of each year. Their retrograde periods are unlikely to be very noticeable unless they are also making difficult aspects to planets in your birth chart while retrograde. The days when they turn retrograde or direct, however, can be tense and unpredictable.

Jupiter's retrograde periods are good times to go back to school, take a long-delayed trip, and re-read favorite books. It's better not to gamble, launch a play or other performance, or begin a teaching career. If you begin a business while Jupiter is retrograde, check your tendency to be too generous, expand too quickly, or otherwise take on more than you can comfortably manage.

When Saturn is retrograde, it's all too easy to say yes when you should say no. These aren't good times to commit to things, but it's fine to review existing commitments. Avoid officially incorporating a business. Address structural problems with your home, organizational problems at work, or problems related to disciplining yourself or others.

Uranus's retrograde periods tend to lend a desire to shake things up, but the changes don't quite happen. Energy and restlessness build until Uranus turns direct again, then spill out in an uncontrolled way. This can be a good time to reconnect with distant friends and former associates and revive old networks of all kinds.

Neptune's retrograde times are good for spiritual retreat and reflection, returning to spiritual places meaningful to you, and psychic and intuitive work. Because Neptune normally makes it harder to see clearly, the opposite is usually true during its retrograde periods. You just have to be willing to accept the reality you see.

Pluto retrograde is excellent for psychological and physical healing and cleansing. It's a time when self-control is easier to harness; you might have better success breaking addictive habits and addressing psychological problems such as phobias, fears, and obsessive-compulsive tendencies. Trying to control others doesn't generally work well now, and in fact will usually backfire—but controlling and empowering yourself is good work for Pluto retrograde.

HOW TO FIND YOUR TRANSITS

At the risk of sounding like a codger who prefaces every statement with, "In my day . . . ," it used to be that every astrologer had a full set of planetary tables, called ephemerides, for at least the current year, and usually for the entire century. In fact, straddling two centuries as we do, many of us have two hundred years' worth of ephemerides on our bookshelves.

Even in this computer age, I recommend investing in a good old-fashioned ephemeris. You can buy them online for a reasonable price or check your local metaphysical bookstore for used copies. If you have an ephemeris, all you have to do is print out your birth chart, flip to the ephemeris entry for the current date, and draw the current transit positions around the outside of your chart:

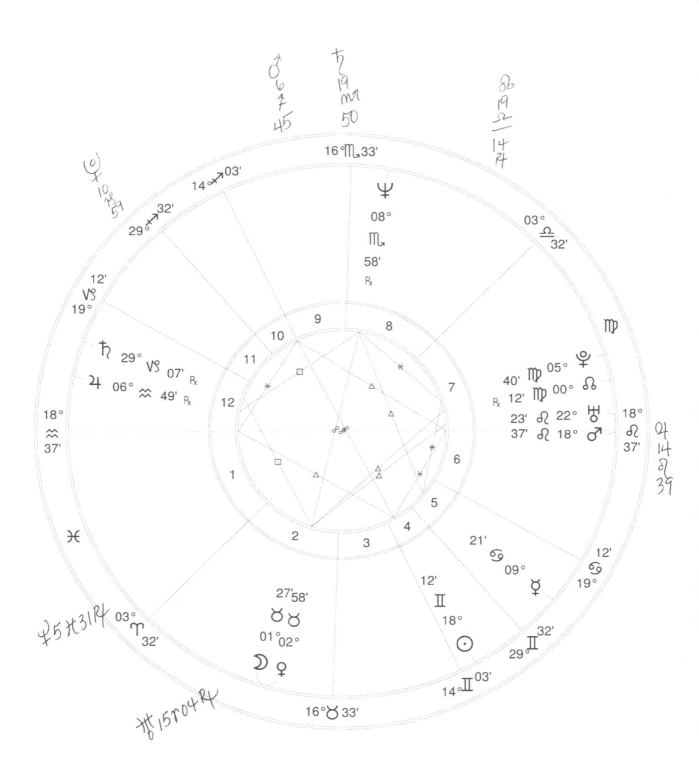

If you prefer, you can calculate the current transits and generate a wheel with your natal chart on the inside and the transits around the outside. Any astrological software does this easily; calculate your chart and a chart for the current date and place, and create a biwheel with your birth chart in the middle.

If you don't have software, you can calculate your birth chart and current transits at Astrodienst:

1. Go to www.astro.com.
2. From the menu, select "Free Horoscopes," then "Extended Chart Selection" under "Horoscope Drawings and Calculations."
3. Enter or select stored birth data. Click "Continue."
4. Under "Methods," expand the drop-down menu labeled "Please select the type of chart you want."
5. Under "Prognostic Methods," select "Transits," then "Natal Chart and Transits."
6. Hit "Click here to show the chart."

The resulting chart shows your birth chart on the inside and the current transits around the outside of the wheel:

Name (9.6.1961)
Born on Fr, 9 June 1961   Time: 0:15 a.m.
In Edmonton, AB (CAN)   Univ. Time: 7:15
113w28, 53n33   Sid. Time: 16:50:49

Natal Chart and Transits (Method: Web Style/Koch)
Date: 1.June 2015
UT: 0:00.00

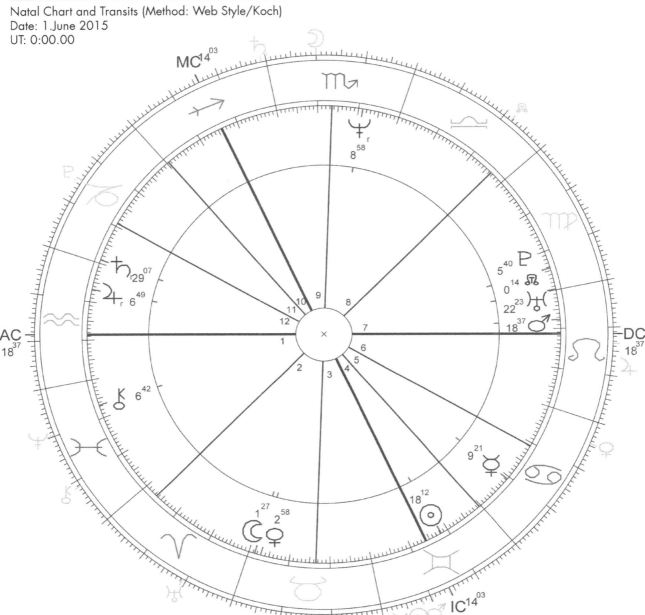

NOT ALL TRANSITS ARE CREATED EQUAL

Transits behave differently for you than for your friends, family, or partner—*because you are different people*. You have different birth charts, with planets placed in different signs, houses, and aspects to other planets.

Imagine you're at dinner with a group of friends. You're the guest of honor, and throughout the evening your friends celebrate with stories about how they met you and adventures you've shared. Some of these stories are familiar, burnished and embellished over years of retelling.

But one friend tells a story that you don't remember at all. Something about the two of you going to a club, many years ago, and meeting a couple of guys. Apparently, the one for whom she felt an immediate, passionate attraction ignored her because he couldn't take his eyes off you. Years of resentment and insecurity came to a head, and soon thereafter, she entered therapy to deal with her feelings of inadequacy.

And you didn't even remember that it had happened.

On the day of the ill-fated club adventure, transiting Venus was crossing Pluto in your birth chart, bringing together themes of affection, attraction, and deep emotion (and, in this case, a jealous female). As we mentioned previously, Venus moves quickly. Every year, it crosses your natal Pluto for a day or so; it's not necessarily a memorable transit.

But for your friend, it was the other way around: Pluto was making an aspect to Venus. Pluto is the slowest-moving of the transiting planets, taking about 248 years to complete a cycle through the zodiac. Not everyone will experience Pluto transiting over Venus in her birth chart at all, and for those who do, the transit might take more than a year to unfold. During that time, relationships will be changed, and your style of relating to others will change, too. Pluto never leaves us unaltered.

In both cases, the symbolism of Venus meets that of Pluto. But a three-day transit from quick-moving Venus to Pluto simply doesn't carry the same clout as a yearlong transit from slow-moving Pluto to Venus.

The effect of a transit is usually much more pronounced if it echoes an aspect in your birth chart. If you were born with Venus and Pluto in difficult aspect to each other, you are extraordinarily sensitive to this combination of planets and the themes it symbolizes. So when transiting Pluto connects with Venus in your birth chart, it's as though a doctor is testing your reflexes with his hammer. Your reaction may seem a little extreme to an observer, but it's because the transit is triggering every Venus/Pluto hurt and betrayal you've ever felt.

HOW TO USE THIS BOOK

This book is designed to let you easily refer to a specific planet, a particular house of the horoscope, or important planetary cycles, including:

- A review of each planet's symbolism
- Identifying the ages when you will encounter important points in each planet's cycle
- A brief description of transiting planets in each zodiac sign
- An examination of each planet's aspects to natal planets
- A description of what to expect when transiting planets are in each house of the horoscope
- Tables and worksheets to help you track and understand transit cycles in your birth chart

I've done my best to make the book user-friendly.

You don't have to be a professional astrologer to work with transits! In fact, every time you take note of a Full Moon or someone's birthday, you're working with transits. That said, you will certainly get more from this book if you have a basic knowledge of astrology, including how to read a chart to locate planets, houses, and aspects, and of the basic meanings of those things. In the Resources section, I've recommended some of my favorite books for learning astrology—check them out!

Key Terms

Here is a brief glossary of some astrological terms that are used often throughout the book.

ANGLES: Four extremely important house cusps—the Ascendant (first house), the Imum Coeli or IC (fourth house), Descendant (seventh house), and Midheaven or MC (tenth house). Transits to the angles of the natal chart are critically important, so you'll see this term used often.

INNER PLANETS: The fast-moving planets—Sun, Moon, Mercury, Venus, Mars.

NATAL: Relates to the birth chart or to a planet or other point in the birth chart. Your birth chart, for instance, is often called your natal chart; Neptune's placement in your birth chart would be called "natal Neptune."

OUTER PLANETS: The slower-moving planets—Jupiter, Saturn, Uranus, Neptune, and Pluto.

RADIX: A chart for a particular moment and place in time other than a birth, such as a chart calculated for an event.

RETURN: The moment when a transiting planet returns to the exact degree and sign that it occupies in the birth or radix chart.

IF IT'S NOT IN THE NATAL CHART . . .

Astrologers often say that if something is not part of the symbolism of your birth chart, you will never experience it through your transits. J. K. Rowling's birth chart includes an extraordinary configuration involving Saturn, Jupiter, Venus, Uranus, Pluto, and likely the Moon; that is no ordinary Saturn! The potential exists in her birth chart for extremes of gain and loss, and for the ability to master both with grace and compassion. During important transits involving Saturn, this natal potential is triggered, and big things happen.

If there's one thing that's really struck me in my career in astrology, it's how often transits work out quite differently than you think they will. When an astrologer, an astrology book, or an astrology website tells you with authority and assurance that a particular transit will absolutely bring something into your life, take it with a grain of salt—the good as well as the bad.

There are so many factors that affect how a particular transit will play out, beginning with nonastrological factors such as age, gender, and other life circumstances. And astrologically, transits don't happen in a vacuum. At any given time, a variety of really interesting and often contradictory transits could be fighting for control over your chart. There are also other predictive factors, such as secondary progressions, that may mitigate or amplify the symbolism of a transit (but that's for another book!).

As with any area of life, it's best to respect those who are knowledgeable about astrology while at the same time acknowledging that you are the expert about your life. You have to get to know the sensitive funny bones of your own chart, your own patterns, and your particular history with a transiting planet to get any sense of what's really coming your way. I've written my book in that spirit and with that in mind.

Not all of us are destined to be insanely wealthy or successful, to be a monarch, a president, or a celebrity. But even the humblest among us have charts that show the potential for astonishing achievement. Understanding your transits can help you recognize the major patterns of your life, overcome difficulties, and make the most of the gifts that are yours.

chapter **2**

UNDERSTANDING PLANETARY CYCLES

have a confession: I don't pay much attention to astrology on a daily basis. I mean, I think about it in an abstract sense. I work with clients and need to know where the current transiting planets are, or I want to post something to Facebook on the astrological tone of the day. But could I tell you where all the planets are in the sky at any moment? Do I consult an ephemeris when I dash out to do errands so I can do them at the "right time"? No, and no.

However, not all days are created equal. A day when you wake up in your own bed, do the sort of work you normally do, and see the people you normally see is quite different from a day when you wake up in an unfamiliar place, start a new job, get married, or face major surgery. On a normal day, you can safely ignore all things astrological (though knowing a few basics can help you enjoy a smoother and more enriching day). On an out-of-the-ordinary day, you need all the help you can get.

WRITE YOUR OWN DAILY HOROSCOPE

There is a lot to be said, little of it good, on the subject of daily horoscopes, the kind you come across in the newspaper or on your favorite astrological website. Horoscopes use the Sun in your chart as a reference point, which is not the worst idea in the world. After all, the Sun is vitally important to life on earth, and symbolically, the Sun in your birth chart is vitally important to a healthy sense of self and purpose. Plus, just about everyone knows his or her sun sign.

But the Sun, however important, is not the only celestial figure in the sky or in your birth chart. Any evaluation of daily affairs will be incomplete if based on only one feature of your birth chart. Is that the end of the world? Most days, there's hardly time to read a paragraph in the newspaper while you gulp down your morning coffee, let alone compare the day's complete transits to your birth chart.

But on one of those out-of-the ordinary days, daily horoscopes begin to look kind of attractive. You might welcome astrology's reassurance on such a day. Here are the most important daily transits to consider.

THE MOON

The transiting Moon is the superstar of daily astrology, because it moves so much faster than anything else. In a little less than one month, it covers the entire zodiac! So the Moon reflects the mood, tone, and rhythms of daily life.

Chapter 9 covers the transiting Moon in great detail, so have a look there for particulars. Meantime, to get a feel for the day ahead, here's what you need to know about the transiting Moon:

- What is the current lunar phase? That tells you whether it's time to move forward (waxing Moon, between New Moon and Full Moon) or time to tie up loose ends (waning Moon, between Full Moon and New Moon).
- What is the Moon's sign today? This will give you a sense of the day's mood, how people instinctively react to situations, and even how to dress.
- What aspects is the Moon making to other planets? A Moon approaching a conjunction with Saturn, for instance, will emphasize a lot of the same matters as a Moon in Capricorn, the sign Saturn rules.

THE SUN

The transiting Sun covers only 1 degree of one zodiac sign each day—it's not exactly tearing up the sky. On a daily basis, it's sufficient to note whether the Sun will make a major aspect to another transiting planet, or a planet in your birth chart.

The Sun describes vitality, self-esteem, and sheer enjoyment of life. If it is making an aspect to a very different sort of planet, such as Pluto, you may feel as though you're a candle that has been carried into a cave so deep and dark, your flame is extinguished.

THE SUN'S DAILY MOTION

One way of thinking of a day is to consider at what time the Sun moves through each part of the sky. The sections of the sky, such as those near the horizon or directly overhead, refer to the houses of the horoscope, so the Sun's predictable daily motion can offer clues to the activities best suited for each time of day.

The Sun's motion, as represented in a chart, is clockwise. This is the opposite direction from transits, which move through a chart counterclockwise (unless they are retrograde). For instance, the Ascendant is the sunrise point of the chart. If you cast a chart for a minute after sunrise, the Sun would be in the twelfth house. About two hours later (depending on time of year and your latitude), the Sun would be in the eleventh house.

The Sun's motion through the sky is, very approximately, something like this:

6 A.M.–8 A.M.	Twelfth house	**6 P.M.–8 P.M.**	Sixth house
8 A.M.–10 A.M.	Eleventh house	**8 P.M.–10 P.M.**	Fifth house
10 A.M.–NOON	Tenth house	**10 P.M.–MIDNIGHT**	Fourth house
NOON–2 P.M.	Ninth house	**MIDNIGHT–2 A.M.**	Third house
2 P.M.–4 P.M.	Eighth house	**2 A.M.–4 A.M.**	Second house
4 P.M.–6 P.M.	Seventh house	**4 A.M.–6 A.M.**	First house

How is this useful? It teaches us about the nature of each hour of the day, the right action for those hours, and helps us understand the houses themselves.

- During the morning hours, our sleepy, unformed Pisces/twelfth house selves move by rote, almost unconsciously, to get ready to meet the world.
- During the first hours of work, we attend to Aquarius/eleventh house social tasks, greeting coworkers and returning emails.
- The last two hours before midday, during Capricorn/tenth house time, we finally dig in to get some work done.
- At lunchtime, during the Sagittarius/ninth house hours, we're ready for a break from the routine. We relish the chance to get away from our work and the freedom to decide where, what, and with whom we will eat.
- Scorpio/eighth house time, during midafternoon, is when the breakthroughs come; we'd nap if we could, so our unconscious minds could work things out.
- Late afternoon is Libra/seventh house time, when we do what needs to be done to "even out" the day before we close up shop and head off to meet our significant other.
- Early evening is devoted to the Virgo/sixth house chores of cooking and eating dinner, throwing laundry in the washer, packing lunches for the next day, helping the kids with homework.
- Then it's Leo/fifth house time, and we watch television, update the blog, have some fun, relax. Most of us hit the hay during the Cancer/fourth house hours, winding down for some rest and retreat.
- In the early Gemini/third house hours, our minds are still active and we haven't yet reached our deepest level of sleep. That comes during the Taurus/second house hours, which are physically restorative and healing. Finally, in the Aries/first house hours before dawn, our brains reinforce important learning and commit new skills to memory, helping us be alert to what's going on.

OTHER EXACT PLANETARY ASPECTS

If other transiting planets will be making an exact aspect to another transiting planet today, changing signs, or moving retrograde or direct it's worth noting. The energy of that planetary combination, sign change, or change in direction will color the entire day.

SUMMARY: HOW TO PLAN YOUR DAY

- Check the Moon's current phase, sign, and aspects to other transiting planets.
- Consider the Sun's aspects to other transiting planets or to planets in your birth chart.
- Use your energy wisely; let the Sun's natural diurnal motion guide your activities.
- Pay attention to transiting planets changing signs, moving retrograde or direct, or making exact aspects to other transiting planets.

YOUR MONTHLY PLANNER

The root of the word *month* is *moon*, and therefore a month refers to the twenty-eight-day cycle of the Moon's orbit around Earth. But modern calendars are based not on the Moon, but on the Sun's path across the ecliptic, which takes 365 days. Our calendar months are a function of cutting the Sun's cycle into twelve intervals of varying lengths, so it makes sense to pay some attention to the Sun as part of your monthly planning.

Note the dates when any planets are changing signs or turning retrograde or direct. On these days you'll notice a significant shift of energy around the matters ruled by that planet.

THE MOON

Note the dates of the New and Full Moon, and in particular the degree and sign of each. Then find which houses of your birth chart those degrees fall in. This will tell you which areas of your life are due for new beginnings (New Moon) and a release of habits or behaviors (Full Moon) during this month.

THE SUN

The Sun changes signs each month, usually within a couple of days of the 20th. See chapter 9 for an in-depth examination of the Sun's sign and aspects to your natal planets. Depending on the sizes of the houses in your birth chart, the Sun will usually spend about a month in each. (If you were born during summer or winter months at a latitude very far from the equator, some houses will be much larger than others.)

MERCURY: CHANGES SIGNS EVERY FEW WEEKS

Within a given month, Mercury will usually change signs at least once. The exception is when Mercury is retrograde and spends a bit longer in a sign. Mercury's transit of a sign brings fresh ideas and a craving for variety and encourages a particular style of communication. It may not sound too exciting—most of us are interested in stuff such as love and money—but trust me: Mercury is a lot more important than you may think, because he influences how you look at the world and how you frame your current circumstances.

VENUS: CHANGES SIGNS EVERY MONTH

Venus's transits describe how you seek enjoyment and pleasure, as well as your changing financial and relationship needs. Venus usually changes signs at least once each month and usually transits one house of your chart in that time.

Note the days when Venus will change sign or move into a new house of your chart. If Venus is retrograde this month, take careful note of the retrograde's beginning and ending dates; avoid major purchases and permanent relationship changes during this period.

SUMMARY: HOW TO PLAN YOUR MONTH

- Note the dates when planets are changing signs or direction (retrograde or direct).
- Find where the New and Full Moons will fall in your chart.
- Consider the Sun's current sign and the house it is transiting in your birth chart.

YOUR YEARLY PLANNER

If you're like many people, you welcome each new calendar year with resolutions, planners, and a big-picture time line for what you'd like to accomplish in the year ahead. If you'd like a little help from astrology, here are the most relevant cycles to keep in mind.

THE SUN'S ANNUAL CYCLE

The year itself is based on the Sun's complete journey through the zodiac. The Sun spends about one month in each sign. During the year, keep an eye out for days when the transiting Sun:

- Returns to its exact position in your birth chart. This happens once each year within a day on either side of your birthday and is called the Solar Return.
- Crosses (makes a conjunction to) the angles of your chart—the Ascendant (first house cusp), IC (fourth house cusp), Descendant (seventh house cusp), and Midheaven (tenth house cusp). These are powerful days when there is a good chance of serious movement in your immediate environment (Ascendant), home (IC), relationships (Descendant), and career (Midheaven). (See chapter 9 for more about the Sun's transits and cycle.)

ECLIPSES

Every six months, the paths of the Sun, Moon, and Earth intersect in exactly the right way and we get a solar eclipse, which is usually accompanied by a lunar eclipse within two weeks before or after.

Eclipses fall in a pair of signs for about a year and a half, which means they also affect a pair of houses in your chart. When eclipses occur within about 4 degrees of a conjunction, square, or opposition of a natal planet, you'll usually see some kind of crisis or moment of truth in the area of life suggested by that planet. Eclipses have eighteen- and nineteen-year cycles. (See chapter 9 for more on eclipses.)

MAJOR RETROGRADE PERIODS

We covered the meaning of individual planetary retrograde periods in chapter 1. The information you'll particularly want to note for your annual planner are periods when Mercury will be retrograde (for about three weeks, three times each year) and when Venus or Mars will be retrograde (this doesn't happen every year).

The houses of your birth chart where these transiting retrograde periods take place are especially important, because they describe where you will experience delays, obstacles, and misunderstandings related to communication (Mercury), money and relationships (Venus), and work (Mars).

JUPITER

Jupiter transits a sign of the zodiac in about one year. Take note of the signs and houses of your chart that will receive Jupiter's adventurous spirit this year.

Approximately every twelve years, transiting Jupiter will return to its position in your birth chart, beginning a new twelve-year cycle of adventures and learning. That sounds saccharine, but not all Jupiter adventures feel very happy at the time. That said, Jupiter crossing over the angles of your chart or moving through your Sun's sign, or a sign in which you have many natal planets, can be one of the nicest periods of your life.

SATURN, URANUS, NEPTUNE, AND PLUTO

Saturn takes about two and a half years to move through a sign of the zodiac. Always keep track of where Saturn is transiting (it will generally be impossible to ignore); it's useful to know if it will change signs or move into a new house of your chart, or make a conjunction, square, or opposition to one or more planets in your birth chart.

Likewise, if Uranus, Neptune, or Pluto is changing signs, moving into a new house of your chart, or making a conjunction, square, or opposition to any natal planets, expect some major life changes.

SUMMARY: HOW TO PLAN YOUR YEAR

- Note the dates when the transiting Sun will conjunct your natal Sun, Ascendant, IC, Descendant, and Midheaven. These are dates when your personal charisma is especially strong.
- Find where the year's eclipses will fall in your birth chart, by house and by close aspect to natal planets, to discover the areas of your life where change is likely and necessary this year.
- Note the dates when Mercury, Venus, and Mars will be retrograde and plan accordingly (see chapter 1 and table 2 of the appendix).
- Note the sign and current house placement of transiting Jupiter, Saturn, Uranus, Neptune, and Pluto. Also note whether you're experiencing a major aspect from one of these planets to their positions in your birth chart (see chapters 3 to 7).
- Note the dates of any conjunctions from Jupiter, Saturn, Uranus, Neptune, or Pluto to an angle of the chart. A month or so on either side of these dates are crucial periods—and some may be among the most important of your life.
- Note any aspects between transiting Saturn, Uranus, Neptune, or Pluto and the natal Sun, Moon, Mercury, Venus, or Mars.

RENDEZVOUS WITH DESTINY

If you want to know when to expect the major transition periods of your life, consider the cycle of the transiting outer planets. The cycle of these planets in aspect to their natal position is very rich and somewhat more universal. Everyone gets a Saturn return around the age of twenty-eight or twenty-nine; everyone endures the Uranian identity crises of ages twenty-one and forty-two; no one enjoys Pluto's square (ages vary depending on Pluto's sign at your birth, but you'll go through it with your age cohort).

Sketch out Saturn's squares, oppositions, and conjunctions with the natal position. Note Uranus's squares and opposition. List Neptune's sextile, square, and opposition. Pin down the dates of Pluto's sextile, square (especially), and trine. Along with these planets crossing the angles of your chart, this will give you a very succinct framework for anticipating the milestones of your life.

The slow-moving transiting planets are really the planets of destiny. They're the big guys whose transits have a deeply—and usually permanently—transformative effect on your life.

Jupiter's returns every twelve years divide your life into important periods of expansion. All things being equal, these are usually years when good breaks come your way. Jupiter's oppositions are a low point in the cycle and represent years with significant setbacks.

When Saturn, Uranus, Neptune, or Pluto crosses one of the angles of your birth chart, the wheel of your life is pulled sharply, and you jolt in a new direction. Other aspects from these planets to the angles of the chart are important, too, but these are the huge, obvious ones. Sketch them out on a piece of paper. Give them a few degrees of orb. You'll quickly glimpse some of the most pivotal moments you'll experience.

Finally, note the years when Saturn, Uranus, Neptune, or Pluto will make a conjunction, square, or opposition to the Sun and Moon in your chart. Their aspects to other natal planets are important, too, of course, but their aspects to the Sun and Moon are particularly crucial, and important transits to these points will usually make for some very interesting years.

SUMMARY: LONG-RANGE PLANNING

- Map out a time line based on the naturally recurring cycles for each planet. See chapters 3 to 7 to find the ages when each slow-moving planet reaches critical points in its cycle.
- Note the years of your Jupiter returns, which occur about every twelve years from your birth.
- Mark the years when Saturn, Uranus, Neptune, and Pluto will cross the angles of your birth chart. Saturn will normally cross every angle at least twice, twenty-nine years apart. Uranus will cross every angle for those who live to age eighty-four. Neptune and Pluto will typically cross a couple of the four angles once in your lifetime.
- Note the years when Saturn, Uranus, Neptune, or Pluto will make a conjunction, square, or opposition to the Sun and Moon in your chart. While these outer planets' aspects to other natal planets are important, their aspects to the Sun and Moon are particularly crucial.

part II:

PLANETARY TRANSITS TO OTHER PLANETS

Transits work on two levels. One is the interaction of transiting planets with individual points in your birth chart. The other is the interplay between transiting planets themselves. I'm writing this, for instance, on a day when transiting Mars is approaching a conjunction with transiting Saturn. They're still separated by 2 degrees, and since Mars moves about 1 degree every two days, the aspect won't be exact for about four more days. But they are within orb of one another, and today my social media feeds are packed with people talking about their frustrations, the obstacles in their way, or not being able to accomplish anything at work.

Simultaneously, both Mars and Saturn are in a square aspect to the natal Sun in my birth chart. I've been battling writer's block for the past few days, which is the last thing a Leo writer on a deadline needs!

Which is more important: the aspects a transiting planet is making to other planets in the sky right now, or the aspects it makes to your birth chart? The answer is that they are probably equally important, with transiting planets in aspect to each other describing the circumstances everyone is dealing with in one way or another, and transiting planets in aspect to your natal planets saying it's no longer a collective experience but one very personal to you.

When a configuration between two planets in your birth chart is replicated by the same two transiting planets, that's something worth watching.

Let's say there is a square aspect in your birth chart between the Sun and Neptune. Since the transiting Sun goes through the entire zodiac annually, it will make two square aspects to transiting Neptune each year. These two days should have an impact on you—*even if neither the Sun nor Neptune is making an aspect to the Sun or Neptune in your birth chart.*

There's a kind of sympathy between what's happening in the sky and what's happening on earth. You are a representative of the gods whose planets are in aspect to each other in your birth chart. And when the gods in the sky quarrel, their representatives on earth feel as though they have a dog in the fight.

THE DIFFERENCE ASPECTS MAKE

I've chosen, in this book, to explore pairs of planets in combination without any reference to the specific aspect between them. If you're getting started with transits, I find that it's best to keep things simple by just considering the natures of the two planets themselves and what might happen when they come together.

If you're more comfortable with aspects, here is a guide to adjusting your interpretation of the planetary combinations based on the aspect:

Conjunction: There is concentrated energy, but possibly a power struggle between the two planets.

Sextile: An opportunity arises to explore the themes presented.

Square: An urge to act is too strong to ignore, or conflict with another person arises.

Trine: Matters proceed without impediment. This is usually, but not always, positive.

Quincunx: An adjustment must be made.

Opposition: Awareness dawns, and objectivity about the matter is gained, often through interaction with another person.

WHICH TRANSITS ARE MOST IMPORTANT

A planet transiting a house of your chart is like a visitor who has come to stay. Depending on the size of the house or the speed of the planet, the duration of its visit could be anywhere from a few days to thirty years.

The transit of a faster-moving planet (the Moon, Mercury, the Sun, Venus, or Mars) is like having a guest stay for a long weekend, or at most like hosting an exchange student for a semester. You become conscious of how small your guest room is, how erratic your antique plumbing, how thin your walls, and how limited the repertoire of meals that you cook. Some of these observations make you uncomfortable, and some rearrangement of your daily routine is inevitable. But because the transit doesn't last very long, the observations don't necessarily lead to permanent change.

The transit of a slower-moving planet (Jupiter, Saturn, Uranus, Neptune, or Pluto), on the other hand, is like undergoing a major home renovation. (In the case of Uranus, Neptune, and Pluto, it can be like a renovation that was not exactly your choice—like rebuilding after a natural disaster!) It begins with destruction, rubble, and a total disruption of your life. In the end, you have something new and different that you (hopefully) like, or at least appreciate.

In evaluating your current transits, begin with the slow-moving planets. That's where the major renovations are happening. These transits are the constant, low-level background noise of your life. Everything else that happens is a reaction to or defined by major transits.

Armed with the knowledge that you'll be dealing with those transits for a while and will eventually come to a deeper and ever-evolving understanding of them, it's fine to turn your attention to the faster transits for a temperature check of your daily and monthly life.

chapter 3

TRANSITS OF JUPITER:
THE LEAP OF FAITH

Planetary Dossier: JUPITER

TIME TO MAKE A FULL CYCLE AROUND THE SUN: 12 years

TIME SPENT IN EACH ZODIAC SIGN: about 1 year

TRANSITING ASPECTS LAST FOR: approximately 3 weeks

STRONGEST SIGNS: Sagittarius, Cancer, Pisces

HAS TO WORK HARDER IN: Gemini, Capricorn, Virgo

KEYWORDS: learning, beliefs, meaning, long-distance travel, big, hope, risk, foreigners, culture

One afternoon in late May 1971, my mother showed up at my elementary school with the family station wagon packed and waiting outside. We were moving, that very afternoon, from our Indiana farm to the suburbs of Los Angeles.

It wasn't a surprise. Mom had been planning this move since soon after my father died in an accident almost exactly one year earlier. Her sister lived near Los Angeles, and we were headed there to get a fresh start.

The problem was that no matter how ghastly it felt to stay in the house where we had lived with Dad, on the land he had lovingly farmed, without him—I didn't want to leave. This was the only home I had ever known, and I wanted to stay where I felt safe.

I didn't know it then, but on that late May afternoon, transiting Jupiter and Neptune were crossing my natal Ascendant in adventuresome Sagittarius, the sign of the traveler. The Ascendant is one of the orienting compass points of the chart, the place where we are pinned to a particular outlook of attitude and geography. Big transits to this angle can often bring a major move. And Neptune can speak of sadness, yes, and grief.

But traditional astrologers called Jupiter "the Greater Benefic." Jupiter is supposed to bring blessings, bounty, and good luck, not a reluctant exodus from the ancestral home. And definitely not tears.

Had I been to see an astrologer in the preceding months, she would probably have told me, with great sincerity, that a grand adventure and great blessings lie ahead. And on the day we left for California, I would have cursed that astrologer as a flat-out liar.

In the years ahead, though, I would have recognized how very right she had been. Indeed, the grandest adventure of my young life began that day. Living in a major city opened up possibilities unimaginable to a girl on a tiny farm. Moving to a bigger place, and a bigger life, absolutely transformed my worldview and my expectations for myself.

I've said, again and again, that moving to California was the best thing that ever happened to me. And had I known about Jupiter back then, I might have recognized that sooner—might have taken a leap of faith and embraced my new adventure with an open heart.

As an astrologer, I spend my days talking to people in all kinds of situations. Often they're in great pain. They need encouragement and hope. Fortunately, even in the midst of the worst that life can dish out and the very hardest astrological transits, there is always Jupiter somewhere in their lives. Somewhere, adventure beckons, and there is a reason to hope . . . even when it doesn't initially look very hopeful at all.

THE NATURE OF THE BEAST

Transiting Jupiter has a twelve-year cycle around the Sun, spending about one year in each sign. He is like a supersized version of the Sun, with its twelve-month cycle and one-month visit in each sign. When we think of the Sun and Leo, the sign it rules, we imagine the king of beasts—but in astrological terms, it's more appropriate to think of Leo as the prince. For in myth, it was Jupiter, Zeus, who was king of the gods.

As king, Jupiter can have anything he desires. He snaps his fingers, and others scurry to do his bidding. All the most beautiful women, all the riches of the realm, are his to command. He is bound only by the limitations of his own kingdom, and he makes it his life's work to expand that kingdom to encompass ever more land, people, and riches.

A good king shares this wealth with his people. He welcomes diversity of opinion and supports education, defends the freedom to practice religion in one's own way (or not at all), and provides open space for people to enjoy the outdoors.

Transits of Jupiter are usually characterized as bringing luck—times when you get to feel like the king or queen of your realm, when nothing is denied you provided you're bold enough to claim it. But these transits can also bring setbacks, usually due to poor judgment or an insatiable appetite for more—more lands to conquer, more wealth, more adulation. You may overeat, overspend, and dominate every conversation with your monologues, refusing to share the stage. Transits of Jupiter are generally terrific, but it's also entirely possible to emerge from them with a bigger waistline, a smaller bank account, and fewer friends returning your phone calls.

USING JUPITER'S CYCLE

Jupiter's transits require a leap of faith and willingness to conquer new frontiers. But Jupiter is also a planet of learning and wisdom, and his transiting cycle gives us twelve years to both make bold leaps and learn from mistakes.

The Jupiter cycle can be divided into four segments of about three years each. Each of these segments represents an important phase of the cycle—initiation, cultivation, review, and adjustment. When Jupiter makes a conjunction with any planet or important point in your chart, an adventure is beginning, though you may not recognize it yet. Next, count forward, three years at a time, and watch the story unfold.

Jupiter is the ruler of Sagittarius and the co-ruler (along with Neptune) of Pisces. Transits of Jupiter have particular significance for you if you were born with the Sun, Moon, or Ascendant in one of these signs, and you will be especially attuned to its twelve-year cycle, making notable changes in your life at your Jupiter returns.

THE JUPITER RETURN

Ages 12, 24, 36, 48, 60, 72, 84, 96

Every twelve years, Jupiter returns to the same degree of the same sign. When it's the same degree and sign it occupies in your birth chart, we call this a Jupiter return. Each Jupiter return marks the beginning of a new growth cycle in the area of life represented by the house, aspects, and sign of your natal Jupiter.

In the tarot, the Fool card depicts a happy-go-lucky fellow who is about to step off a cliff. This is more or less how the beginning of a Jupiter cycle feels. You're stepping off a familiar cliff into the unknown, initiating a new twelve-year cycle and moving your life's story a bit further along.

Jupiter returns happen every twelve years, so any age divisible by twelve is one when you'll begin a new cycle of personal growth, when a part of you yearns to push past your comfort zone and expand your realm.

THE OPENING JUPITER SQUARE

Ages 3, 15, 27, 39, 51, 63, 75, 87, 99

At the first square of the Jupiter cycle, you begin to better understand the nature of the adventure you embarked on three years prior. Now it's time to take an active role in determining the direction it will take.

Let's imagine that Jupiter is in the tenth house of your birth chart. You might expect a Jupiter return in the tenth house, the House of Career, to bring tremendous career success. But for a client of mine, Tom, it brought the loss of his job. For the next couple of years he felt lost, trying to imagine what to do next. To pass the time, he built a website and began posting articles and tips.

When Jupiter made a square to his natal Jupiter three years later, he realized he had found a line of work that he enjoyed immensely and began to establish a credible consulting business. The nature of his new career adventure was coming into focus, and now he could channel his energy in a specific direction.

THE JUPITER OPPOSITION
Ages 6, 18, 30, 42, 54, 66, 78, 90

At the Jupiter opposition, it's time to take a long look at your progress. Are you taking the right kinds of chances? Do you have more to learn about your career? How are others in your field doing? The Jupiter opposition feels like the low point in the cycle. Even if you've done everything right, the breaks just don't seem to come your way. Fortunately, Jupiter comes bearing the gift of optimism and philosophy. From this perspective, you can see that there are actually more things you could try. You come to a better understanding of any mistakes that you've made along the way. After reaching this low point in its point in the cycle, Jupiter bounces back and so does your optimism, along with some lucky breaks.

THE CLOSING JUPITER SQUARE
Ages 9, 21, 33, 45, 57, 69, 81, 93

You may feel ready to burst out of your shell. You're getting close to the finish line, and it's time to make the final push. Some lose heart now, give up, act out, and sabotage their chances for success. But when it comes to Jupiter, go big or go home, as the saying goes. Jupiter wants the big win! Whatever you started nine years ago, don't give up now.

TRANSITING JUPITER BY SIGN

Jupiter urges you to grow, expand, take risks, and seek meaning. His transits through the twelve signs of the zodiac prescribe the avenues through which all of us, simultaneously, seek to expand our horizons. The extent to which this affects you directly will depend on planets you may have in that sign, and the house through which Jupiter is transiting (see part III for an exploration of the transiting planets in the houses of the horoscope).

TRANSITING JUPITER IN ARIES ♈

Persecuted for their faith, a group of English pilgrims migrates to the New World. A family who have lost everything in the Great Depression and watched their Oklahoma home subsumed by the Dust Bowl packs up a truck and heads west. Pioneers launch themselves into the unknown for an opportunity to improve their lot in life and to be more fully themselves.

Aries is the sign of the pioneer, the indomitable spark of individuality. While Jupiter is in this sign, fortune favors the brave. It is time to claim your true self, usually through meeting challenging and even threatening circumstances.

It is time to break free from any situation that makes it impossible for you to truly be yourself. Accept challenges, even if you're not sure you can meet them. The rule of thumb while transiting Jupiter is in Aries is, if you think something can't be done, by all means, do it!

Biggest rewards: Aries, Leo, Sagittarius

Pressure to take risks: Cancer, Libra, Capricorn

Significant opportunities: Gemini, Aquarius

Jupiter in Aries (2000–2050): Oct. 22, 1999–Feb. 14, 2000; June 5–Sept. 8, 2010; Jan. 22–June 4, 2011; May 10–Oct. 27, 2022; Dec. 20, 2022–May 16, 2023; Apr. 21, 2034–Apr. 29, 2035; Apr. 4, 2046–Apr. 13, 2047

TRANSITING JUPITER IN TAURUS ♉

Jupiter awakens the urge to grow, explore, and seek meaning. In Taurus, Jupiter seeks ways to increase prosperity, security, and pleasure, and for meaning in nature, in the enjoyment of the world's bounty, and in the senses. Gradual, steady growth is favored over sudden, dramatic growth spurts.

For thousands of years, cultures have revered the cow or bull as a symbol of wealth and of Earth's bounty. The blessings of Jupiter in Taurus are many: a sense that anything is possible, that security is within reach, and that pleasures are abundant. But the combination of Jupiter's respect for doctrine and Taurus's conservatism has a potential downside: the unwillingness to confront needed change. The idiom *sacred cows* (based on the reverential treatment of cows by Hindus and in other cultures) refers to something that is considered immune from question or criticism. While Jupiter is in Taurus, we are unlikely to rethink entrenched attitudes or policies, however inconvenient, outmoded, or even harmful they may be.

Commit to Jupiterian endeavors, such as education or writing, that require Taurus's patience and stamina. Invest in knowledge. Grow a garden. Spend time in nature. Hug a cow.

Biggest rewards: Taurus, Virgo, Capricorn

Pressure to take risks: Leo, Scorpio, Aquarius

Significant opportunities: Cancer, Pisces

Jupiter in Taurus (2000–2050): Feb. 14–June 30, 2000; June 4, 2011–June 11, 2012; May 16, 2023–May 25, 2024; Apr. 29, 2035–May 9, 2036; Apr. 13, 1947–Apr. 22, 2048

TRANSITING JUPITER IN GEMINI ♊

Jupiter is at something of a disadvantage in Gemini. At first glance, the two have lots in common: a love of travel, learning, communicating. But scratch the surface and you'll find that they approach this common ground from opposite points of view. Jupiter rules higher education, but Gemini prefers self-directed learning and practical knowledge and skills. Jupiter favors long-distance travel to exotic places; Gemini prefers shorter journeys by car, train, or on foot.

While Jupiter transits Gemini, you may not be sure whether to finish your novel or write letters to friends, or whether to apply for a passport or purchase a rail pass. One thing is certain, though: Jupiter's transit through Gemini is a tremendous time for socializing. You may have opportunities to connect with people you haven't seen for many years, or online friends you've never met in person.

Biggest rewards: Gemini, Libra, Aquarius

Pressure to take risks: Virgo, Sagittarius, Pisces

Significant opportunities: Aries, Leo

Jupiter in Gemini (2000–2050): June 30, 2000–July 12, 2001; June 11, 2012–June 25, 2013; May 25, 2024–June 9, 2025; May 9, 2036–May 23, 2037; Apr. 22–Sept. 23, 2048; Nov. 12, 2048–May 5, 2049

TRANSITING JUPITER IN CANCER ♋

It may seem odd that the planet of travel and adventure should have been considered by traditional astrologers to be particularly strong in Cancer, the sign of home and family. But think about it. After you've traveled to a foreign country or lived in a city far from your birth home, you've got one more place in the world that feels familiar to you. Spend a little time sharing a meal with people from a different world, and you begin to understand that they're not that different from you after all.

"Travel is broadening," the old saying goes. And it is—but not because of the novelty of visiting unfamiliar places and eating weird food. Travel is broadening because it enlarges the boundaries of what feels safe and familiar to you. While Jupiter is transiting through Cancer, open your home and heart and venture out to claim more territory. The more you see of the world, the more of it feels like home to you, and the more of its people feel like your family.

Jupiter in Cancer can also be a favorable time to enlarge your home or renovate (but mind your budget). You may find new members joining your family as well, through birth or marriage.

Biggest rewards: Cancer, Scorpio, Pisces

Pressure to take risks: Aries, Libra, Capricorn

Significant opportunities: Taurus, Virgo

Jupiter in Cancer (2000–2050): July 12, 2001–Aug. 1, 2002; July 25, 2013–July 16, 2014; June 9, 2025–June 29, 2026; May 23, 2037–June 12, 2038; Sept. 23–Nov. 12, 2048; May 5–Sept. 27, 2049

TRANSITING JUPITER IN LEO ♌

Like a good yoga teacher, Jupiter pushes you to expand your reach, to do more than you thought you could, to trust. This year's yoga lesson is about opening up your creative Leo side. Adulthood often means preoccupation with serious concerns such as making a living, and it's easy to overlook the value of having fun and being yourself. It's also risky to put your heart on display and chance rejection. But turning your back on your playful side is much more precarious than the possibility of being rebuffed, ignored, or ridiculed, because once you stop engaging creatively, you're near enough to dead.

While Jupiter is in Leo, dust off your dancing shoes, tune your guitar, unearth those acrylics from the closet, and tell us your story. Engage in artistic expression, and share it with someone you trust—or maybe even people you don't know. Don't be bashful; not everyone will love your efforts, but I've always found that as long as you communicate truthfully and from the heart, you will eventually find your audience.

Look your best, be yourself, do your very best work, and take a bow. As you open your arms and lift your head high, I'll bet you'll hear a round of applause.

Biggest rewards: Leo, Sagittarius, Aries

Pressure to take risks: Taurus, Scorpio, Aquarius

Significant opportunities: Gemini, Libra

Jupiter in Leo (2000–2050): Aug. 1, 2002–Aug. 27, 2003; July 16, 2014–Aug. 11, 2015; June 29, 2026–July 25, 2027; June 12–Nov. 16, 2038; Jan. 16–July 7, 2039; Sept. 27, 2049–Jan. 13, 2050; May 22–Oct. 18, 2050

TRANSITING JUPITER IN VIRGO ♍

In the Northern Hemisphere, the Sun is in Virgo at harvest time. In a year when Jupiter's grace touches Virgo's harvest energy, the potential payoff is richer than it has been in more than a decade.

Virgo is the sign of work and health, but more importantly, it is the sign of the rituals and habits behind them. Someone once said that "work is love made visible"; Virgo is the sign of craft, of precise and loving work, and during this Jupiter cycle you're called to examine the work you're doing. Have you outgrown your work? Have you been thinking too small, when what you have to offer the world through your work is really very large? Or perhaps you planted a seed twelve years ago, when Jupiter was last in this sign, and now it has grown so strong and lush and is bearing so much fruit that you're ready to retire and move on to something else.

While Jupiter is in Virgo, enjoy the fruits of your labor and make peace with the seeds that didn't bear fruit. Plant new crops, for you know better now which crops are right for you and how to cultivate them. Love your work. Improve your skills. Enlarge your résumé. Tend your fields with care, and you can look forward to a rich harvest the next time Jupiter is in Virgo!

Biggest rewards: Virgo, Capricorn, Taurus

Pressure to take risks: Gemini, Sagittarius, Pisces

Significant opportunities: Cancer, Scorpio

Jupiter in Virgo (2000–2050): Aug. 27, 2003–Sept. 24, 2004; Aug. 11, 2015–Sept. 9, 2016; July 25, 2027–Aug. 23, 2028; Nov. 16, 2038–Jan. 16, 2039; July 7–Dec. 12, 2039; Feb. 19–Aug. 5, 2040; Oct. 18, 2050–Feb. 26, 2051

TRANSITING JUPITER IN LIBRA ♎

The luckiest planet in the solar system transiting the sign of partnership—what could be better for those looking for a happy, committed relationship, right?

Well, yes . . . but it's not as though a happy marriage is something you stumble across at the mall, gift-wrapped and ready to go. It's something you build, one day at a time. It's a relationship that helps you grow, and it's a relationship that you grow into.

Maybe you'll take a leap of marital faith when Jupiter is in Libra. (I did!) But if you're in a relationship that isn't letting you explore and have the adventures that you want to have, maybe it's time to leap off the sinking ship. Maybe love won't be on the menu at all; that doesn't mean you won't grow through relationship this year. Your dearest friends and your open rivals will provide plenty of opportunities for figuring out whom you want to be in relationship with, what you want from the people closest to you, what they want from you—and how to balance it all.

Biggest rewards: Libra, Aquarius, Gemini

Pressure to take risks: Aries, Cancer, Capricorn

Significant opportunities: Leo, Sagittarius

Jupiter in Libra (2000–2050): Sept. 24, 2004–Oct. 25, 2005; Sept. 9, 2016–Oct. 10, 2017; Aug. 23, 2028–Sept. 23, 2029; Dec. 12, 2039–Jan. 19, 2040; Aug. 5, 2040–Jan. 11, 2041

TRANSITING JUPITER IN SCORPIO ♏

You think you're married after you stand up in front of a legally sanctioned officiant and say "I do," or maybe after your wedding night. But I'm here to tell you, you're not *really* married until you've combined bank accounts with another person.

Okay, that's an exaggeration. Many, many couples maintain separate finances and consider themselves well and truly married, thank you. But my larger point is: Unless you also maintain separate households, at some point the subject of shared property and merged finances comes into play—and the way you manage the dynamics of shared resources very much determines the level of true intimacy and honesty in your relationship.

When Jupiter is in Scorpio, the required leap of faith takes us into the heart of sharing. As a sign, Scorpio has a reputation for being suspicious, even paranoid, and very secretive. Well, how do you feel when someone in your life asks to borrow money from you? Or your car, a favorite pair of shoes, or even a book? How about your most important possession: your body?

When Jupiter is in Scorpio, it is time to take a chance and trust people. That doesn't mean you have to be silly about it and trust total strangers. It does mean, though, that it's time to reward the people who have been there for you, who are loyal and honest, with a bigger piece of your heart.

Biggest rewards: Scorpio, Pisces, Cancer

Pressure to take risks: Taurus, Leo, Aquarius

Significant opportunities: Virgo, Capricorn

Jupiter in Scorpio (2000–2050): Oct. 25, 2005–Nov. 23, 2006; Oct. 10, 2017–Nov. 8, 2018; Sept. 23, 2029–Oct. 22, 2030; Jan. 11, 2041–Feb. 8, 2042; Apr. 24–Oct. 4, 2042

TRANSITING JUPITER IN SAGITTARIUS ♐

Ever get in one of those tedious conversations with someone who gives you an interminable monologue about his pet subject, delivered with bombast and a bellicose self-righteousness?

While transiting Jupiter is in Sagittarius, don't be that guy. Instead, learn more things. Go someplace new. For one year, continually place yourself in situations where you are not an authority, where you may not even speak the native language.

If you have been timid about adventure, this year will be a tremendous gift to you. New experiences are healthy: They keep you from believing that you know everything. They keep you from becoming that guy.

Biggest rewards: Sagittarius, Aries, Leo

Pressure to take risks: Gemini, Virgo, Pisces

Significant opportunities: Libra, Aquarius

Jupiter in Sagittarius (2000–2050): Nov. 23, 2006–Dec. 18, 2007; Nov. 8, 2018–Dec. 2, 2019; Oct. 22, 2030–Nov. 15, 2031; Feb. 8–Apr. 24, 2042; Oct. 4, 2042–Mar. 1, 2043; June 9–Oct. 26, 2043

TRANSITING JUPITER IN CAPRICORN ♑

Jupiter is not at his best in Capricorn. His naturally exuberant, expansive nature feels confined and oppressed in serious Capricorn.

But that doesn't have to mean it won't be a good year. In fact, it can be a fantastic year . . . for Capricorn things. Things such as business, maturity, organization, and long-range planning. If you are considering opening or expanding your own business, for instance, Jupiter in Capricorn is just the investor you need. If you are becoming a parent for the first time, Jupiter can give you the confidence (and fantastic shower gifts) to get you started.

If on the other hand you spend this year spinning your wheels, wasting your time, and hanging around waiting for everyone else to do the heavy lifting, Jupiter in Capricorn can make things very uncomfortable for you, even humiliating. So balance your checkbook, stand up straight, and make every effort to improve your situation!

Biggest rewards: Capricorn, Taurus, Virgo

Pressure to take risks: Aries, Cancer, Libra

Significant opportunities: Scorpio, Pisces

Jupiter in Capricorn (2000–2050): Dec. 18, 2007–Jan. 5, 2009; Dec. 2, 2019–Dec. 19, 2020; Nov. 15, 2031–Apr. 11, 2032; June 26–Nov. 29, 2032; Mar. 1–June 9, 2043; Oct. 26, 2043–Mar. 14, 2044; Aug. 9–Nov. 4, 2044

TRANSITING JUPITER IN AQUARIUS ♒

Even the most gregarious among us have moments when we feel we just don't fit in. While transiting Jupiter is in Aquarius, one of two things will usually happen. One is that you find your people—the friends and groups with which you feel you truly belong. The other is that you remain an outsider but learn to embrace that and make it work for you.

Either way, you'll be a happier human.

Jupiter in Aquarius is a year for appreciating others and letting them appreciate you. It doesn't mean you have to marry them or even like them all that much, just that you grow in your ability to appreciate others exactly as they are and peacefully coexist.

Put yourself in situations where you are most likely to encounter people who speak your language. Even if you're an extreme loner, try to find a club or meet-up that speaks to one of your dearest interests. This year, joy and good breaks come from acknowledging that, while you are your own person, there's nothing wrong with being part of society as well.

Biggest rewards: Aquarius, Gemini, Libra

Pressure to take risks: Taurus, Leo, Scorpio

Significant opportunities: Sagittarius, Aries

Jupiter in Aquarius (2000–2050): Jan. 5, 2009–Jan. 17, 2010; Dec. 19, 2020–May 13, 2021; July 28–Dec. 28, 2021; Apr. 11–June 26, 2032; Nov. 29, 2032–Apr. 14, 2033; Sept. 12–Dec. 1, 2033; Mar. 14–Aug. 9, 2044; Nov. 4, 2044–Mar. 25, 2045

TRANSITING JUPITER IN PISCES ♓

Are you judgmental? Do you lack compassion for people enduring hardships? Do you find it difficult to spend time around those who are ill and suffering? Are you uncomfortable around the poor or members of minority groups?

Here is your opportunity to overcome those limitations. While Jupiter is in Pisces, experiment with acceptance, forgiveness, compassion, and empathy. You don't have to commit to them for the rest of your life. Just try it for one year, and like Dr. Seuss's famous Grinch, feel your heart grow three sizes.

Here are the guidelines: (1) Don't judge. (2) Go barefoot as much as possible. (3) Give money to people on the street. I know, they're just gonna spend it on booze. Doesn't matter. Do it. (4) Don't criticize. Criticism is judgment. We're not doing that this year. (5) Take naps. You cannot be mean when you've just woken from a nap.

Biggest rewards: Pisces, Cancer, Scorpio

Pressure to take risks: Gemini, Virgo, Sagittarius

Significant opportunities: Taurus, Capricorn

Jupiter in Pisces (2000–2050): Jan. 17–June 5, 2010; Sept. 8, 2010–Jan. 22, 2011; May 13–July 28, 2021; Dec. 28, 2021–May 10, 2022; Oct. 27–Dec. 20, 2022; Apr. 14–Sept. 12, 2033; Dec. 1, 2033–Apr. 21, 2034; Mar. 25, 2045–Apr. 4, 2046

TRANSITING JUPITER IN ASPECT TO NATAL PLANETS AND ANGLES

Jupiter moves at the rate of about 1 degree of the zodiac per week. Generally, his transits are experienced most strongly for about three weeks: one week in advance of the exact aspect, the week it is exact, and (to a lesser extent) the week after the aspect is exact.

Jupiter's square, opposition, and quincunx aspects to natal planets can suggest overconfidence, excessive spending, unwise risk-taking, and overindulgence in food and drink. The same can happen under Jupiter's transiting conjunctions, trines, and sextiles, but usually with less deleterious results. Usually a harmonious aspect from Jupiter to the natal chart is good news indeed, though occasionally it may not look that way at first.

TRANSITING JUPITER IN ASPECT TO THE NATAL SUN

These transits are among the best for putting yourself forward, exploring your creativity, getting the attention you deserve, and generally having fun. Good opportunities present themselves, sometimes out of nowhere; on the whole, you have more confidence, feel more popular, and are willing to take risks. But be a bit cautious. Jupiter in combination with the Sun can be too much of a good thing! Don't become too full of yourself. Share some of the spotlight with deserving others. Jupiter's transits to the Sun benefit you most in the areas where your confidence and luck need shoring up; where you are naturally blessed, Jupiter may cause you to overdo it.

TRANSITING JUPITER IN ASPECT TO THE NATAL MOON

It's time to pry open your home and the other private spaces in your life. These are mainly favorable transits, especially for travel, hosting houseguests, and offering any kind of educational or philosophical gatherings in your home. If you decide to embark on home improvement projects now—which is quite possible—be sure they are truly needed and that your budget is realistic. (In the digital age, you can apply this advice to, say, building a new website or app.)

Jupiter's transiting aspects to the Moon can be overwhelming if you are private by nature and enjoy a quiet life. A hectic home and daily life during this transit usually means you need some practice saying no. It's tempting to imagine your life is infinitely expandable, but you have to respect your limits. This transit brings more of everything to your door—people, money, and new opportunities and experiences. Whether you invite them inside is entirely up to you.

TRANSITING JUPITER IN ASPECT TO NATAL MERCURY

To me, these transits always seem to work like an inverted funnel: There are so many ideas and impressions coming your way that you feel they can't possibly squeeze through the tiny aperture that leads to your brain!

I had this transit while writing this book, and I found that regular changes of scenery helped with inspiration and organizing my thoughts. I embarked on a self-funded Amtrak "residency," taking several daylong trips and writing on the train! Jupiter loves travel and welcomes adventure, so just exposing yourself to something new and inspiring (such as gazing out at the Pacific Ocean while you work) can open up your mind and get it firing on all cylinders.

TRANSITING JUPITER IN ASPECT TO NATAL VENUS

These transits are designed to yield more of the things that bring you pleasure and satisfaction. Initially, your attention will likely be called to things you're lacking or the ways that you're not enjoying what you already have. During this transit, you can remedy that. But as always with Jupiter, it's important to determine how much of a good thing is too much. Venus symbolizes what we enjoy, but not necessarily what we need. There is a difference. Anyone who has left a mall with both hands full of shopping bags and a maxed-out credit card knows the sinking sensation of buyer's remorse! While transiting Jupiter aspects Venus, learn to appreciate what actually makes you feel good and happy; it is usually a balance between having some of what you want without sacrificing too much money, space, or peace of mind in the process.

TRANSITING JUPITER IN ASPECT TO NATAL MARS

Even if you're not competitive by nature, this transit will probably awaken your desire to conquer! Confidence, physical vitality, and initiative are at a peak, and you can make great strides toward specific goals. This can be an excellent time to initiate a serious exercise program or get involved in sports, because you're willing to push yourself to become stronger, faster, and as full of oats as a racehorse. When Jupiter and Mars are through with you, simply moving your body will feel glorious. Just be careful not to push too far, too fast.

Jupiter's tendency toward exaggeration can cause problems during these transits, particularly if you have trouble managing anger and frustration. The tendency will be to blow slights out of proportion. Though it's fine to assert yourself and go after what you want, don't lose sight of the importance of good sportsmanship and generosity toward others.

TRANSITING JUPITER IN ASPECT TO NATAL JUPITER

You have reached an important point in Jupiter's cycle of growth and learning. If it's a conjunction, you are having a Jupiter return and beginning a new twelve-year cycle. The trines and sextiles support your natural disposition and beliefs around travel, religion, and education; the squares and opposition are moments when, through conflict, you see another point of view. (See "Using Jupiter's Cycle" on page 38 for more about these aspects.)

TRANSITING JUPITER IN ASPECT TO NATAL SATURN

Challenging and flowing aspects alike allow Jupiter's optimism and joy to lighten the weight of Saturn's responsibility and tendency to worry. In some cases, this begins by exaggerating Saturn's misery until we realize how ridiculous that is and ease up on ourselves.

These can be tremendously inspiring transits for career success, coaxing you to venture out of your carefully delineated professional path to look for other opportunities. If you have been setting the bar too low for yourself, Jupiter will encourage you to push for bigger things.

TRANSITING JUPITER IN ASPECT TO NATAL URANUS

Imagine you are in prison, armed with a bomb that could help you break out, but without a match to light the fuse. Uranus is the bomb, and Jupiter is more than happy to provide the match. At this time, there may be a dramatic break with a job, relationship, or living situation. Ultimately, it's probably for the best, but Jupiter isn't particularly careful about looking before it convinces you to leap.

Both Jupiter and Uranus are extremely fond of freedom. Jupiter hates limits, and Uranus loathes the status quo. When the two come together in your chart, they hold the keys to unlock nearly any door. Just be sure that when you walk through the door you choose to open, you're moving toward something better, and not just away from something oppressive.

TRANSITING JUPITER IN ASPECT TO NATAL NEPTUNE

It's time to face your fears. All the secrets and disappointments that you strive to hide away are brought out into the open, and Jupiter will help you make friends with, heal, and generally overcome them.

Your fears are potentially your greatest source of strength, and as transiting Jupiter touches Neptune by any aspect, you come closer to claiming that strength. You may feel as though you have been thrown into the ocean without knowing whether you can swim. Paddle too hard, and you'll go under. Now is the time to stop struggling and float a little.

TRANSITING JUPITER IN ASPECT TO NATAL PLUTO

You may naturally be a person of great purpose, focus, and determination. If you're not, though, you may be a little shocked by just how formidable you become during these transits. The combination of Jupiter's strong beliefs and Pluto's ruthless determination makes this an excellent time for marshaling your forces and accomplishing amazing things.

Be warned: Pluto's determination can be a mixed blessing. You may get what you wanted and come to regret it. The combination of Jupiter and Pluto can also make for overzealousness bordering on fanaticism. If you find yourself believing that your point of view is the only one that could possibly be right, you're likely wandering into dangerous territory. Take care to be a wise steward of your power without becoming overly attached to it; there are always other ways of seeing the world, and believe it or not, they might be just as valid as yours.

TRANSITING JUPITER IN ASPECT TO THE NATAL LUNAR NODES

A couple years ago, on the day transiting Jupiter made an aspect to my natal Lunar Nodes, I was enjoying a fabulous anniversary dinner with my husband in New Orleans. A few days earlier, I'd presented my first lecture for a large and influential astrology conference. I was with my favorite person in a fabulous city I'd always wanted to visit and had just reached a significant career milestone. Add the three desserts we shared after dinner, and it was pretty much a peak experience.

A lot of transits are difficult, and even Jupiter's transits aren't always a cakewalk. But transiting Jupiter's aspects to your natal Nodes are the closest thing astrology has to a sure bet. So pause for a moment. Welcome what comes your way. Appreciate these little messages of hope that say you're moving in the right direction, and let your heart cry out, "More, please!"

TRANSITING JUPITER IN ASPECT TO THE NATAL ASCENDANT

These transits can be a little overwhelming; you may feel as if you're walking out of a dark movie theater into bright, blinding sunlight. Too much freedom and change at one time can be disorienting.

Jupiter wants to take you on an adventure. You may well move, perhaps even someplace far away (particularly if Uranus, Neptune, or Pluto is making an aspect to your Ascendant at the same time). Always, transiting aspects to the Ascendant call for reinvention. It's time for a fresh start in a new place, and a chance to be a new and hopefully happier self.

TRANSITING JUPITER IN ASPECT TO THE NATAL MIDHEAVEN

Regardless of the aspect, this transit ushers you to the winner's circle. It is time to claim the career opportunities and accolades that have long eluded you. Your reputation is enhanced; it's like being invited to the court of Henry VIII and making a big splash. But remember: Anne Boleyn made a big splash at King Henry's court and ended up without her head. Don't lose yours by overreaching and grabbing for too much during this transit.

chapter 4

TRANSITS OF SATURN:
THE ABILITY TO RESPOND

Planetary Dossier: SATURN

TIME TO MAKE A FULL CYCLE AROUND THE SUN: 29.5 years

TIME SPENT IN EACH ZODIAC SIGN: 2.5 years

TRANSITING ASPECTS LAST FOR: approximately 6 weeks

STRONGEST SIGNS: Capricorn, Aquarius, Libra

HAS TO WORK HARDER IN: Cancer, Leo, Aries

KEYWORDS: maturity, wisdom, discipline, work, authority, mastery, limits and boundaries

She was an African American girl born to an unmarried teenage mother in the mid-1950s, in impoverished, rural Mississippi. A survivor of childhood sexual abuse, she gave birth at the age of fourteen to a baby who died several days later. She was fired from her first television reporting job because her boss declared she was "not suitable for television."

Just before her Saturn return, Oprah Winfrey landed her own morning talk show. By the age of thirty-two, she was a millionaire. By the time Saturn transited her Midheaven and she retired from *The Oprah Winfrey Show*, she had a net worth of $2.9 billion, owns her own cable network, and is regularly cited as one of the world's most influential women.

Born with the Sun in a close aspect to Saturn, Oprah Winfrey is the model of a self-made woman. Her tenacity, hunger to succeed, and determination to overcome adversity are all hallmarks of a successful response to Saturn. Because she was not hardwired to expect life to be easy, she works hard. And when Saturn's transits push her into challenging situations, she pushes back. That's the key to earning Saturn's respect.

THE NATURE OF THE BEAST

The beginning of a Saturn transit is a bit like living in a cloudy, rainy place where the sun never shines. You know Saturn is overhauling you when find yourself waking up tired every single day, when nothing excites you, when everything feels difficult and takes too much effort.

But assuming the universe is a benevolent place, you can bet that tenderness lies beneath this tough Saturnine surface. What does Saturn want from you? He wants work and maturity, diligence and responsibility; he wants to see you behind the wheel of your own life, eyes on the road, foot on the accelerator. And he wants you to consult a GPS before ever hitting the road. In other words, he wants your life to have a plan, and he wants it to be a plan you came up with yourself. (Eyes on your own paper, missy!)

I won't lie to you: Saturn's transits can bring frustration, deprivation, and loneliness. However, they are a means to an end, not the end itself. Saturn has no interest in abandoning you in a pit of despair. Rather, these transits teach you what you're made of and force you to create a life that is more nurturing and supportive of the real you.

Suffering through hardships doesn't feel good. It hurts—and it is *supposed* to hurt! There is a reason for it, just as there is a reason the physical body feels pain: to alert you that something is endangering your well-being, that something isn't right, so that you can avoid or fix it. So it is with your heart and your spirit: If you hurt, it's because you are *supposed* to hurt when your life is moving in the wrong direction.

USING SATURN'S CYCLE

You inherited many circumstances when you came into the world: a particular set of parents; a socio-economic status; a world in war, peace, prosperity, or poverty; a genetic predisposition to particular diseases or weaknesses; innate talents.

These elements comprise a structure that you inhabit before you're old enough to realize that they don't represent the totality of human experience. The external structures impose themselves onto your insides as well, building mazes of entitlement, limitation, and expectation that perfectly mirror what's on the outside. You came into the world as molten goo in search of a form. As child development experts like to say, children need structure. At some level, they are grateful for even the most dysfunctional forms and structures of their early lives, and look to those structures for a sense of who they are and what is possible for them.

Life is one long process of unmolding yourself from these earliest forms. Like a cake liberated from a pan, you are made in a particular shape, of particular ingredients—but a lot can still be done to alter the flavor, configuration, and presentation. A cake can be frosted and decorated, cut into shapes, served on lovely plates, or eaten right out of the refrigerator as a midnight snack. We are cakes made of particular stuff, all right, but our lives are a process of creating interesting shapes and forms, and flavorful offerings, from our basic makeup.

Each time Saturn in the sky hits a degree of the zodiac that resonates with your birth chart, you become dissatisfied with the shape of your life. It seems to need something—perhaps a new layer, or a different frosting. How you respond to this dissatisfaction, this challenge, highly depends on how you were taught to respond. Are you fearful, resistant, angry, or excited to get to work?

THE SATURN RETURN

Ages 29, 58, 87

The Saturn return occurs when this planet symbolizing maturity, responsibility, career, and limitations comes back to its position in your birth chart. This huge event—which happens only every twenty-nine years—is a time to stand back and take a cold, hard look at your life. Are you happy with your career? Do you have a sense that life is moving in the right direction? Do you feel like a grownup? When Saturn returns to its natal position, you become uncomfortably aware that you are mortal. Life has an expiration date. A panic sets in. Is it too late to do the things you want to do?

At the initial Saturn return, you realize for the first time that it is already too late for some things. "Olympic gymnast" or "child prodigy" are roads that are firmly closed to you. But really, the first Saturn return is a wake-up call that comes just as you're entering your prime—when it's still early enough in the game to change course, even if you do have to adjust some of your expectations.

At the second Saturn return, around the age of fifty-eight or fifty-nine, begins the transition into what is traditionally considered "retirement." This doesn't mean that no work will be done; it doesn't take long to turn up examples of exalted figures who produced their finest work later in life. What it does mean is that your most important role becomes that of teacher, of tribal elder. In modern America, unlike in other cultures that revere elders as keepers of wisdom, this role is not well defined and is even less respected.

You must find a way to make the transition to elder a graceful and meaningful one. It's tempting at midlife to feel sad about what we haven't accomplished, and hard to accept that we may never reach the heights of our profession. But none of us reaches our fifties without having learned an enormous amount. The key to a happy second half of life is a balance between learning new things and sharing what we've already mastered. And so the whole concept of career becomes much different in your midfifties than it was ten years earlier. The focus is less toward striving and more toward sharing.

THE OPENING SATURN SQUARE

Ages 7, 35, 63, 91

These are the ages of reason, when awareness of responsibility, maturity, and mortality comes into clearer focus, catalyzed by some external event. Life pushes you, and you have to push back, hard, to open the door to the next chapter. Achieving something in particular is not the point; simply making a serious effort to move forward is enough to satisfy Saturn.

THE SATURN OPPOSITION

Ages 14, 42, 70, 98

All is clear; at the top of the mountain, you can see for a hundred miles. When transiting Saturn is opposed your natal Saturn position, you have come to the halfway point in the cycle of maturity. You can see where you started out, and in the distance you can pinpoint where you will end up if you continue along your path. This is the moment to weigh your options: Is it time to correct your course?

THE CLOSING SATURN SQUARE

Ages 21, 50, 78

The first closing Saturn square at age twenty-one dovetails with the first transiting Uranus square, so this is an age marked by tremendous tension between fitting into society and the urge to rebel against everything you've known. The second closing Saturn square at age fifty can bring a pinnacle of career achievement if you've been working hard toward a particular goal, but of course you're also beginning to feel your age. At the third Saturn square, you can review your career, consider your legacy, and mentor others to continue your work.

TRANSITING SATURN BY SIGN

Saturn does not want to hear excuses. All that matters is results. Saturn's sign is not just about style but also about the nature of the work assigned to us.

The first step in handling Saturn's sojourn through any sign is not to panic, but to take stock. Figure out what structures of your life have been neglected and draft a plan for shoring them up. It doesn't have to happen overnight. Saturn simply asks that we acknowledge responsibility—determine the ways we are able to respond to a situation—and then do what we can to improve.

TRANSITING SATURN IN ARIES ♈

Some people blame others for their failures and misfortunes—and then there are those who are successful.

When Saturn is moving through Aries, it is tempting to be the first kind of person. We can enumerate chapter and verse of the ways other people and cruel circumstance are holding us back. *If only I were better looking, born to a rich family, had married my high school sweetheart. If only people treated me fairly instead of giving everything to somebody else. If only, if only, if only . . .*

The real "if only" goes something like this: *If only I had the courage to go after what I want. If only I had the gumption to keep trying every time I fail. If only I treated other people as well as I expect to be treated, and I worked hard to earn the breaks I feel that I deserve.*

When Saturn is in Aries, we are charged with accepting total personal responsibility for our lives. Saturn will not accept excuses, complaints, or blame. You are the author of your life, so write it the way you want to, and then turn the book into the movie you want to live in.

Most challenging for: Aries, Cancer, Libra, Capricorn

Earned rewards for: Leo, Sagittarius

Advancement opportunities for: Gemini, Aquarius

Saturn in Aries (1950–2050): Mar. 1967–Apr. 1969; Apr. 1996–Mar. 1999; May 2025–Apr. 2028

TRANSITING SATURN IN TAURUS ♉

How is your relationship with the physical world? Are you treating your possessions with care and respect? How about your money? Your body?

While Saturn transited Aries, survival was the order of the day. As Saturn enters Taurus, all appears to be in a hopeless state of entropy. Taurus's season, regardless of the planet transiting there, is devoted to strengthening your position. While Saturn is here, you'll need to work hard to make sure you've got everything you need and that it's all in good, working order.

If you have been lazy about organizing your house, balancing your checkbook, getting exercise, or having your car serviced regularly, Saturn will get a bit harsh with you. Establish new goals and routines devoted to getting your life in order so it can support you on the road ahead.

Most challenging for: Taurus, Leo, Scorpio, Aquarius

Earned rewards for: Virgo, Capricorn

Advancement opportunities for: Cancer, Pisces

Saturn in Taurus (1950–2050): Apr. 1969–Feb. 1972; June 1998–Apr. 2001; Apr. 2028–June 2030

TRANSITING SATURN IN GEMINI ♊

Impeccability is Saturn's defining trait. It is the stern inner taskmaster that insists we can do better, be better. Like your favorite teacher from school, Saturn expects great things from you. And while Saturn transits through Gemini, you are expected to master Gemini matters—communication, learning new things, and building social networks. Should you refuse to apply yourself to these things, Saturn will not hesitate to rap your knuckles with a ruler and keep you after school for two years of detention.

Saturn in Gemini reminds us to honor and respect purely Gemini processes and skills by doing our best to respond to them with integrity. But don't imagine you need to spend the next two years tediously crossing *t*'s and dotting *i*'s. Go ahead—be sociable, be a terrific conversationalist, communicate! But do your research so you can ask the right questions.

Be Saturn-impeccable in your word while employing Gemini's gift of tact. Return phone calls and emails promptly, and be scrupulous about sending thank-you cards and acknowledging birthdays. Keep good to-do lists, and actually do the things on them. Perform routine maintenance on your car. Be a good neighbor and sibling. Ask the older people in your life to tell you their stories; they've been waiting a long time to be asked. Go back to school and learn something new. Two years is plenty of time to accomplish good work—but a long time to spend in detention!

Most challenging for: Gemini, Virgo, Sagittarius, Pisces

Earned rewards for: Libra, Aquarius

Advancement opportunities for: Aries, Leo

Saturn in Gemini (1950–2050): June 1971–Apr. 1974; Aug. 2000–June 2003; June 2030–July 2032

TRANSITING SATURN IN CANCER ♋

When Saturn transits through Cancer, you are likely to feel overwhelmed by Cancerian responsibilities for your home and family, and by your need for security. That feeling of crushing weight is a natural consequence of awakening to the enormous responsibility we bear for these things.

The impulse is to furiously create vessels in which to save every drop of security against the lean and dry times. The temptation is strong to delegate responsibility for your well-being to someone else. But Saturn never approves of delegating responsibility. It's up to you to protect yourself and the ones you love.

But don't overdo it. Security is important, but so are freedom and breathing room. Beware of smothering your loved ones in your desire to protect them.

Most challenging for: Cancer, Libra, Capricorn, Aries

Earned rewards for: Scorpio, Pisces

Advancement opportunities for: Taurus, Virgo

Saturn in Cancer (1950–2050): Aug. 1973–June 1976; June 2003–July 2005; July 2032–May 2035

TRANSITING SATURN IN LEO ♌

When Saturn transits through Leo, it's time to come to terms with the reality of aging and mortality. Abruptly, the Leo party of self-celebration and preoccupation with the good life is over: The aging playboy finds he is no longer attractive to the youngest, most desirable women; the spendthrift with a closet full of shoes realizes she's bankrupt.

Those who don't respond well to Saturn's challenge become tyrannical children, waving their arms and hollering in impotent fury. This is a tough transit for leaders. Gaining a prominent position requires an enormous ego, and such egos are not happy about being put aside for the general good. It's not easy for artists, either, since Leo is the sign most associated with creative self-expression. Saturn in Leo insists that we express ourselves creatively despite indifference, criticism, and obstacles.

The biggest challenge of this transit is to figure out how to be truly yourself, respect what you are, and let yourself age gracefully. Those who seem at ease with themselves and who laugh effortlessly are the ones succeeding.

Most challenging for: Leo, Scorpio, Aquarius, Taurus

Earned rewards for: Aries, Sagittarius

Advancement opportunities for: Gemini, Libra

Saturn in Leo (1950–2050): Sept. 1975–July 1978; July 2005–Sept. 2007; Aug. 2034–Oct. 2036

TRANSITING SATURN IN VIRGO ♍

Like a good editor, Virgo takes the wild, heartfelt creative urges of Leo and cleans up the grammar and punctuation. If Leo is about letting it all hang out, Virgo's job is to rein you in and tighten things up.

Saturn is the world's toughest boss, and his tutelage and discipline can be truly miserable to endure. Place Saturn in a sign such as Virgo—already inclined to overdo it in attempting to make things better—and you have a recipe for a demanding transit.

So take it easy on yourself. You will not become perfect in two and a half years—or ever. The goal of Saturn in Virgo is to teach you to recognize and move in the direction of quality. Forgive yourself when you fall short of your standards, but don't lower those standards. All the attention to detail seems trivial, but it's moving you in the direction of greatness.

Most challenging for: Virgo, Sagittarius, Pisces, Gemini

Earned rewards for: Taurus, Capricorn

Advancement opportunities for: Cancer, Scorpio

Saturn in Virgo (1950–2050): Sept. 1948–Aug. 1951; Nov. 1977–Sept. 1980; Sept. 2007–July 2010; Oct. 2036–Sept. 2039

TRANSITING SATURN IN LIBRA ♎

Libra is the sign in which Saturn is thought to be "exalted"—that is, he does some of his best work here. Libra is the sign of fairness, balance, and collaboration. Saturn's transit through Libra illustrates what's fair and what's not, where your life is out of balance, and everything that's wrong with your closest relationships.

Libra brings out the best in worldly Saturn, contesting single-minded ambition with the question, What good are achievements if you have no one to share them with you? Even when it's been pointed out to you that your ambitions are having a bad impact on your relationships, or that your inflexibility is making you old before your time, it can be hard to correct course.

What's needed to check these tendencies are the strong and dissenting voices of those who know us best—whether because they love us, or because they've traveled the same road. Marriages and business partnerships, in particular, must either be reinforced or, like an old building, "brought up to code," lest they crumble completely.

Most challenging for: Libra, Capricorn, Aries, Cancer

Earned rewards for: Gemini, Aquarius

Advancement opportunities for: Leo, Sagittarius

Saturn in Libra (1950–2050): Nov. 1950–Oct. 1953; Sept. 1980–Aug. 1983; Oct. 2009–Oct. 2012; Sept. 2039–July 2042

TRANSITING SATURN IN SCORPIO ♏

The good news is that Saturn in Scorpio encourages us to form intimate, sharing, and supportive relationships; to trust our own judgment; and to learn to let others give to us. The bad news is, Saturn's particular form of encouragement tends to be a little rough. "Just how badly do you want to form intimate, sharing, and supportive relationships?" he asks. "Let's throw every possible impediment in your path and see whether you still want those relationships." Or the ever popular, "How's about you make a real whopper of a bad decision—trust somebody you really shouldn't—and see whether you're still able to trust your own judgment?"

When outer planets transit Scorpio, stuff gets *real*. There's no use sugar-coating it. But each sign has its blessings as well as its curse, and Scorpio bestows the kind of strength that comes from knowing the truth—about ourselves, about others, and about the way the world works. From there, we'll eventually move forward into Saturn in Sagittarius and construct a belief system that helps put it all in a larger perspective.

One thing that Saturn's passage through Scorpio throws into bold relief is the value of having supportive friends and loved ones, and of learning to accept their support with grace and humility when it's needed. Saturn in Libra showed you who your friends are and gave you a good look at your enemies as well. Now it's time to trust those friends, and to heed the little voice inside that tells you to flee when you see Godzilla stomping toward your heart.

Most challenging for: Scorpio, Aquarius, Taurus, Leo

Earned rewards for: Cancer, Pisces

Advancement opportunities for: Virgo, Capricorn

Saturn in Scorpio (1950–2050): Oct. 1953–Oct. 1956; Nov. 1982–Nov. 1985; Oct. 2012–Sept. 2015; Nov. 2041–Oct. 2044

TRANSITING SATURN IN SAGITTARIUS ♐

What do you know, and how do you know it? When Saturn transits Sagittarius, the pressure is enormous to *know* things, to have opinions, and if possible, to legislate your opinions to become the law of the land. Usually public opinion skews very conservative when Saturn transits Sagittarius—for example, the transits of the late 1950s and late 1980s were among the most conservative in American culture and politics. These can be times when those with strong opinions dominate the media, making convictions seem obnoxious.

But don't let that dissuade you from owning *your* beliefs. While Saturn toured Scorpio, you got a behind-the-scenes look at human nature, and a lot of it wasn't pretty. But it also put you in a much stronger position to determine for yourself what you believe and what you stand for. While Saturn transits Sagittarius, draft your very own code of ethics to subscribe to. Remember that you're human and fallible: You will occasionally fall short of your standards.

I remember reading that Navajo weavers deliberately work tiny imperfections called *spirit lines* into their designs. Among other explanations, it's said that the spirit line allows the weaver's spirit to escape the rug, so any negative emotions she might have been feeling during her work will not be passed on to the owner. Likewise, while Saturn is in Sagittarius, weave a beautiful tapestry of beliefs—but include an escape valve for imperfection.

Most challenging for: Sagittarius, Pisces, Gemini, Virgo

Earned rewards for: Aries, Leo

Advancement opportunities for: Libra, Aquarius

Saturn in Sagittarius (1950–2050): Jan. 1956–Jan. 1959; Nov. 1985–Nov. 1988; Dec. 2014–Dec. 2017; Feb. 2044–Oct. 2047

TRANSITING SATURN IN CAPRICORN ♑

Saturn is at his most powerful in Capricorn, so during these transits he flexes his muscles and holds nothing back in his quest for world domination. Many of us begin Saturn in Capricorn transits feeling like failures and unable to own our lives. To transcend your misguided notions of inadequacy, take your cue from Capricorn's totem animal, the goat. He scales unlikely peaks slowly, deliberately, putting one hoof steadfastly in front of the other. It looks as though he isn't getting anywhere, but by minding his own business and refusing to give up, he eventually reaches the summit. Keep trudging along, step by step, and by the time Saturn leaves his home turf you could have an entirely new career—or simply a higher status and more respect in your existing one.

Most challenging for: Capricorn, Aries, Cancer, Libra

Earned rewards for: Taurus, Virgo

Advancement opportunities for: Scorpio, Pisces

Saturn in Capricorn (1950–2050): Jan. 1959–Jan. 1962; Nov. 1988–Feb. 1991; Dec. 2017–Dec. 2020; Jan. 2047–Jan. 2050

TRANSITING SATURN IN AQUARIUS ♒

Before the discovery of Uranus, Saturn was considered the ruling planet of Aquarius. In fact, many astrologers still consider this to be so. So we can assume that Saturn is very strong in Aquarius, almost as much as in Capricorn.

Aquarius's goals, however, extend beyond earthly achievements. You may work hard to build a career during this transit, but more important, you are building a legacy. Change is in the air, but some of it is superficial—new window dressing to disguise old ideas. To get through this transit successfully, challenge not just society's rules but also your own.

Most challenging for: Aquarius, Taurus, Leo, Scorpio

Earned rewards for: Gemini, Libra

Advancement opportunities for: Aries, Sagittarius

Saturn in Aquarius (1950–2050): Jan. 1962–Dec. 1964; Feb. 1991–Jan. 1994; Mar. 2020–Mar. 2023; Jan. 2050–Jan. 2053

TRANSITING SATURN IN PISCES ♓

Remember when you were a kid and your mother overheard you saying something nasty about someone? Hopefully she made you realize the value of empathy, encouraging you to stand awhile in another's moccasins before judging.

So it goes while Saturn is transiting through Pisces, the sign of the underdog. As adults, we are judged, and rightly so, by how we treat those who are smaller or weaker than we are. And here's the not-so-well-kept secret: We judge others based on our own fears and inadequacies. If you ridicule people based on their clothing, their color, their weight, their sexual orientation, or the car they drive, you are an insecure mess. You are seeking a scapegoat.

While in Pisces, Saturn intends to put an end to such nonsense. Grown-ups are kind to others. For that matter, they know when to give themselves a break, too.

Most challenging for: Pisces, Gemini, Virgo, Sagittarius

Earned rewards for: Cancer, Scorpio

Advancement opportunities for: Taurus, Capricorn

Saturn in Pisces (1950–2050): Mar. 1964–Mar. 1967; May 1993–Apr. 1996; Mar. 2023–Feb. 2026

TRANSITING SATURN IN ASPECT TO NATAL PLANETS AND ANGLES

Transiting Saturn moves at the rate of about 3 degrees of the zodiac per month. Its transits are generally experienced most strongly for about six weeks—or more if Saturn moves retrograde within a couple of degrees of a natal planet.

Saturn's conjunction, square, opposition, and quincunx aspects to natal planets can suggest times of struggle, blockage, exhaustion, and feeling as if too much responsibility has been placed on your shoulders. The same can happen under Saturn's transiting trines, and sextiles, but these also bring a feeling that you are getting an opportunity to take your game to the next level, especially professionally.

TRANSITING SATURN IN ASPECT TO THE NATAL SUN

This can be a productive, character-building transit, but rarely a cheerful one. You will generally feel as though you're carrying the weight of Saturn itself on your shoulders. Further, you will feel you're not getting credit for all this heavy lifting; on the contrary, others may accuse you of being a killjoy. It's tempting to say that the trine or sextile from Saturn to the natal Sun is not so bad, but really, those transits don't feel all that wonderful, either. If you're looking for a good transit for tackling projects that require confidence and popularity, this is not one of them.

So what are Saturn/Sun transits good for? They're unsurpassed for building strength and endurance and for proving to yourself that you can stick it out when times get tough. Through these transits, you'll develop strength and character that lasts because it has been truly earned. So show up, put your behind in the seat, keep your head down, and do your work.

TRANSITING SATURN IN ASPECT TO THE NATAL MOON

Saturn is the tough daddy who insists on your best effort and shows no sympathy when you fail. The Moon is your inner mommy, the one you run to when someone makes you sad or beats you up for your lunch money. When transiting Saturn aspects your natal Moon, mom and dad negotiate about the best way for you to parent yourself.

If Saturn is making a conjunction, square, or opposition to your natal Moon, the dialogue is rough, with Saturn insisting you need to toughen up and the Moon maintaining that you need to be protected. Often an authority figure in your life—a boss, a coach, a parent—makes life difficult for you during these transits. If the aspect is a gentler one, a trine or a sextile, a satisfying compromise between the two approaches is more easily reached. Either way, this transit demands that you learn important lessons about protecting yourself. Usually the lessons learned are about creating healthier boundaries in relationships and structuring your life in a way that allows you to grow while still feeling safe.

TRANSITING SATURN IN ASPECT TO NATAL MERCURY

This transit usually happens within a few weeks of transiting Saturn's aspect to the natal Sun, which overshadows everything else. But there are distinct differences between that one and Saturn's aspects to Mercury. The Sun is about who you are or are learning to be; Mercury, on the other hand, is about who you *tell yourself* that you are, how you frame the epic saga of your personal development. When transiting Saturn aspects Mercury, a reality check is in order: Are you telling the truth about yourself, your goals, your life? Are you trying so hard to spin reality that you no longer know what the truth is?

For each of us, there are stories about ourselves that we would prefer to forget. Sometimes Saturn's transits of Mercury offer opportunities to revisit them, perhaps with renewed perspective and understanding. Relationships with siblings and neighbors are the province of Mercury, and these are relationships that can help you come to a clearer understanding of yourself during these transits.

TRANSITING SATURN IN ASPECT TO NATAL VENUS

As this transit begins—especially the conjunction, square, or opposition—you may feel unloved or as though you will never have enough money.

But Saturn has a plan. Saturn wants you to feel good about yourself. Really good. Authentically good. He wants you to have a financial goal, a vision. He is forcing you into the driver's seat in this area of your life. He is saying, "No more pretending that you are powerless to resist the siren song of ill-advised love affairs or sad stories from people who are broke. No more using money as a way to distance yourself from other people."

So make a plan, then take the steps necessary to implement it. Manage what you have more wisely. When life gets tough, sometimes the most responsible action is to ask for help—from family, friends, even the universe. As astrologer Caroline Casey says, the universe wants to help, but spiritual etiquette requires that we ask. Ritual, even something as simple as burning a candle while stating our intention for the month ahead, is a way of politely asking the universe for the aid we seek. And sometimes the best thing that comes out of a Saturn transit is clarity about what we need versus what we simply want. Often, simply understanding what you need to the extent that you are able to articulate it is very powerful, very Saturnian magic.

TRANSITING SATURN IN ASPECT TO NATAL MARS

When transiting Saturn aspects natal Mars, your inner guard dog springs to life, straining against its leash, escaping from the backyard fence, and menacing the neighbors. During a relatively benign sextile, I had a lecturer at school (a Saturn authority figure) who wrote disparaging comments on one of my papers and made "corrections" to grammar that was, according to Strunk and White, already entirely correct. My rage was incendiary.

The soundtrack for this transit is the Bobby Fuller Five oldie "I Fought the Law (and the Law Won)." Saturn will win in the end; quick-tempered Mars is simply overpowered and outlasted. But you have the choice of what lesson to take away from these transits: Will you impose more control and discipline over your temper, impulsiveness, and physical drives? Or indulge in chronic rage against "The Man"?

TRANSITING SATURN IN ASPECT TO NATAL JUPITER

This is one transiting combination in which the type of aspect involved makes a big difference. A hard aspect from transiting Saturn to natal Jupiter can make you feel like the unluckiest person in the world. A nice trine or sextile, however, can bring your fondest hopes to fruition, because Saturn gives form and structure to Jupiter's pie-in-the-sky dreams.

When the transiting aspect is a conjunction, square, or opposition, Jupiter simply experiences Saturn as a buzzkill. Saturn, for his part, has lost all patience with Jupiter's big ideas and lack of follow-through, and starts to get a little bit mean.

Luckily, Jupiter is smart enough to know that his huge ambitions need a little discipline and practicality to become reality. And Saturn loves nothing more than to roll up his sleeves and sort out a huge mess. So a trine or sextile between the two can bring your dreams to reality.

TRANSITING SATURN IN ASPECT TO NATAL SATURN

These transits are milestones in your evolving, lifelong journey with Saturn. Look for events, people, and circumstances that awaken your ambition, responsibility, and authority.

You have reached an important point in Saturn's cycle of maturity, responsibility, and authority. If the aspect is a conjunction, you are having a Saturn return and beginning a new twenty-nine-year cycle. The trines and sextiles support your self-discipline and attitude toward career, reputation, and achievement; the squares and opposition represent moments when, through conflict, you gain perspective that encourages greater maturity. (See "Using Saturn's Cycle" on page 51 for more about these aspects.)

TRANSITING SATURN IN ASPECT TO NATAL URANUS

A part of each of us doesn't want to conform or live according to anyone's rules; that's the part we call *Uranus*. There is an equally compelling urge to be respected and recognized by society, to achieve stature; that urge is called *Saturn*. When the two collide, we must decide whether to indulge one side or the other, or to find a compromise. During a conjunction or square, you may feel like a hopeless outcast. Everyone close to you seems to be reaching milestones beyond your grasp. The opposition, interestingly, seems to have just the reverse effect, allowing you to conform without losing your individuality. And the trine and sextile can make you feel about as popular as you'll ever feel, as your distinctive brand of wackiness suddenly finds its place in society.

TRANSITING SATURN IN ASPECT TO NATAL NEPTUNE

Saturn trine or sextile Neptune marks some kind of honeymoon period, where the status quo feels wonderful. When Saturn opposes or squares Neptune, the honeymoon is over, the clouds disappear, and grim reality is revealed. The conjunction between the two is pretty difficult: What happens when you have no refuge from reality? It's like torture by sleep deprivation, discordant music blaring at all hours.

If you're of a certain age and haven't been taking care of yourself, this is when your health gremlins can come home to roost. If you're young and robustly healthy, you're more likely to experience serious disillusionment about something or someone in your life. Ultimately, the purpose of the transit is to make us face reality and acknowledge our limits; only then can we begin to understand the potential beauty of things as they truly are.

TRANSITING SATURN IN ASPECT TO NATAL PLUTO

From time to time, you will find that you have climbed to the next level in your life. You have achieved some kind of success, reached an important developmental milestone, and you feel good about yourself. Until suddenly you don't. Some people can't stand to see others achieve; on the Internet, we call them "trolls," miserable sorts who crawl out of the muck to spew invective in blog comments.

There is a troll inside you, too—a nasty little creature who whispers that you're insignificant, a deep disappointment to your family, to yourself, and potentially to humanity. This troll is awakened when Saturn transits Pluto. Will you let yourself be successful, or will you let others tear you down because you don't believe you deserve your success?

TRANSITING SATURN IN ASPECT TO THE NATAL NORTH NODE

We're taught that transits of Saturn deny us whatever we want as a kind of character-building exercise. Sometimes that happens. But sometimes, usually after we have struggled and worked and sacrificed for a very long time, Saturn transits bring us something very precious. Especially Saturn's transits of the Moon's North Node.

The North Node represents a sort of brass ring that, if you reach for it, delivers profound happiness. Saturn's transits to your North Node can bring truly life-changing success. Sometimes you succeed in a way that you have envisioned, down to the last, most unlikely details; sometimes the success comes in a form you never could have imagined but makes perfect sense in hindsight. However, if you've been working all along toward the things that make your heart sing, this is a transit that will open doors for you. All you have to do is walk through them.

TRANSITING SATURN IN ASPECT TO THE NATAL ASCENDANT

The Ascendant symbolizes the threshold between you and the rest of the world. It's the body that defines you as an individual, with your own appearance and name. It's the style and personality you put together to impress others, set yourself apart, and cope with what the world throws at you. It's even your literal threshold, the front door to your house and what you see when you first walk outside.

When Saturn aspects the natal Ascendant, a significant adjustment is made to your threshold. You might move to a new house, change your appearance or your name, or adopt a new style; all of these will generally be of the nature of Saturn: serious, classic, mature.

There may be loss, or a feeling of mortality. The Saturn-ruled parts of the body (i.e., joints, bones, teeth) may suffer. When Saturn comes to your door, he's not peddling magazines or religion. He's reminding you in every way he can that none of us lives forever, and that it's up to you to create the environment you want for yourself while you're here.

TRANSITING SATURN IN ASPECT TO THE NATAL MIDHEAVEN

As transiting Saturn makes an aspect to the Midheaven, it may seem that the earthly goals you set for yourself are out of reach or not bringing you as much happiness as you'd hoped. You might find yourself at a moment when the people you thought were your closest friends seem to be turning away from you. You may feel tired and fed up, frustrated, and constrained by obligations. Everyone has limits, and you may very well feel that you've reached yours.

But by the end of this transit, you'll realize that what's important in your life is still alive and well. You have learned what doesn't work for you. You're learning that the more you respect yourself, the more you will attract people who also respect you. Real success in life doesn't depend on what you do, but how you do it—with dignity, honor, self-respect, enthusiasm, and respect for others.

chapter **5**

TRANSITS OF URANUS:
THE SHOOTING STAR

Planetary Dossier: URANUS

TIME TO MAKE A FULL CYCLE AROUND THE SUN: 84 years

TIME SPENT IN EACH ZODIAC SIGN: about 7 years

TRANSITING ASPECTS LAST FOR: approximately 3 months

STRONGEST SIGNS: Aquarius, possibly Scorpio

HAS TO WORK HARDER IN: Leo, possibly Taurus

KEYWORDS: awakening, invention, originality, science, the future, electricity, revolution, rebellion, unexpected events, natural disasters

One day, you're a plain, awkward, middle-aged woman living a quiet and slightly lonely life in a small village. Precisely one day later, your extraordinary singing voice has made you an overnight sensation. Suddenly you are adored by millions—not only for your lovely voice, but also for your unpolished charm and unpretentious spunk. But now, the pressure is on. Will you be just a flash in the pan, a novelty act . . . or can you build an actual career, with real staying power?

It's the stuff of fairy tales, but it actually happened to vocalist Susan Boyle. Just before her forty-eighth birthday, Boyle stepped onto the stage as a contestant on *Britain's Got Talent*. Taking in her dowdy frock, frizzy hair, and makeup-free face, the judges and audience tittered as Boyle shared her dream of becoming a Broadway star. Then she opened her mouth and began to sing, and no one was laughing. By the time she sang the third line of her song, the audience was cheering. When she finished, there wasn't a dry eye in the house.

In just under three minutes, one unassuming but spunky Scotswoman had broken through the world's cynicism, capturing attention, awakening hearts, and offering inspiration.

On the night the program aired, transiting Uranus, the planet of surprise and change, was making a square aspect to Boyle's natal Ascendant, the point of the chart that symbolizes physical appearance and personality. However lovely her singing voice, the impact of Boyle's performance would not have been the same had she been more elegantly groomed or more conventionally attractive. It was the contrast between her magical voice and the audience's expectations, based on her appearance, that stunned the crowd. Someone who looked like Susan Boyle was not supposed to be talented; she was supposed to be ignored.

Transiting Uranus did not make Susan Boyle a star. Without natural talent that had been refined over years of practice, she would have performed without distinction, earned more ridicule, and never been heard from again. What transiting Uranus did was signal a moment, an opportunity, for the whole weird, wonderful Susan Boyle package to break through and surprise the world.

Astrologers usually say that transits of Uranus bring change and unexpected events. That's not untrue, and it would be disingenuous of me to suggest that every Uranus transit is positive. Even positive change comes with complications. It isn't always easy to deal with being noticed, because there is a fine line between being recognized as unique and feeling like a misfit. When Uranus comes along, you may feel lonely. You may feel weird. Within months of her television debut, Susan Boyle was hospitalized for emotional stress. It was an extreme consequence of a Uranus transit—but then, hers was a dramatic Uranus transit!

Uranus transits can have a dark side. But they also nearly always offer the opportunity to break out of your shell, live a different kind of life, and reinvent yourself.

THE NATURE OF THE BEAST

Early astrologers relied on a simple and elegant system comprising the visible planets, the Sun, and the Moon. Saturn represented the "city limits" of our solar system, and so it came to symbolize boundaries of all kinds and even death.

Then, in 1781, this elegant system was set on its ear by the discovery of a new planet: Uranus.

Not only did Uranus crash a very exclusive party, but it didn't even try to fit in. Unlike a proper, respectable planet, Uranus orbits the Sun while lying on its side. There are at least three different ways to pronounce its name, a name which was decided on only after a couple of failed attempts to disrupt the tradition of naming the planets for mythological figures.

In these simple facts about the planet Uranus, we see several key facets of its astrological symbolism:

- Uranus is associated with breaking the rules and disrupting the established order.
- Uranus is associated with people who don't fit in.
- Uranus represents tension between tradition and innovation.

In your birth chart, Uranus symbolizes how you are different, innovative, and perhaps a bit rebellious; how well you fit in, or don't; and how well you coexist with tradition and rules. By transit, Uranus generally indicates that you are being asked to change, innovate, or consider whether to fit in.

But that sounds dry, and it's inadequate. "Being asked to change" sounds as though the universe has sent you an invitation to an unexpected but generally agreeable soirée. The reality is that Uranus's disruptions can indeed be extremely exciting and welcome, depending on your disposition and the nature of the disruption. But very often, Uranian transits are a volatile mixture of exhilarating excitement and unsettling disorientation. They are the reminder that you are not static; you are not a statue. You might have forgotten that, imagining yourself as just one, unchanging thing. Uranus is here to wake you up and remind you that all things change, and so can you.

USING URANUS'S CYCLE

Uranus's transits require a willingness to reinvent yourself at the expense of your security and comfort. The seasons of its eighty-four-year cycle describe the process of that reinvention.

The Uranus cycle can be divided into four segments of about twenty-one years each. Each of these segments represents an important phase of the cycle—initiation, cultivation, review, and adjustment. It is a story of dissatisfaction with the status quo. It is a story about learning to celebrate the untamed, eccentric, one-of-a-kind you.

On the day you were born, and on the day any important event happened in your life, Uranus occupied a specific degree of a particular sign. About every eighty-four years, Uranus returns to that degree of the same sign, called the Uranus return.

In the tarot, the Tower card—which many associate with Uranus—shows a castle turret being struck by lightning. That's as good a metaphor as any for the beginning of a Uranus cycle. Your world is suddenly turned upside down. The circumstance that capsizes you may be a natural disaster or car accident, an exciting new romantic interest, sudden fame, or a midlife crisis. Whatever the nature of the event that strikes your tower, the requirement is the same: that you improvise, innovate, and adapt to your new reality.

THE FIRST URANUS SQUARE

Age 21

At twenty-one, we all experience the first square from transiting Uranus to our natal Uranus position, and most of us go a little bit nuts. We cut our hair in some extreme way, move far from home, get involved with bad relationships and sketchy behavior. There is often the unsettling feeling of no longer knowing who you are or what you want from life.

But there is a positive impulse at work here too: the desire to throw off the rules and constraints with which you were raised and claim a life that is uniquely yours. Everything seems possible, past restrictions are thrown away with both hands, and if you wish to, you can create a life that's absolutely different from the one you inherited from your parents.

THE URANUS OPPOSITION

Age 42

When you experience transiting Uranus's opposition to its natal position, you'll be about forty-two years old—truly middle-aged. The need for rebellion is still strong, but the pressures to act out or the ways of doing so are usually pretty different. Oh, people who've walked the straight and narrow for twenty years might cut loose and perform the sad little midlife crisis drama—ditch the older partner for the younger one, get a red sports car, whatever. But most of us have a quieter sort of awakening. One that says, "Yikes, I really am not getting any younger, am I?"

I had my Uranus opposition when I was a forty-two-year-old college junior at a state university. I spent my days sitting in lecture halls with people who were having their Uranus squares. It was the perfect setting for a midlife crisis, actually, because Uranus transits call for an examination of the ways we don't fit in, and I certainly didn't fit in there. But unlike at the Uranus square of age twenty-one, at the opposition you know who you are. You just don't know whether you *want* to be that person anymore.

THE SECOND URANUS SQUARE

Age 63

When you're about sixty-three, transiting Uranus makes one last square to your natal Uranus position. Traditionally, this was the age when most people began their transition into retirement. Today, many people are choosing to remain in the workforce well into their sixties and even seventies, for financial reasons or simply because they still feel they have plenty of energy and wisdom to contribute.

If you do transition out of the workforce at this age, the new freedom may be disconcerting. Living life without your usual schedule, rules, and social infrastructure is a huge adjustment. However confining your life may have been, the freedom to spend your days in any way you choose can be overwhelming at first. Since Uranus is also associated with social networks, it can be helpful to cultivate at least one or two group-centered activities to help keep you connected and involved.

THE URANUS RETURN

Age 84

Uranus returns to its position in your natal chart only once in your lifetime, when you're at age eighty-four. It's only recently that an upward trend in longevity has made it more common for individuals to experience a Uranus return. If you are lucky enough to reach your Uranus return, it can be a time when you reinvent yourself one last time, particularly if you enjoy reasonable health and financial security. This time, the urge for freedom manifests itself as a rejection of societal preconceptions about old age. It may be necessary to fight for your independence and freedom to live on your own, or at least on your own terms.

TRANSITING URANUS BY SIGN

Uranus urges change and liberation from the constraints that make life dull. Its transits through the twelve signs of the zodiac prescribe the avenues through which all of us, simultaneously, seek more liberty, autonomy, and opportunity for innovation. The extent to which this affects you directly will depend on planets you may have in each sign, and the house of your chart through which Uranus is transiting (see part III).

The years of Uranus's most recent and next transits through each sign are given. These include retrograde periods when Uranus might back into a previous sign for a short time.

TRANSITING URANUS IN ARIES (1927–1934; 2010–2018) ♈

Aries has a can-do spirit and the ability to survive in the face of societal upheaval and even revolution. However, it can be an excessively self-absorbed and aggressive sign. I'm writing this during Uranus's transit through Aries, and what is striking is a certain wild-west spirit and a regrettable emphasis on the primacy of the individual. "Me first," and in fact "me only," is the spirit of the times.

Upheaval for: Aries, Cancer, Libra, Capricorn

Awakenings for: Leo, Sagittarius

Unexpected opportunities for: Gemini, Aquarius

TRANSITING URANUS IN TAURUS (1934–1941; 2018–2025) ♉

In the 1930s, Uranus's transit of Taurus, a sign closely associated with money, was reflected in the Great Depression, a devastating disruption of economic and societal stability. Some argue, however, that this kind of disruption can be necessary when too many resources have been concentrated in too few hands. The consequences of Uranus transiting Taurus can be the dispersal of wealth and property more equally through society, as was the case in the United States following World War II.

Upheaval for: Taurus, Leo, Scorpio, Aquarius

Awakenings for: Virgo, Capricorn

Unexpected opportunities for: Cancer, Pisces

TRANSITING URANUS IN GEMINI (1941–1948; 2025–2032) ♊

Previous transits of Uranus in Gemini have seen revolutionary advances in technology and transportation, both ruled by this sign. Gemini also rules communities and neighborhoods, and in the postwar United States, the emergence of suburbs created an automobile culture, disrupted existing communities, and led to a more isolated and fragmented society. Gemini is one of the signs associated with the mind, and radical ideologies can prosper while Uranus transits here.

Upheaval for: Gemini, Virgo, Sagittarius, Pisces

Awakenings for: Libra, Aquarius

Unexpected opportunities for: Leo, Aries

TRANSITING URANUS IN CANCER (1948–1956; 2032–2040) ♋

While Uranus is in Cancer, families, food, and nationalism all begin to change shape. Technology affects the way we nourish ourselves; caretakers are liberated by innovations that make their daily tasks easier.

During the most recent transit of Uranus in Cancer in the late 1940s to mid-1950s, a radical reconfiguration of the traditional family unit was under way. Birth control offered women reproductive control and helped open the door to new opportunities outside the home. The flight to the suburbs and the decrease in multigenerational households changed the way we thought about family and community.

Upheaval for: Cancer, Libra, Capricorn, Aries

Awakenings for: Scorpio, Pisces

Unexpected opportunities for: Virgo, Taurus

TRANSITING URANUS IN LEO (1955–1962; 2039–2046) ♌

Uranus in Leo is characterized by shocking upheavals in popular culture, unorthodox attitudes toward parenting and young people, and the rebellious embrace of individualism and self-expression. Uranus's most recent transit through Leo introduced the beatniks and the beginning of an artistic revolution. Though mainstream culture was still listening to crooners from the Big Band era, a rich subculture of shaggy poets and aggressively nonglamorous musicians, movie stars, and writers was blossoming. Dr. Benjamin Spock's then-controversial views on child-rearing were adopted by parents wishing to prepare their children to be stronger individuals.

Upheaval for: Leo, Scorpio, Aquarius, Taurus

Awakenings for: Sagittarius, Aries

Unexpected opportunities for: Libra, Gemini

TRANSITING URANUS IN VIRGO (1961–1969; 2045–2052) ♍

Uranus transiting the sign of work, health, and service introduces dramatic adjustments in the workplace and the technology of everyday life. Uranus was transiting Virgo during the 1960s, one of the most tumultuous recent periods in U.S. history. The civil rights movement disrupted political agendas and created the most profound schism between North and South since the Civil War. Meanwhile, technology became part of daily life, the workforce was shaken up by the entry of more women and minorities, and it was becoming evident that mechanization was going to eventually liberate—or more frighteningly, displace—many workers.

Upheaval for: Virgo, Sagittarius, Pisces, Gemini

Awakenings for: Capricorn, Taurus

Unexpected opportunities for: Scorpio, Cancer

TRANSITING URANUS IN LIBRA (1968–1975; 2051–2059) ♎

The last transit of Uranus in Libra, the sign of relationships and of balance, coincided with the sexual revolution and the rise of the women's liberation movement. Widely available birth control and the Supreme Court decision in *Roe vs. Wade* that legalized abortion transformed sexual relationships; women could now explore sexual freedom with far less likelihood of unwanted pregnancy. In 1972, the Equal Rights Amendment cleared both houses of Congress and, while it failed to receive ratification from enough states, demonstrated that the balance of power had shifted away from male dominance and closer to equality. The divorce rate rose dramatically, and women entered the workforce in record numbers.

Upheaval for: Libra, Capricorn, Aries, Cancer

Awakenings for: Aquarius, Gemini

Unexpected opportunities for: Sagittarius, Leo

TRANSITING URANUS IN SCORPIO (1974–1981; 2058–2065) ♏

Uranus calls for liberation, and Scorpio knows where all the taboos are hidden; it's no wonder this transit brings all manner of skeletons spilling out of society's various closets. Scorpio rules sexual intimacy, and Uranus's most recent transit of Scorpio began when sexual liberation was at its peak. The transit closed with an epidemic of a deadly sexually transmitted disease, AIDS, which disproportionately affected gay men. Many were shocked when actor Rock Hudson died from AIDS, and his death led to mainstream discussions about the epidemic and gay culture.

Uranus's transit of Scorpio was also a time widely regarded as a golden age of cinema, with gritty dramas confronting the horror of Vietnam and the effects on those who fought there, and a spectacular assortment of stories set in space, exploring the possibility of extraterrestrial life. In New York, a nascent punk rock movement, shocking and ugly to mainstream audiences, would explode at the end of the 1970s.

Upheaval for: Scorpio, Aquarius, Taurus, Leo

Awakenings for: Pisces, Cancer

Unexpected opportunities for: Capricorn, Virgo

TRANSITING URANUS IN SAGITTARIUS (1981–1988; 2065–2072)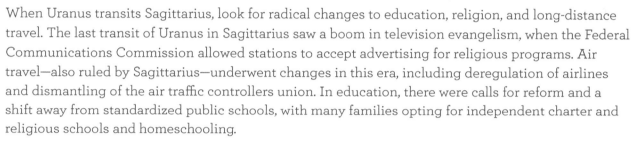

When Uranus transits Sagittarius, look for radical changes to education, religion, and long-distance travel. The last transit of Uranus in Sagittarius saw a boom in television evangelism, when the Federal Communications Commission allowed stations to accept advertising for religious programs. Air travel—also ruled by Sagittarius—underwent changes in this era, including deregulation of airlines and dismantling of the air traffic controllers union. In education, there were calls for reform and a shift away from standardized public schools, with many families opting for independent charter and religious schools and homeschooling.

Upheaval for: Sagittarius, Pisces, Gemini, Virgo

Awakenings for: Aries, Leo

Unexpected opportunities for: Aquarius, Libra

TRANSITING URANUS IN CAPRICORN (1904–1912; 1988–1995; 2072–2079)

When Uranus transits Capricorn, the world changes in measurable ways with long-reaching consequences. Say good-bye to the established order as governments and other institutions are set on their ears. The most recent transit of Uranus through Capricorn, the sign of the establishment, saw the fall of the Berlin Wall and the end of the Cold War; the Black Friday stock market crash; the first fully televised military conflict (the first U.S. invasion of Iraq); racial unrest and riots in Los Angeles after police officers were acquitted of brutalizing Rodney King; the release of Nelson Mandela from prison and the end of South African apartheid; the Oklahoma City bombing; and the revolts in Tiananmen Square. The previous transit of Uranus in Capricorn gave birth to popular film, revealed Einstein's theory of relativity, saw San Francisco leveled in an epic earthquake and fire, welcomed Ford's Model T, and brought down the "unsinkable" Titanic.

Upheaval for: Capricorn, Aries, Cancer, Libra

Awakenings for: Taurus, Virgo

Unexpected opportunities for: Pisces, Scorpio

TRANSITING URANUS IN AQUARIUS (1995–2003; 2079–2087) ♒

Uranus is considered particularly strong in Aquarius, so these tend to be years of great technological advances and revolutionary ideas. Emerging technologies, such as the Internet, to use an example from the most recent transit of Uranus through Aquarius, connect the entire world, both for good and for ill. The world becomes smaller, access to information is more democratic, and social and business connections become possible among people who are separated by great physical and even ideological distances.

But these are also transits that accentuate disruption, such as war and pandemics. Radical political movements flourish, and intractable ideologies are reinforced. Rather than understanding each other better, some people become more stubbornly entrenched in their own worldview.

Upheaval for: Aquarius, Taurus, Leo, Scorpio

Awakenings for: Gemini, Libra

Unexpected opportunities for: Aries, Sagittarius

TRANSITING URANUS IN PISCES (2003–2010; 2087–2095) ♓

Innovative breakthroughs in genetics and physics, but also an emergence of racism, fascism, and radical religious movements are likely with Uranus in Pisces. Pisces is related to disease, and widespread outbreaks of infectious disease may occur (as with the 2009 flu pandemic) or lead to dramatic changes in society (the end and immediate aftermath of the 1918 Spanish flu pandemic).

Pisces is the sign of faith, of the things we believe even in the absence of evidence. During the most recent transit of Uranus in Pisces, logic and science were often disregarded in favor of creating one's own reality. Diseases that had been eradicated reemerged as parents declined to vaccinate their children.

Pisces rules minorities, and during the most recent transit of Uranus in Pisces, many U.S. states legalized marriage between same-sex couples, and the country elected its first African-American president.

Upheaval for: Pisces, Gemini, Virgo, Sagittarius

Awakenings for: Cancer, Scorpio

Unexpected opportunities for: Taurus, Capricorn

TRANSITING URANUS IN ASPECT TO NATAL PLANETS AND ANGLES

Uranus moves at a rate of a little less than 1 degree of the zodiac per month. Its transits are generally experienced most strongly for about three months: one month in advance of the exact aspect, the month it is exact, and the month after the aspect is exact.

However, Uranus is retrograde for half of each year. It is very likely that if transiting Uranus forms an aspect to a natal planet or angle, it will repeat that aspect several times: once when direct, then again when retrograde, and a third time when it has moved direct again. You may very likely experience a transiting Uranus aspect for up to one full year.

Uranus's conjunction, square, opposition, and quincunx aspects to natal planets can suggest rebelliousness, dramatic disruptions, sudden endings to career or relationships, and instability. The same can happen under Uranus's transiting trines and sextiles, but these can also bring a feeling that you are getting an exciting fresh start.

TRANSITING URANUS IN ASPECT TO THE NATAL SUN

The Sun and Uranus serve completely different and mutually antagonistic functions: The Sun symbolizes a strong and healthy ego, and Uranus transits usually demand that you reinvent yourself to some degree. It can certainly be liberating to open yourself up to new ways of being, but it can also be disorienting.

Much depends on the relationship between the Sun and Uranus in your birth chart. If they are in good aspect or even just in the same sign, you may actually enjoy these transits, feeling revitalized and able to function well in environments that have previously made you uncomfortable. In poor aspect to each other, they can trigger a chronic struggle between nurturing your sense of personal identity and avoiding becoming too inflexible and missing exciting opportunities.

TRANSITING URANUS IN ASPECT TO THE NATAL MOON

You will probably feel itchy about where you live and your deepest relationships during this transit. You may be in situations that make you feel insecure and emotionally unsafe, or that you don't have enough privacy. Your normal patterns of connecting with others no longer work for you. You may move to a new place under these transits—and if you don't or can't, you at least want to, and will often spend extra time away from home or try to significantly alter your home.

If the Moon has many challenging aspects to any other planets in the birth chart, and in particular to Uranus, your sense of safety and security is constantly under threat. The pressure of a Uranus transit to the Moon gives you the opportunity to free yourself from these often unconscious patterns and motivate you to develop more inner security independent of external circumstances. It isn't necessarily an easy path, but in the long run it can be an extremely liberating one.

TRANSITING URANUS IN ASPECT TO NATAL MERCURY

When transiting Uranus aspects natal Mercury, you may feel it's hard to get people to listen. It may be hard to speak out because you feel different from the people around you, or you may be living in a new area where you don't know your neighbors. But these transits can also augur periods in your life when your words have tremendous impact on others and you have many opportunities to make yourself heard.

John F. Kennedy, born with Mercury square Uranus, was considered one of the most inspiring orators who ever served as president of the United States. One of his famous speeches was delivered on the occasion of his inauguration, when he memorably urged, "Ask not what your country can do for you. Ask what you can do for your country." On the day of the inauguration, transiting Uranus was 4 degrees from an exact square to his natal Mercury.

TRANSITING URANUS IN ASPECT TO NATAL VENUS

Venus is the planet of relationships and money, but more generally it's the planet of *want* (versus *need*, represented by the Moon). When transiting Uranus connects with natal Venus, you may find that you have or are motivated to achieve more financial freedom. Relationships that begin under this influence may be unconventional, surprising, or even shocking. Longtime relationships can suffer as both parties desire more freedom or, in extreme cases, to leave altogether. Close friendships may be disrupted, yet your popularity overall may reach a high point as you find acceptance among people with whom you feel you really belong.

Seeming to bring enhanced popularity (or in some cases, notoriety), this transit will likely bring the breakthrough you've been wishing for if you have been trying to get attention for your style or artistic talents.

TRANSITING URANUS IN ASPECT TO NATAL MARS

These transits awaken the impulse toward self-preservation. If you are reasonably safe and your basic needs are being met, this will be a transit that brings forth your competitive spirit. You may gain a promotion (or more) at work. Technological and interpersonal skills will have an important impact on the direction of your career.

Mars's symbolism is physical and sexual, and you may experience new feelings or transitions in these areas of your life. You may suddenly develop an interest in a particular sport, and your level of sexual awareness or activity may change. The combination of Uranus and Mars can also, in extreme situations, suggest accidents, as changes in your usual patterns meet increased impulsiveness and recklessness.

TRANSITING URANUS IN ASPECT TO NATAL JUPITER

Jupiter is the planet of wide-open spaces, both of place and of mind. Transiting Uranus in aspect to Jupiter awakens your desire to make your life larger, to expand your perspective, and to seek meaning. During these transits, you may appear to others to be rash and impulsive; usually it's closer to the truth to say that you've been bored or confined for too long, and now that you have a chance to be free, you'll waste no time in taking it.

You may travel during these transits, particularly if you're the kind of person who normally likes staying close to home. You may decide to pursue a degree or certification, or you could have a religious experience that involves either suddenly converting to another religion or leaving a church. All are ways of making yourself more free by breaking down self-imposed limitations.

TRANSITING URANUS IN ASPECT TO NATAL SATURN

Imagine that you have spent half your life in prison, then suddenly someone shows up with a key and a pardon from the governor and sets you free.

Transits of Uranus to Saturn can be among the most exhilarating you'll experience. Saturn represents your deepest insecurities and fear of failure, and Uranus transits give you a chance to see what life would be like without them. For the duration of the transit, you get to feel truly free from the bondage, often self-imposed, that has made you feel like a prisoner in your own life.

If you have done the work Saturn asked of you, such as pursuing worthwhile career goals or other ambitions and being reputable and responsible in your dealings, then transits of Uranus leave you free to move on to the next level in your life. Even if you eventually lose some of the sense of freedom when this transit is finished, your eyes will have been opened. Now you know that you are the one who holds the key to your own prison door.

TRANSITING URANUS IN ASPECT TO NATAL URANUS

These transits are milestones in your evolving, lifelong journey with Uranus. Look for events, people, and circumstances that awaken your rebelliousness, unconventionality, and desire for freedom. (See "Using Uranus's Cycle" on page 68 for more.)

You have reached an important point in Uranus's cycle of individuation. The trines and sextiles support your desire to break away from conformity and explore new avenues; the squares and opposition represent moments when, through conflict, you see another point of view that can encourage greater personal freedom.

TRANSITING URANUS IN ASPECT TO NATAL NEPTUNE

If you are a musician, artist, dancer, mystic, or spiritual seeker, this could well be a transit that catapults you into the limelight. It can also be a time of unexpected loss or surprising spiritual awakening. During the sextile from transiting Uranus to my natal Neptune, I returned to musical performance after a long hiatus, started my professional astrology career, and found I had a completely unexpected psychic talent.

Neptune also symbolizes the desire to retreat from life's difficulties, often through potentially damaging escapes such as alcohol and drugs. Uranus's transits to Neptune can launch you on such a hazardous journey but can also awaken you to the destructive nature of denial. This can be the addict's "hitting rock bottom" transit. Uranus is the liberating planet, and if you wish to free yourself from self-destructive behavior or relationships, Uranus's transits to Neptune can be extremely helpful.

TRANSITING URANUS IN ASPECT TO NATAL PLUTO

These are transits during which you may rebel in ways that have very serious permanent consequences. You absolutely refuse to submit to others' control; sometimes it is an obsession (an intense relationship, perhaps an addiction) that becomes the vehicle for liberating yourself. If you have had a very difficult time facing the darker side of your character, this transit will probably change that. Self-awareness becomes the key to breaking free from self-defeating behaviors and situations.

Groups of friends, professional networks, or societies and clubs related to your interests, especially those associated with metaphysics, technology, or science, can awaken insecurities, jealousies, and battles for control and power. You will become aware of the extent to which these difficult emotions are holding you back from making the sorts of beneficial connections that will help you succeed in the future.

TRANSITING URANUS IN ASPECT TO THE NATAL NORTH NODE

You have a dream. Some days, it feels truly unreachable. You take tentative steps toward it, but something stops you, or there are disappointments, or you end up stopping yourself just short of your destination.

The Moon's North Node represents the dream, the brass ring that seems to perpetually elude your reach. When transiting Uranus makes an aspect to the natal North Node, you reach out again, hopeful that this will be the time that the dream comes true. And surprisingly often, it will.

That's because Uranus is a rule breaker and refuses to agree with your internalized beliefs about why achieving your dreams simply isn't possible. You may not realize the entire dream in precisely the way that you'd imagined you would. Sometimes you simply grab something else that's wonderful, that you never went looking for but that presented itself nonetheless. But reaching for the dream means you're getting closer to it. And when you eventually get there, Uranus will be cheering you on.

TRANSITING URANUS IN ASPECT TO THE NATAL ASCENDANT

A few of my dearest friends have been older ladies who were unapologetically blunt and a little bit eccentric. In your eighties and nineties, you can get away with saying things no one else would dare. You're free to blurt out the embarrassing things everyone is thinking but no one will say.

That's how I see Uranus's transits to the Ascendant. The Ascendant symbolizes your personality, the socially sanctioned mask that you wear; Uranus liberates you from your inhibitions and lets you drop the mask. But this comes with a caveat: To be more yourself, you have to be willing to sacrifice your comfort. It feels good to hide behind a mask when you walk into a party where you don't know many people. You can pretend to be whatever you want to be, and no one's the wiser. But once Uranus opens up the bottle and the real you spills out, there's no putting it back.

Transiting Uranus is freeing. You get to be the feisty, opinionated senior who tells it like it is because really, who does she need to impress? But being yourself is like a high-wire trapeze act; it takes a lot of courage to work without a net.

TRANSITING URANUS IN ASPECT TO THE NATAL MIDHEAVEN

Transiting aspects to the Midheaven simultaneously aspect the IC, or fourth house cusp. Uranus's transits to this axis symbolize opportunities to advance in your career, pursue a calling at odds with what might be expected of you, or adjust your life in such a way that your career is better in sync with your family life, or simply with the demands of your heart.

Rebelling against your history and moving in the direction of a bright, new future is the promise of transiting Uranus in aspect to the Midheaven. This could be a transit that moves you away from the family business and into a business of your own, or into retirement. You might move or make major changes to your home. It could be a time of difficulty with or for your parents. Overall, these transits generally place you at odds with the people who have previously been, or considered themselves, authorities over your life.

chapter 6

TRANSITS OF NEPTUNE:
THE TIDE

In 1976, twenty-eight-year-old Steven Georgiou nearly drowned off the coast of Malibu, California. As he struggled for his life, he recalls shouting, "Oh God! If you save me, I will work for you."

Three years later, on November 22, 1979, Steven Georgiou performed his final concert under his stage name, Cat Stevens. Georgiou had converted to Islam the previous year, adopting the name Yusuf Islam, and decided to leave behind a thirteen-year career as a highly successful folk singer/songwriter. He would spend the next twenty-seven years devoting his time (and royalties from his recordings) to philanthropic and educational causes.

The story of Cat Stevens's dramatic transformation from pop idol to Yusuf Islam spanned the three-year period when transiting Neptune was approaching a conjunction with his natal Jupiter. Neptune is the planet that baptizes us into a spiritual view of the world, and when the planets of spiritual purpose (Neptune) and religious dogma (Jupiter) converge, it's not surprising to have a profound religious experience. However, the baptism and religious conversion are seldom quite so literal!

Some Neptune transits can be as subtle as a slow leak from a punctured tire. Perhaps you find it a bit hard to concentrate; your energy and motivation are low. Other Neptune transits can act like a tsunami, washing away all remnants of your former life and carrying you out to sea. Your Neptune transits may not be quite as dramatic as Cat Stevens's, but they will, in some way, wipe clean the slate of your life.

THE NATURE OF THE BEAST

Transits of Neptune are like a trip to the beach. You've set up your beach chair and umbrella, your radio, book, and snacks just the way you want them. Then the tide comes in, washing all manner of lovely and unexpected treasures onto the sand: sea glass and bottles and license plates from faraway states you haven't visited. But when the tide goes out, it takes some things with it, such as your beach towel, your iPod, or your car keys.

Neptune tells us, "Look: Life brings us gifts, glittering treasures with beauty we never could have imagined. But it takes things from us, too. That's the way of the sea. That's the way of life."

During Neptune's transits, things are coming in, and many of them will go right back out. "Don't get attached" is Neptune's lesson—that and learning to sift through the sand after the tide goes out, to see what small, glittering jewels might have been left behind.

In the midst of a Neptune transit, the temptation to escape can be strong. Eating or drinking too much, watching hours of TV, even reading compulsively can all be ways of avoiding reality. You may feel confused and fuzzy-headed, and your physical energy may be low. Astrologer Caroline Casey likes to compare Neptune transits to the familiar experience of walking into a room and realizing you have no idea what you came for!

While transiting Neptune makes aspects to your natal planets, you're likely to experience a lack of focus and attention. Forgetfulness can be a sign that Neptune is begging for an end to denial and a celebration of the spiritual values that bring meaning to your life.

USING NEPTUNE'S CYCLE

Because Neptune takes an incredibly long time to make a complete tour of the zodiac, you won't experience its full cycle in your lifetime. You can, however, reasonably expect to experience four major aspects between transiting Neptune to your natal Neptune.

Neptune's cycle is characterized by evolving spiritual awareness. The catalysts for this vary, but they may be related to loss, illness, or emotional suffering. Neptune's transits are often associated with fogginess, implying you'll simply sleepwalk through these transits. Certainly the way forward may not be clear, but perhaps that's because Neptune is calling you to walk an unfamiliar path—one that is not straight and unambiguous, but that nevertheless leads to a place you need to visit.

THE NEPTUNE SEXTILE

Age 27

The transiting Neptune sextile to natal Neptune happens around age twenty-seven, just a year or two before Saturn's return. The sextile is an opportunity aspect; this is an age when you may choose to accept or reject invitations that lead to a clearer understanding of yourself, the world, and your place in it. The urge to hide from reality has ended in tragedy for more than one twenty-seven-year-old (for example, Jim Morrison, Janis Joplin, and Jimi Hendrix, all of whom died of drug overdoses). To navigate this transit successfully, take the opportunity to retreat from the pressure of daily life. The strain of the impending Saturn return (age twenty-nine), however, can make it difficult to step off the merry-go-round and give yourself some quiet time.

THE NEPTUNE SQUARE

Age 42

This is one of the major transiting aspects that converge around the ages of forty-one and forty-two, which astrologers call the "midlife crisis" aspects. Calling for a rather painful reexamination of beliefs that you've held sacred, this transit calls faith into question. Disillusionment with a relationship, a mentor or spiritual leader, or your career is likely. It can be a disorienting transit, but it is healthy to examine beliefs in light of new information or life experiences.

THE NEPTUNE TRINE TO NATAL NEPTUNE

Age 55

The trine does not force a crisis of faith, but you may find yourself having to make peace with your accomplishments so far and let go of dreams that didn't come true. The intense quest for worldly achievement that dominated your thirties and forties is beginning to lose its fascination. Giving something back to your profession and your community begins to seem more important than buying a second home or a new car. You feel that it's time to put your life into a spiritual context, and this can be a time of exploring religion, philosophy, or metaphysics. Art, meditation, and travel can help connect you with a feeling of being part of something greater and more lasting.

THE NEPTUNE OPPOSITION

About age 82

If you've navigated the previous transiting Neptune aspects gracefully and consciously, you'll have summited your personal spiritual mountain. Your wisdom and perspective are at their peak; you inspire those who are younger and less sure of themselves. But there are still lessons to learn from Neptune, and this can be an age when physical and mental challenges begin to play a larger role in your daily life. Acceptance of diminishing physical and mental vitality leads to an appreciation of the spirit, which grows stronger as other faculties weaken.

TRANSITING NEPTUNE BY SIGN

What will save the world? What sort of music and art is inspiring? How can we feel less alone? Neptune's approximately fourteen-year passage through each sign refers to what we might call each generation's "prevailing dream"—as well as its potential for delusion.

The years of Neptune's most recent and next transits through each sign are given. These include retrograde periods when Neptune might back into a previous sign for a short time.

TRANSITING NEPTUNE IN ARIES (1861–1875; 2025–2039) ♈

The dream of Neptune in Aries is that an individual, or perhaps a nation, can save the world. But with so much emphasis on the individual, territorialism can damage humanity's innate tendency toward building societies and working together. Deluded thinking lacking balance and insight is typical of Neptune in Aries, leaving some reaching for weapons to solve problems.

Disillusionment for: Aries, Cancer, Libra, Capricorn

Spiritual awakening for: Leo, Sagittarius

Spiritual questing for: Gemini, Aquarius

TRANSITING NEPTUNE IN TAURUS (1874–1889; 2038–2052) ♉

The dream is that wealth, luxury, art, and all the monetary rewards of the good life will lead to happiness and security. But these transits end up demonstrating the illusory nature of security and the societal instability that follows when socioeconomic classes become unbalanced.

Disillusionment for: Taurus, Leo, Scorpio, Aquarius

Spiritual awakening for: Virgo, Capricorn

Spiritual questing for: Cancer, Pisces

TRANSITING NEPTUNE IN GEMINI (1888–1902; 2051–2066) ♊

The dream of Neptune in Gemini is that if we could all speak the same language and get from place to place easily, all of our problems would be solved. This was the dream of L.L. Zamenhof, the creator of Esperanto, who envisioned a universal language uniting the world. The first volume written in Esperanto was published during Neptune's last transit of Gemini. The disillusionment of these transits, however, is the awareness that language and physical distance are usually the least of the problems that separate us from one another.

Disillusionment for: Gemini, Virgo, Sagittarius, Pisces

Spiritual awakening for: Libra, Aquarius

Spiritual questing for: Leo, Aries

TRANSITING NEPTUNE IN CANCER (1901–1915; 2065–2079) ♋

The illusion of Neptune in Cancer is that family and country will keep us safe and give meaning to our lives. As World War I demonstrated during the last transit of Neptune in Cancer, however, safety is an illusion. A benefit of this transit, though, was the uniting force of the shared war experience, making some countries feel more like families.

Disillusionment for: Cancer, Libra, Capricorn, Aries

Spiritual awakening for: Scorpio, Pisces

Spiritual questing for: Virgo, Taurus

TRANSITING NEPTUNE IN LEO (1915–1929; 2078–2093) ♌

Neptune in Leo dreams of life as a nonstop party with glitter, glamour, free-flowing champagne, and continuous entertainment. This transit was a golden age of literature, and cinema brought the magic of flickering images into the mainstream. But as the world found with the market crash of 1929, eventually the party comes to an end—sometimes abruptly. The reality is that there is more to life than fun, glamour, and indulgence.

Disillusionment for: Leo, Scorpio, Aquarius, Taurus

Spiritual awakening for: Sagittarius, Aries

Spiritual questing for: Libra, Gemini

TRANSITING NEPTUNE IN VIRGO (1929–1943; 2092–2107) ♍

In this dream, anyone who works hard and practices thrift and self-reliance can make something of his life. But during Neptune's transit through Virgo during the Great Depression, the reality was that many couldn't find work and had nothing left to sacrifice—until many sacrificed their lives in World War II.

Disillusionment for: Virgo, Sagittarius, Pisces, Gemini

Spiritual awakening for: Capricorn, Taurus

Spiritual questing for: Scorpio, Cancer

TRANSITING NEPTUNE IN LIBRA (1943–1955; 2105–2120) ♎

Peace prevails, economic extremes are evened out, and good manners triumph over all. If we don't rock the boat, all will be well. But this polite, peaceful equality comes at the price of vigorous individualism and the suppression of unpleasant realities.

Disillusionment for: Libra, Capricorn, Aries, Cancer

Spiritual awakening for: Aquarius, Gemini

Spiritual questing for: Sagittarius, Leo

TRANSITING NEPTUNE IN SCORPIO (1956–1970; 2119–2134) ♏

The dream of Neptune in Scorpio is that the world will be a better place if we all just *get real*. If we speak openly and bluntly about sex, death, and anything else that's considered taboo, our secrets will cease to control us. But rob people of their sacred illusions without offering a replacement, and you end up with many bitter, cynical people.

Disillusionment for: Scorpio, Aquarius, Taurus, Leo

Spiritual awakening for: Pisces, Cancer

Spiritual questing for: Capricorn, Virgo

TRANSITING NEPTUNE IN SAGITTARIUS (1970–1984; 2134–2148) ♐

Dreams of unlimited possibilities and liberation for all characterized Neptune's transit through Sagittarius in the 1970s and early 1980s. It seemed the 1960s had truly introduced a new era of love, acceptance, and freedom. The transit ended in disillusionment about public leaders and the political process, and a terrible illness that brought the era of free love to a screeching halt.

Disillusionment for: Sagittarius, Pisces, Gemini, Virgo

Spiritual awakening for: Aries, Leo

Spiritual questing for: Aquarius, Libra

TRANSITING NEPTUNE IN CAPRICORN (1984–1998; 2148–2162) ♑

Neptune in Capricorn's dream was that money equals success, that "greed is good" (in the words of *Wall Street*'s Gordon Gecko, in one of the breakout films of this era), and that free trade and globalization will save the world. Disillusionment came with the 1987 stock market downturn and intensified as economic opportunities for the middle class began to dwindle.

Disillusionment for: Capricorn, Aries, Cancer, Libra

Spiritual awakening for: Taurus, Virgo

Spiritual questing for: Pisces, Scorpio

TRANSITING NEPTUNE IN AQUARIUS (1998–2012; 2161–2176) ♒

Neptune in Aquarius dreams that technology will save the world. Automation would free us from drudgery, everyone would telecommute, and computers and other technology would be the great equalizer, providing opportunity for all. But the most recent transit ended amid concerns about income inequality, massive unemployment, and technology endangering privacy.

Disillusionment for: Aquarius, Taurus, Leo, Scorpio

Spiritual awakening for: Gemini, Libra

Spiritual questing for: Aries, Sagittarius

TRANSITING NEPTUNE IN PISCES (2012–2025; 2175–2190) ♓

The dream of Neptune in Pisces is that the whole world is one, nations will come together in peace, and a cure is found for all of the world's ills. But this transit has been characterized by denial of inconvenient reality, increased xenophobia, and a culture that blames the disadvantaged for being a drain on society.

Disillusionment for: Pisces, Gemini, Virgo, Sagittarius

Spiritual awakening for: Cancer, Scorpio

Spiritual questing for: Taurus, Capricorn

TRANSITING NEPTUNE IN ASPECT TO NATAL PLANETS

You were boiling a pot of stew on the stove before you got a phone call. When you hang up the phone and turn back to your stew, you've got a sticky, charred mess on your hands. You may be tempted to trash the whole pot. Instead, fill it with water and walk away. A few hours later, all that mess will slide down the drain.

Neptune is as powerful as water, but it takes time to perform its magic. By transit, it travels only 2 degrees in an entire year. This means that a transiting Neptune aspect to a planet or angle in your birth chart goes on for a very long time—at least a couple of years.

We make messes as we go through life, messes of the heart, messes of the mind, messes at work, even our houses become messes. Periodically, we become overwhelmed by it all. We wonder how to clean the slate and start over.

Then Neptune comes along and reminds us: Just apply Neptune to the sticky mess. In a while, it will all slide down the drain.

Neptune's transits are generally experienced most strongly for about two years. Its conjunction, square, opposition, and quincunx aspects to natal planets and angles emphasize disillusionment, denial, confusion, certain kinds of illness, and difficulty handling daily affairs. All of this is possible under Neptune's transiting trines and sextiles, but these are also likely to bring spiritual awareness through religion, art, or service to others.

TRANSITING NEPTUNE IN ASPECT TO THE NATAL SUN

We all need someone we can look up to. When we're young, it's usually our parents. When we're older, we might look to those who have made great achievements in their professions, who are successful and glamorous, or who always seem to be ethical and kind. Somewhere out there, we imagine, is a savior.

When transiting Neptune aspects the natal Sun, especially by square or opposition aspect, you will discover that these people have feet of clay. We all do. Saints do not, as a general rule, walk the earth. Mistakes are made, sometimes in public. People will let you down—politicians, religious leaders, the guy you hired to rebuild your website. Even those who are generally kind and supportive are hiding an unattractive side, because they're only human.

It's fine to admire people, to be inspired by their talents and their uplifting messages. But as transiting Neptune aspects your Sun, you see that no one has all the answers. No one else can lead you to the promised land. Making something of your life and your world falls on your shoulders. You have to be your own hero and create your own dream.

TRANSITING NEPTUNE IN ASPECT TO THE NATAL MOON

We are creatures of habit. We have needs and cravings without examining them too closely. We perform little rituals that we hardly notice. We feel uncomfortable around some people without quite knowing why. All of these unconscious habits and instincts are represented in your chart by the Moon.

It's no wonder that the people closest to us are the ones who connect in some way with our lunar needs and habits. We project the Moon onto them so that we can see it, objectively, and wrestle with it.

When transiting Neptune makes an aspect to your natal Moon, especially when you're young, you are highly likely to meet someone who seems to embody all your longings, hopes, and dreams, someone whom you feel you absolutely cannot live without. It's an alluring idea that one person can be everything to another. It's as irresistible as falling into a feather bed at the end of a long, tiring day.

Of course, this enchanting creature is a fellow human. The day will come when reality will intervene. This is when Neptune's enchantment often gives way to disillusionment—but remember, Neptune also offers compassion as an option.

TRANSITING NEPTUNE IN ASPECT TO NATAL MERCURY

Neptune is like a sponge, and Mercury is a happy little gatherer of words, images, and experiences. Now, the music you listen to, the books you read, the movies you see will stay with you for a long time. So be careful about what you take in.

These transits can be troublesome for extremely rational, practical personalities. If your work requires sharp analysis and logic, you will be frustrated. But these transits also heighten intuition and make needed breakthroughs possible.

The urge is strong during these transits to make music, turn words into poetry, take evocative photographs, or paint something. Sometimes you'll process experiences logically, but sometimes you'll have to settle for a wild surmise. "What if?" is a perfectly reasonable question while Neptune transits your natal Mercury; answer it with a song, an image, a poem.

TRANSITING NEPTUNE IN ASPECT TO NATAL VENUS

Once, when transiting Neptune opposed my friend's natal Venus, she fell madly in love with a completely inappropriate man. So deeply ingrained were her misconceptions about her attractiveness and value that it took several romantically disastrous years for her to learn, once and for all, that she deserved better than a hopeless relationship with a man who was a mess.

Not all Neptune transits to Venus are that bad, but partnerships (ruled by Venus) often do take a beating. Usually it's because one of you entered the relationship with far too many illusions about what you needed or what was going on. Sometimes a relationship entered in good faith dissolves because one or both partners realize they've simply changed, irrevocably.

Typically your relationship with money will also come under review. When I had a trine from transiting Neptune to natal Venus, I let go of a source of income that had been a mainstay of my business for a decade. It was absolutely terrifying to give up what had been a sizable percentage of my earnings, but I found that by the end of the year, I had earned just as much as the year before. The idea that I couldn't afford to let go turned out to have been an illusion.

All Venus problems begin with a lack of faith in yourself. Neptune is determined to heal that. At the end of its transits to Venus, you'll know what you're worth, and you'll let go of what drains you and those who don't appreciate you.

TRANSITING NEPTUNE IN ASPECT TO NATAL MARS

Overall, Mars is a fairly self-serving planet. Think of him as your personal bodyguard, defending your physical and emotional safety, as well as your ego. When transiting Neptune makes an aspect to your natal Mars, it's as though someone has slipped him a mickey.

These can be good transits for putting your Mars skills to work for a good cause. You might devote a few years to volunteering for your favorite charity or coaching a sports team of underprivileged kids. These can be effective transits for bringing a spiritual, artistic, or gentling influence into your work or physical pursuits, such as practicing meditation or yoga, or getting involved in dance.

What these transits are not good for are any pursuits requiring strong drive or intense focus, or that mostly benefit just you. If you try to make great strides in your career during this transit, you'll likely meet with failure. It's better to dedicate your energy to pursuits that "give back" to your profession or that build a sense of community. If you decide to train for a sporting event that requires strength and stamina, you are likely to come up short in both areas. Instead, cultivate flexibility and know when to step back and take a break.

These don't have to be negative transits, but you have to approach them in the right spirit. Now is not the time for you to achieve spectacular individual goals. Instead, contribute to the betterment of your community, your society, and your planet.

TRANSITING NEPTUNE IN ASPECT TO NATAL JUPITER

There are more things in heaven and earth, Horatio,
Than are dreamt of in your philosophy.
—*Hamlet* (1.5.167–8), Hamlet to Horatio

Neptune and Jupiter have a lot in common. They are like two guys who run in the same circles and show up at a lot of the same meetings and parties, whose mutual friends say things like, "Oh, Jupiter, you must be great friends with Neptune!" A bit like astrologers and astronomers, in fact.

But there are fundamental differences between them that can make transits of Neptune to natal Jupiter anything from awkward to disastrous. Both planets are associated with beliefs, but Jupiter is a fan of theology and Neptune prefers faith. Jupiter's beliefs are usually based in doctrine, research, or philosophy; Neptune, like Hamlet, understands that there is more to the universe than can be explained by conventional methods.

During these transits, Neptune plays Hamlet, struggling to convince Horatio/Jupiter that life holds ineffable mysteries that science, academia, and religion can't explain. Neptune celebrates this—it makes life more confusing, but also more beautiful; but Jupiter is a fan of *knowing*, not simply believing.

During these transits, expect to doubt your beliefs and be forced to rely, instead, on faith. Doubt is brought by any number of experiences—failure, disillusionment, illness, grief, even visiting a different country for the first time and realizing how limited beliefs are when they're based on a narrow experience of the world.

TRANSITING NEPTUNE IN ASPECT TO NATAL SATURN

The dance between Saturn and Neptune is similar in tone to that moment in the movie *The Wizard of Oz* right after the cyclone ends, when Dorothy opens the front door of her house and the black-and-white imagery of her life in Kansas is magically transformed to lush color. Saturn sees things in black and white, and while that can be starkly beautiful, it can be monotonous, too. When you've overdosed on Saturn, it can be nice to have an injection of Neptune—a sort of organic hallucinogenic experience that makes everything prettier and more interesting for a while.

But the spiritual promise of Neptune is not about escape or inoculating yourself from everyday life. Rather, it's the promise that beauty can be seen in the starkest of landscapes. Grace can be mined from the dreariest and most mundane daily tasks.

Saturn's world of jobs, school, career success, reputation, and authority is so formidable that it constantly threatens Neptune's imaginative connection with the world of spirit. You can feel this imbalance building when you find yourself forgetting names, facts, and details; when you discover yourself growing absolutely enraged toward people who are helpless victims; when you lose your temper when a friend is late for your lunch date. The tyranny of time, schedules, and minutiae is the tyranny of Saturn. Neptune transits are designed to depose the tyrant and make your world a little lovelier.

TRANSITING NEPTUNE IN ASPECT TO NATAL URANUS

There's a reckless, rebellious, restless place inside you that astrologers associate with the planet Uranus. Even the mildest person has a bone to pick with some part of the status quo. That same rebellious side is related to the feeling you might have when you show up alone to a party, like a lonely misfit. Both are Uranian traits.

Neptune's transits to Uranus tend to be confusing and painful. There is a stronger-than-usual sense of the ways that you don't quite fit in with your peers. You don't want to lose the qualities that make you unique, but it hurts to feel like an outcast.

While Neptune transits this place in your chart, he invites you to stop struggling so hard to be one of a kind and instead go with the flow. Often Neptune offers something such as music, art, dance, spiritual questing, or (less positively) drugs and alcohol as a means to feeling less alone. The objective is to open yourself up to being a conduit for collective spiritual energy, but you have to choose your escapes wisely during these transits and be a little wary about the opportunities that offer a sense of belonging.

TRANSITING NEPTUNE IN ASPECT TO NATAL NEPTUNE

These transits are milestones in your evolving, lifelong Neptune journey of spiritual growth. Look for events, people, and circumstances that awaken your compassion and humility. (See "Using Neptune's Cycle" on page 81 for more.)

TRANSITING NEPTUNE IN ASPECT TO NATAL PLUTO

Are you in control of your life? If you answered yes, you've probably got a very strong Pluto in your chart. Sure, we can control plenty. But there are absolutely things that we can't manage, and eventually we will confront them. These transits usually bring a couple of them your way.

You *can* reliably control the way you choose to see and react to things. These transits help by leading you to seek a spiritual context for what can't be controlled. How can troubles help you grow, particularly in compassion for others? How can you train your mind and spirit to transcend pain, fear, or rage?

Sometimes during these transits, you'll fantasize about escaping your life and starting over, someplace far away, perhaps under an assumed name. Practically speaking, that's not an option for most of us. But seeking meaning in hardship and cultivating faith in that meaning is an option available to everyone.

TRANSITING NEPTUNE IN ASPECT TO THE LUNAR NODES

The Lunar Nodes represent the tension between comfortable, familiar patterns (South Node) and the drive to reach toward something challenging yet rewarding (North Node). During transiting Neptune's aspects to the Lunar Nodes, you're faced with a choice between floating along with what's safe and actively sailing your ship into unknown waters.

When you are called to a particular course of action, to remake your life in a significant way, fear is a completely reasonable response. Pursuing a meaningful life can be a lonely business. During these transits, faith is your greatest ally. You won't be certain that what you're doing will work out. All you can be certain of is that for you, at this moment in time, it feels like exactly the right path to take.

TRANSITING NEPTUNE IN ASPECT TO THE NATAL ASCENDANT

In the Ascendant, we find all the smoke and mirrors and sleight-of-hand tricks you've mastered to influence how the world sees and reacts to you. When Neptune aspects this point, it's as though a tidal wave has crashed ashore, washing away all the footsteps you had left in the sand—you can no longer retrace your steps home.

Your personality is fluid now, like molten metal assumes any shape it comes in contact with. You're re-creating yourself. It doesn't really feel like that, of course. It just feels as though all your old tricks no longer work, leaving you naked and exposed, washed as smooth as a piece of sea glass. A series of crises buffet you like fierce waves, knocking you down as soon as you stand up. Instead of struggling so hard to keep your head above water, plunge deeper into the sea. That's the only way to wipe the slate clean and to keep you from hardening too soon into the wrong shape.

TRANSITING NEPTUNE IN ASPECT TO THE NATAL MIDHEAVEN

Once, looking through an old trunk, my mother found one of my school projects from second grade, an outline of what I wished for the future. "What do you want to be when you grow up, and why?" asked one of the questions. I had responded, "A secretary, because they type so fast."

At the time mom unearthed evidence of my childish dream, I in fact *was* an executive secretary (and a very fast typist). But I'd had no memory whatsoever of wanting to do that in second grade. I felt my career choice had all been a mistake, something to fall back on until I could be a musician or an astrologer.

I was born with Virgo on the Midheaven, the career angle of the chart. I suppose you could say it was my destiny to have a career that involved organization and helping others. But there are a lot of ways to accomplish that. I wasn't doomed to remain in a job I disliked just because my second-grade self had been impressed by Mr. Drysdale's secretary on *The Beverly Hillbillies*.

A couple of years later, as Neptune made a supportive trine aspect to my Midheaven, I left my secretarial job to be an astrologer, and I never looked back.

When Neptune makes an aspect to your Midheaven, you may be disillusioned with your career. It's time to dream a new dream about what you want to be when you grow up—no matter how old you are!

chapter 7

TRANSITS OF PLUTO:
THE UNDERTOW

Planetary Dossier: PLUTO

TIME TO MAKE A FULL CYCLE AROUND THE SUN: about 248 years

TIME SPENT IN EACH ZODIAC SIGN: varies; between 14 and 30 years

TRANSITING ASPECTS LAST FOR: varies, but at least several years

STRONGEST SIGN: Scorpio

HAS TO WORK HARDER IN: Taurus

KEYWORDS: power, control, transformation, obsession, hidden things, dictatorships, generation, regeneration, and degeneration

Every astrologer's favorite keyword for Pluto seems to be *transformation*. But I consider that a euphemism, a consolation prize for enduring Pluto's transits. "Oh, it'll be great. You'll be transformed!" But who among us asks the universe for transformation? We want money and sex and acclaim!

It is not inaccurate to say we're transformed by Pluto's transits. It's just a tad incomplete. That's because humans are fairly stubborn creatures, and it generally takes some fairly dramatic life experiences to lead us kicking and screaming toward personal evolution. We'd like the ends, but the means can be daunting.

Some people are hardwired to cope with Pluto. The late Maya Angelou, born with the Sun, Moon, Mercury, Venus, and Jupiter all in close aspect to Pluto, knew a little something about transformation. During her eighty-six years on the planet, she transformed herself into an acclaimed poet, author, civil rights activist, and one of the world's most admired women.

But that's not the whole story. There was her parents' divorce, her sexual assault at the hands of her mother's boyfriend at the age of eight. There was the perpetrator's murder after Angelou had identified him for the crime. There was agonizing guilt as she blamed herself, and specifically her voice, for his death. There were five silent years when she stopped speaking altogether, lest others die.

On the road to her eventual career, Angelou married several times, bore a beloved child, and worked at various times as a calypso singer, a prostitute and madam, a dancer, and the first black woman cable car conductor in San Francisco.

She had fascinating—and devastating—stories to tell. And in 1968, with transiting Pluto opposed her natal Mercury, the planet of storytellers, she was offered an opportunity to tell them. Suffering a deep depression following the murder of her friend Reverend Martin Luther King Jr., Angelou resisted at first. But when her memoir *I Know Why the Caged Bird Sings* was published the following year, it launched a brilliant literary career. More importantly, it demonstrated that the girl who had once feared the power of her voice was now in full command of her own story. Her distinctive work and her self-possession inspired others for the next forty-five years.

Pluto's transiting aspects are not for the faint of heart. Sometimes bad things happen; sometimes it's just a blue period; other times, fantastic success presents itself. Fearing what Pluto might bring is unproductive. It's better to focus on what Pluto wants from you, which is always, and above all, honesty. Pluto's transits reveal what we're made of, good and bad. They give us no choice but to become more than we thought we could be—stronger, braver, more candid, more authentic versions of ourselves. Pluto will stand for nothing less.

THE NATURE OF THE BEAST

Astrologer Caroline Casey has described Pluto's transits as having three phases. The first is the total disruption of your world. The second is not knowing. And the third is the emergence of the authentic self.

In the meantime, the valley. The cave. The craving to withdraw from the world during a Pluto transit is very strong. To the extent that you can, honor it. You are retreating to adjust to what has happened to you. Grief is a physical process as well as an emotional one, and this is never more true than when you are grieving the death of immediate blood relations. Give yourself time and space to come to terms with your situation.

TRANSITING PLUTO BY SIGN

Pluto takes the longest of any planet to make a full transit of the zodiac—about 248 years. Its orbit is irregular, and it spends a lot more time in some signs than in others. You'll experience Pluto's transit of between four and six signs of the zodiac during your lifetime.

Like Uranus and Neptune, Pluto is in a single sign for so long that everyone born in the same fourteen-to-thirty-year period will share the same Pluto sign. More than any other planet, Pluto seems to characterize entire generations, from the Greatest Generation to the baby boomers to generation X. Each generation faces its own distinguishing challenge, shepherding the world through a massive sea change of cultural mores, political trends, technological advancements, and societal values.

The years of Pluto's most recent and next transits through each sign are given. These include retrograde periods when Pluto might back into a previous sign for a short time.

TRANSITING PLUTO IN ARIES (1822–1851; 2066–2097) ♈

Aries is the sign of rugged individualism, courage, and pioneer spirit, and these transits further progress and exploration at all costs. Pluto's previous transit in Aries in the early nineteenth century coincided with the settlement of the perilous American West, the Industrial Revolution, and the introduction of Darwin's theory of evolution. But while Pluto in Aries furthered progress in industry, transportation, and exploration, it also reveals a shadow side of impulsive, self-serving violence, genocide, and exploitation.

Reality check for: Aries, Cancer, Libra, Capricorn

Empowerment for: Leo, Sagittarius

Deep insights for: Gemini, Aquarius

TRANSITING PLUTO IN TAURUS (1851–1884; 2095–2129) ♉

Spanning the golden age of agriculture through the Gilded Age of the late nineteenth century, this era saw enormous wealth and ease for privileged landowners. It often came, however, at the cost of others' freedom. For example, the Indian Mutiny resulted in transfer of rule to the British crown, settlers in New Zealand waged a war over property rights against the indigenous Māori, and America went through civil war and bloody reconstruction to settle the matter of whether the privilege of the few justified the misery of many.

Reality check for: Taurus, Leo, Scorpio, Aquarius

Empowerment for: Virgo, Capricorn

Deep insights for: Cancer, Pisces

TRANSITING PLUTO IN GEMINI (1882–1913) ♊

Automation enabled the widespread adoption of the telephone and automobile, transforming travel, communication, and commerce. Technological advances led to the gradual introduction of electricity in homes.

Reality check for: Gemini, Virgo, Sagittarius, Pisces

Empowerment for: Libra, Aquarius

Deep insights for: Leo, Aries

TRANSITING PLUTO IN CANCER (1912–1939) ♋

These years saw World War I, a global flu pandemic, and the Great Depression. Deteriorating economic conditions contributed to the rise of fascism and, eventually, World War II. This era was characterized by a fight for the survival and security of clan and country.

Reality check for: Cancer, Libra, Capricorn, Aries

Empowerment for: Scorpio, Pisces

Deep insights for: Virgo, Taurus

TRANSITING PLUTO IN LEO (1937–1958) ♌

This era included World War II, the birth of the nuclear age, and the baby boom. The generation born during these years rode the wave of a mighty youth culture that emphasized the supremacy of the individual and eternal youthfulness. Negatively, the baby boomers have been branded as self-absorbed and reluctant to accept conventional adult responsibilities and the inevitability of aging.

Reality check for: Leo, Scorpio, Aquarius, Taurus

Empowerment for: Sagittarius, Aries

Deep insights for: Libra, Gemini

TRANSITING PLUTO IN VIRGO (1956–1972) ♍

These years saw the rise of the middle class, good conditions for working people, social programs for the elderly and the poor, efforts to correct lingering racial inequalities, and dawning awareness of environmental issues. However, a disastrous war in Vietnam, cultural divides between generations, and disillusionment with government were also profound influences on this generation.

Reality check for: Virgo, Sagittarius, Pisces, Gemini

Empowerment for: Capricorn, Taurus

Deep insights for: Scorpio, Cancer

TRANSITING PLUTO IN LIBRA (1971–1984) ♎

The challenge of negotiating fair and equitable resolutions to conflicts, including wars, political scandals, and the escalating battle for gender equality, defined this transit. Divorce became increasingly common and would influence an entire generation of children to view divorce as almost inevitable. Pluto, planet of power, in Venus-ruled Libra, a sign closely associated with women, saw the election of Great Britain's first woman prime minister, Margaret Thatcher, as well as the first woman in space (Sally Ride).

Reality check for: Libra, Capricorn, Aries, Cancer

Empowerment for: Aquarius, Gemini

Deep insights for: Sagittarius, Leo

TRANSITING PLUTO IN SCORPIO (1983–1995) ♏

The AIDS pandemic entered mainstream consciousness in the early 1980s, serving as a dreadful punctuation mark at the end of the 1970s "free love" era. Never before had sex carried such a death sentence. Culture wars that divided Americans on sexuality, abortion, and religion emerged. Videos and cable television brought previously taboo subjects to a wider audience.

Reality check for: Scorpio, Aquarius, Taurus, Leo

Empowerment for: Pisces, Cancer

Deep insights for: Capricorn, Virgo

TRANSITING PLUTO IN SAGITTARIUS (1995–2008)

Sagittarius is the sign of world travel, and this transit was defined by the explosion of the Internet and pervasive globalism, which changed the way we viewed the world and our place in it. Maintaining privacy became challenging. Sagittarius also rules beliefs. This transit also saw the rise of religious fanaticism, mistrust of those who are different, and extreme polarization between groups with different political opinions.

Reality check for: Sagittarius, Pisces, Gemini, Virgo

Empowerment for: Aries, Leo

Deep insights for: Aquarius, Libra

TRANSITING PLUTO IN CAPRICORN (2008–2024) ♑

I'm writing this book six years into Pluto's transit of Capricorn, a sign of government and big business, and the story of this transit is still being written. So far, it has been characterized by a devastating financial collapse, exposure of governmental secrecy and spying, a U.S. Supreme Court decision that granted corporations the right of unlimited political campaign contributions, and a widespread distrust of government and corporations.

Reality check for: Capricorn, Aries, Cancer, Libra

Empowerment for: Taurus, Virgo

Deep insights for: Pisces, Scorpio

TRANSITING PLUTO IN AQUARIUS (1778–1798; 2023–2044) ♒

The last transit of Pluto in Aquarius corresponded with the war for American Independence and its establishment as a republic, and the era ended with the French Revolution. It seems likely that the next Pluto in Aquarius transit will find nations in rebellion and transition as well. After the Pluto in Capricorn transit, seemingly destined to deconstruct existing societal structures, it will be time to reinvent society and nations.

Reality check for: Aquarius, Taurus, Leo, Scorpio

Empowerment for: Gemini, Libra

Deep insights for: Aries, Sagittarius

TRANSITING PLUTO IN PISCES (1797–1823; 2043–2068) ♓

The last transit of Pluto through Pisces in the first quarter of the nineteenth century saw the Napoleonic Wars and the rise of the British and Russian empires, mass migration, and significant advances in science and transportation. Pisces is the sign associated with immigrants and minorities, so it's likely another shift in the world's population will occur with Pluto in this sign, possibility as a consequence of climate change, disease, or contamination.

Reality check for: Pisces, Gemini, Virgo, Sagittarius

Empowerment for: Cancer, Scorpio

Deep insights for: Taurus, Capricorn

USING PLUTO'S CYCLE

Pluto's cycle is characterized by awareness and acceptance of reality. The catalysts for this vary, but they may be related to loss, illness, emotional suffering, or dramatic shifts in societal paradigms.

Pluto has a fearsome reputation, and it is well deserved. Looking back on the most dramatic milestones of your lifetime, you will find Pluto nearby. Not every Pluto transit brings disaster; indeed, there are sometimes spectacular dividends when Pluto comes for a visit. But if the natal planet is poorly aspected, these can honestly be some of the most challenging transits of your life.

Because Pluto takes so long to complete a tour of the zodiac, you won't experience its full cycle in your lifetime. You can, however, reasonably expect to experience the sextile of transiting Pluto to natal Pluto, the square, the trine, and perhaps the opposition. Pluto spends much longer in some signs (twenty-seven years in Cancer!) than in others (only twelve in Scorpio, thank goodness), so the age when you have these transiting aspects will be the same as other people born within a few years of you, but could be quite different from people of other generations.

TRANSITING PLUTO SEXTILE NATAL PLUTO

About Age 25

The transiting Pluto sextile to natal Pluto offers opportunities, if you're willing to do a little work. If not, these can be lost years, when you can still afford to mope a bit and deny the fact that you're getting older. That option disappears in a few years, when your Saturn return gets under way. If you are willing to work, though—and at this age, that usually includes not putting up with poor treatment from others—you'll be in a better position to feel in control of your life at the Pluto square, about a decade from now.

TRANSITING PLUTO SQUARE NATAL PLUTO

Between Midthirties and Midforties

This is the opening shot fired in the battle of midlife. Sometimes there are devastating external events that bring about a crisis and a heightened awareness of mortality—the death of an elder, the end of a marriage, a serious illness, a child leaving the nest. For some, the Pluto square rolls in like a dark, wet fog that saps the color and energy out of life. It's hard to get out of bed; everything seems pointless, and a dull depression sets in. At the Pluto square, we cast a cold, fishy eye at our youthful dreams, ideals, and ambitions and decide we've been fools to think any of it meant anything. It's a grim, difficult rite of passage that often leads people to do foolish things, to prove to themselves they're still alive.

Eventually the transit passes, the clouds part, and the sun begins to shine again. But there will always be a little scar where the shrapnel entered.

TRANSITING PLUTO TRINE NATAL PLUTO

Early Fifties

You are at the peak of your personal power. If you've positioned yourself in a life, career, and relationships that are honest and supportive of your true self, you will impress the world during this transit. You will feel respected and appreciated.

If, on the other hand, you managed to squelch the astrological noise of the midlife crisis, this transit is very likely to be the one that brings you to your knees. The square is not subtle, and if you are very strong and very stubborn, you may be able to dig in your heels and weather the storm. But the trine sneaks up on you. The birthday cards ribbing you about getting older actually carry a sting. You're haunted by the thought of everything you've missed and all the opportunities that passed you by.

There is only one way out of the situation: Surrender. Let yourself be changed. Your life is not over yet, and if you can let yourself live more honestly and authentically, what is left will be much more worth living.

TRANSITING PLUTO OPPOSED NATAL PLUTO

Because of Pluto's erratic orbit, not everyone will live long enough to see transiting Pluto in opposition to natal Pluto. If you do, however, it will be in your eighties and can be a powerful transit. You no longer have anything to hide; you have no falseness about you. Your life is entirely honest. You are facing mortality, but you aren't afraid, because what frightens us most is not what the world can throw at us or take from us, but the things we try to hide from ourselves. At this point in your life, you conceal nothing, so there is nothing to fear.

TRANSITING PLUTO IN ASPECT TO NATAL PLANETS AND ANGLES

Pluto is the slowest moving of all transiting planets. Some years his net movement is actually minus a degree or two. If Pluto makes a major transiting aspect to a planet or angle of your chart, find a way to make peace with it, because he will be staying for a good long time, spending a couple of years within close orb of the aspect.

Pluto's conjunction, square, opposition, and quincunx aspects to natal planets are times when it can be hard to see the light at the end of the tunnel. You feel like a fish on a hook, wiggling and thrashing without hope of escape. The same can happen under Pluto's transiting trines and sextiles, but these can also bring a sense that you have an opportunity to achieve a more profound under-standing of yourself and your motivations, and perhaps empowerment.

Much depends on the relationship between natal Pluto and the natal planet being aspected. If, for instance, you have a square aspect between the natal Sun and natal Pluto, transiting Pluto's aspects to the natal Sun will usually create a much stronger reaction.

TRANSITING PLUTO IN ASPECT TO THE NATAL SUN

Pluto's terrible reputation makes us fearful when we see him lumbering down the ecliptic toward us. Sometimes difficult transits of Pluto converge with difficult outward events in your life; this is most often the case when Pluto is close to an angle of your chart at your birth, or in difficult aspect to the angles. Just as often, Pluto is experienced on a quieter, more psychological level. When Pluto con-nects with the natal Sun, it can feel as though the color and contrast are turned down on the televi-sion of your life. It can be difficult to feel very engaged, to find meaning or purpose.

We associate depression with Saturn, but I think of Saturn as the state of being in pain. Depression, on the other hand, deadens feeling. A small burn stings like hell for days. A deep, life-threatening burn may not cause any sensation because all the nerves are dead. That's the kind of burn Pluto gives us.

Being a Jupiterian type myself, I assume the universe has something in mind for us with every transit, rather than just enjoying our suffering. For Pluto's transits, it's the chance to rid ourselves of falseness. It's the chance to rid ourselves of what we no longer need. When Pluto connects with the Sun, the dead, outgrown parts of the self are burned away. Letting go of waste is cleansing. Having nothing to hide is empowering.

TRANSITING PLUTO IN ASPECT TO THE NATAL MOON

The Moon is astrological shorthand for security, a word that can evoke images of an elderly woman snug in her rocking chair, crocheted blanket on her lap and cat dozing at her feet. If you are young, adventurous, and even a bit reckless, security may not speak to you much.

Let me reframe the idea of the Moon as a symbol of what and whom you rely on. Even as you gal-livant boldly through life, making your mark, still there is something you rely on. It may be a loving family waiting for you back home, money in the bank, or your physical and mental health. Perhaps you've never been seriously threatened, have always had a safe home or true friends.

Until we lose something or someone that we have relied on, we may not realize what was holding us up all along. In *Gone with the Wind*, even ferocious Scarlett O'Hara discovered her hated rival was actually her dearest friend and supporter. Scarlett didn't realize it until the woman was on her death-bed, though, assuming Scarlett alone was the font of her own strength.

Pluto's transits to the natal Moon take away something that you depend on. And this is a permanent loss, which is a scary prospect. Sometimes this loss may make you doubt your faith in life and in human nature. You could lose a person, a place, a thing, or even your anonymity, as some people can become fa-mous with this transit. Whatever you lose, the challenge is to use what's left to rebuild a strong, true life.

TRANSITING PLUTO IN ASPECT TO NATAL MERCURY

Mercury symbolizes how we think and communicate, and how we frame what happens to us. Pluto's transiting aspects to Mercury can influence us to see our lives in the worst possible terms.

The optimist in me wants to encourage you to think positive thoughts so you can create a more uplifting reality—but this ignores the necessity of Pluto's transits, as necessary as a forest fire in renewing the growth of the forest.

So instead I'll say this: A lot of what you've been telling yourself for years, about yourself and other people, is wrong. Either they were wrong from the start, or they've become wrong over time. For a while, as Pluto transits Mercury, you'll be unable to hide from these truths.

Healthy, repetitive, absorbing activities are the best outlet I've found for these transits. Knitting. Puzzles. Running. Otherwise, the obsessive qualities of Pluto can lead to unhealthier pursuits, compulsions, and addictions.

TRANSITING PLUTO IN ASPECT TO NATAL VENUS

A few years ago, transiting Pluto opposed my natal Venus. A veteran of a long string of Pluto transits, I watched this one coming with anxiety, certain I'd lose all my money or my husband would run away with someone half my age.

Instead I increased my business income significantly and fell obsessively in love with all things pink, a color associated with Venus. My marriage came through just fine. All in all, it was a pretty nice transit.

Venus, ruler of Taurus and Libra, represents the enjoyment of life and its pleasures, and our connections with other people. Pluto, ruler of Scorpio, symbolizes the knowledge that nothing lasts forever, and that part of life is learning how to disconnect from what we've lost. When the two symbols collide, the challenge is to learn how to reconcile their very different messages: how to love life and people even though we know they won't last forever and will surely change, and how to let ourselves grieve our losses without forfeiting our appreciation for what is good about life.

You might find yourself challenged financially. Venus rules what we value and what we collect around us in order to feel secure. In this scenario, Pluto encourages us to separate our sense of security and our own value from things such as possessions and good looks and lots of money; sometimes it does this by letting us experience financial blows such as a business setback, a loss of property, or an investment that doesn't work out.

Of course, you might find yourself challenged in your relationships. What does it mean when people close to us change—do we still have a contract to be in a relationship with those people? Does the loss of relationships mean we are less valuable and lovable? Can we still love someone we discover is flawed and capable of awful behavior, or love ourselves when we find out we are capable of treating our loved ones badly?

TRANSITING PLUTO IN ASPECT TO NATAL MARS

Mars's lessons are primal, lessons of survival. Survival means protecting yourself from threat and having the confidence to compete with other people for the same resources. When Pluto and Mars come together, it is possible to become absolutely ruthless in your pursuit of what you want.

Without a healthy outlet for your energy and ambition, however, you may experience feelings of impotence and inadequacy. The haunting question is, do you have what it takes to succeed? Or will you—as is often the case when natal planets aspect Pluto—simply give up? Astrologer Donna Cunningham said that where we have Pluto is an area of life where we tend to "fail for spite." Sometimes giving up feels like the only way to regain control. If none of your efforts will make a difference, it's tempting to just take your toys and go home—at least then you're in charge of how the game ends.

These transits often bring career difficulties, usually related to a career change or a difficult boss that creates an intolerable workplace. Mars also rules the men in your life, so a partner, father, or other important male might suffer a crisis of confidence or a career setback.

As always with Pluto's transits, the message is about the limits of your personal power. No matter how hard Mars fights, how angry you get, or how hard you work, things sometimes happen that are beyond your control. In those situations, what matters most is how you handle weakness, anger, and frustration.

TRANSITING PLUTO IN ASPECT TO NATAL JUPITER

This transit likely brings a significant improvement in your fortunes. You might find yourself in a new job with a better salary, or living in a new place with a greater range of opportunities. Sometimes, if you've been through a particularly tough time, you might find yourself strongly drawn to religion.

Pluto was the wealthiest of the gods, so when he comes together with Jupiter, the luckiest of the gods, big things can happen for you financially. Powerful forces combine to bring wealth to you. It's not always earned wealth, either. Marrying into money, winning the lottery, making a killing in the stock market—a transiting Pluto in Jupiter won't make these things happen, but when they do occur, you'll see Pluto/Jupiter on the scene.

TRANSITING PLUTO IN ASPECT TO NATAL SATURN

Transiting Pluto in aspect to Saturn teaches healthy skepticism about the forms and structures you look to for moral guidance and a sense of purpose, or see as exemplars of success. It could be that every authority in your life—parents or other elders, teachers, the church, the government—has been revealed as imperfect. Or it could be that some empowering insight has enabled you to see beyond the small structure you've built around your life, to see that no one else, however wise or accomplished, can make your decisions for you—that kind of power and authority you must reserve for yourself.

Conversely, if you've been playing fast and loose with the rules, that is likely to come to light now. When Pluto trined my natal Saturn at age eight, I (ironically) cheated to get a bunch of Girl Scout merit badges. My mother, a shrewd judge of my character, picked up on the unlikelihood of my having done all of the work necessary to earn them. She didn't make me give back the badges, but she personally saw to it that I completed every requirement. That was, in all honesty, the last time I cheated for anything.

Saturn represents the ethical framework of your entire life, the part of you that personally contributes to upholding society and the rule of law. Pluto needs you to be a true and worthy role model. Pluto cannot let you get away with doing and being less than your best. If he has to tear you down and personally see to it that you earn every merit badge, he will. Society depends on it.

TRANSITING PLUTO IN ASPECT TO NATAL URANUS

You probably understand by now that Pluto can be a drag. He would have us believe that nothing is worth doing. It's all meaningless. We are but a void in an unfeeling universe. Pluto square Uranus, however, has a particularly nasty message: "You might as well just do what you're doing. Give up trying to do anything different. This is your life and you're stuck with it."

There is a silver lining to this dark Pluto cloud, if you can ignore its discouraging messages. Pluto transits indicate change on a massive and societal scale—and Uranus is a planet that really appreciates change. If you are willing to rebel not only against the powers that be, but also against your notions of who you are, how you thought your life would turn out, and what you're capable of accomplishing, you will have some of the most amazing opportunities of your life during this transit. Lend your most innovative talents to a cause bigger than yourself, and Pluto will place you in a position of considerable influence.

TRANSITING PLUTO IN ASPECT TO NATAL NEPTUNE

Neptune can be a planet of illusions, or of disillusionment. But as always with Pluto, there can be empowerment as well. The key is to give yourself over with passion to your dreams. Transiting Pluto in aspect to natal Neptune is especially well suited to spiritual, metaphysical, and artistic pursuits, but I've known people who have experienced significant success in their dream careers during these transits, too.

When Pluto transits Neptune, you may realize a cherished dream or become more achingly aware of the dreams that have not yet come true. The promise of these transits, though, is discovering which dreams are really yours and which were taught to you by other people or society. Pluto doesn't insist that your dreams be realistic, only that they be honest and true.

TRANSITING PLUTO IN ASPECT TO NATAL PLUTO

These transits are milestones in your evolving, lifelong Pluto journey. Look for events, people, and circumstances that help you develop greater authenticity and accept the limits of your control. (See "Using Pluto's Cycle" on page 97 for more.)

TRANSITING PLUTO IN ASPECT TO THE NATAL LUNAR NODES

Missteps during these transits seem to be caused by grasping at what appears to be your only option, even as part of you knows, deep down, that it's not right for you. The Lunar Nodes represent a path to what is good and fits you, and Pluto's transits here can derail you from that path with a bad relationship, bad job, or career opportunity that seems good but ends up a disappointment.

The grasping comes from fear and a need to feel in control. Once you understand that, it is more likely you'll be able to correct course and make better decisions. Releasing your fearful mind-set, and accepting your bad decisions without punishing yourself for them, will help you get back on track and move forward with greater self-knowledge.

TRANSITING PLUTO IN ASPECT TO THE NATAL ASCENDANT

From birth, we adopt, devise, and refine a series of survival techniques that we use to interact with the world. We call this collection of techniques "the personality." It's not necessarily false, but it doesn't reveal the full scope of your character. It's the way that, given your particular upbringing and environment, you learned to charm the checkout girl at the supermarket into accepting your expired coupon.

When transiting Pluto makes an aspect to your natal Ascendant, something unsettling happens. Your old bag of tricks is no longer sufficient for your circumstances, which may for various reasons be suddenly and irrevocably altered. If you've always been outgoing, you might become wary; a nice guy will turn nasty; a weakling, formidable; a great beauty, suddenly not so stunning. The more dramatic the external events that rattle your cage, and the less your personality reflects your true self, the more exaggerated the change in your personality. You need new weaponry. You need a new identity. You need to throw away the tricks and the charm and act like the person you are on the inside.

Transits in aspect to the Ascendant also aspect the Descendant. Pluto here can mean changes in your relationship status, major transitions involving your spouse or partner, or deepening ties or breaks with close friends.

TRANSITING PLUTO IN ASPECT TO THE NATAL MIDHEAVEN

The older I get and the longer I practice astrology, the more respect I have for the idea of destiny. It's not that I believe you have no agency whatsoever over where you end up or how you get there, but I do feel more and more that just as there is a place where you begin, there is also a place where you're headed. The Midheaven gives a strong indication of the qualities of that destiny: What will it look like when you arrive? What are the characteristics that will get you there?

When transiting Pluto makes an aspect to your Midheaven, destiny calls. Sometimes it shows up with a wrecking ball. Pluto has very specific ideas about what your destiny should look like, and if the career, reputation, and standing you've built for yourself are not in keeping with Pluto's ideas, down they will come.

Transiting aspects to your Midheaven also aspect your IC (fourth house cusp). Pluto's aspects to this axis will often bring a significant move, major work to your home, or important transitions related to members of your family.

chapter 8

TRANSITS OF MERCURY, VENUS, AND MARS: PLANETARY TRIGGERS

The transits of Mercury, Venus, and Mars fall somewhere between the epic, life-altering transits of the big boys—Jupiter, Saturn, Uranus, Neptune, and Pluto—and the familiar and fleeting cycles of the Sun and Moon. These planets move through the zodiac quickly; the slowest, Mars, takes only two and a half years. So their transits don't represent major and lasting change in your life. They can and do, however, act as triggers to detonate the ticking time bombs of the slower planetary transits.

Most people born within a year or two of you will have Jupiter, Saturn, Uranus, Neptune, and Pluto in the same sign you do. But Mercury, Venus, and Mars move quickly enough that they can be in quite different condition from one week to the next. Schoolmates born a month after you are likely have these three planets in different signs and aspects to other planets. This makes them very significant in analyzing your birth chart.

But their transits go by so fast that they hardly rate a mention when an astrologer reads your chart. And so the three of them share this chapter. They are far from unimportant, but their transits act mostly as catalysts for other, slower-moving planets.

TRANSITS OF MERCURY: MEETING AND COMMUNICATING

Planetary Dossier: MERCURY

TIME TO MAKE A FULL CYCLE AROUND THE SUN: 88 days

TIME SPENT IN EACH ZODIAC SIGN: roughly 3 weeks

TRANSITING ASPECTS LAST FOR: about 2 days

STRONGEST SIGNS: Gemini, Virgo, Aquarius

HAS TO WORK HARDER IN: Sagittarius, Pisces, Leo

KEYWORDS: thinking, learning, skills, ideas, communication, conversation, perception, listening, gossip

The rosebush at the end of my driveway is actually a newspaper. I know this because each time a neighbor walks by with a dog, the pooch cannot resist stopping and sniffing. I'll bet if a dog could talk, he could go on for half an hour about everything he was picking up from that bush.

On my own morning walk, I notice tiny, informal libraries are springing up, housed in little birdhouse-style boxes in front yards throughout my neighborhood. You can take or leave a book, or scratch a friendly message in a notebook the "librarian" left there.

I notice that a nearby house is gathering yellowed newspapers and fliers on the front porch. Are the neighbors away, sick, or indifferent? A few doors down, another home is freshly painted. Are those owners getting ready to sell?

The world is talking to us all the time, every day. Even a quiet walk around your neighborhood is a kind of conversation with your environment. You notice things; everywhere, there are clues and signs. In the simplest, seemingly unchanging details of daily life, there are tiny variations to interest the observant person.

Mercury is the planet of perception. Where Mercury transits your chart, you are curious, awake, noticing things you normally would not. You want to learn more.

But not much more. Mercury's transits are the equivalent of bookmarking an interesting website so you can go back and take a closer look later when you're not so busy. Like Curious George, Mercury wants stimulation and new experiences. So let him guide you, and pay attention to what he shows you.

HOW TO WORK WITH TRANSITS OF MERCURY

Mercury moves quickly by transit, whipping through each sign of the zodiac within a few weeks (unless it's retrograde, which happens three times each year for several weeks at a time). Transiting Mercury's aspects to natal planets move quickly and are only influential for a couple of days.

TRANSITING MERCURY BY SIGN

TRANSITING MERCURY IN ARIES ♈

Impressions are formed very quickly and are usually incomplete. When it comes to written communications, even more than usual, no one wants to read anything that's more than a few lines long. You'll have to spoon-feed information to people in tiny chunks. On the plus side, this is an excellent transit for dealing with situations that require quick decisions. If you normally dislike conflict, it will be a little easier for you to speak your mind during this transit.

TRANSITING MERCURY IN TAURUS ♉

You are slow to notice things, but you pay close attention to whatever does capture your interest. A slow, well-modulated delivery helps others get the most from what you're saying. This is a good time to analyze problems requiring patience and tenacity and to formulate financial plans and strategies. You may be more sensitive than usual to sounds, smells, and touch.

TRANSITING MERCURY IN GEMINI ♊

This is one of Mercury's strongest signs, and the pace of life seems to accelerate during these few weeks. There are so many distractions! If you're a person who likes to pay attention to and complete one task at a time before moving to the next, this could be a frustrating transit for you. It's a terrific transit for brainstorming, however. Bright ideas are floating everywhere—your only problem will be finding a way to hold on to them all.

TRANSITING MERCURY IN CANCER ♋

This is a good transit for improving your memory, finding language for your feelings, and communicating with others on an emotional level. It can be a melancholy transit, too, with nostalgia overtaking you at odd moments. This is not a good transit for dispassionate communication; either you display more emotion than you had intended or you react with strong emotion to what other people say. It's a good transit for investigating the past, especially genealogy.

TRANSITING MERCURY IN LEO ♌

There is an old joke about an egotist who, having talked his friend's ear off for ages, finally stops and says, "But that's enough about me. Let's talk about you. What do *you* think of me?" This sums up Mercury in Leo—both in the birth chart and by transit—pretty well! Like a newspaper reporter, Mercury works best when it is a little bit objective; Mercury in Leo, however, is completely subjective: "What do *I* think?" Anyone can be charmed simply by asking him to talk about himself. Creative impulses are awakened, too, but this is a better transit for brainstorming creative ideas than actually doing anything with them.

TRANSITING MERCURY IN VIRGO ♍

If Virgo has a flaw (which I am not prepared to concede), it's a predilection for criticism to an unhealthy degree. Perfection is an unreasonable standard for mere humans, unless we decide to see everything as perfect simply by virtue of it being what it is. While Mercury is in Virgo, another of its strongest signs, perception is keen. Intellect is sharp. But compassion and tact may be lacking. Time spent in solitary pursuits that require a good deal of attention and craft is time well spent while Mercury is in Virgo.

TRANSITING MERCURY IN LIBRA ♎

This is one of the nicer transits of Mercury, because Libra brings qualities of grace, balance, and tact to interactions. But the Libran desire for balance can also lead to argumentativeness. If you say no, the other will say yes, and so forth. It's not a strong transit for assertiveness or decisiveness, but it's great for negotiations, handling sticky interpersonal situations, and persuading others to see things your way.

TRANSITING MERCURY IN SCORPIO ♏

Mercury is ruthless in Scorpio, seeing everything in the pitiless detail of a tintype photo. It can make most of us a bit raw. You may be a bit blunt in how you deliver information, so it's a good time to resolve matters that require exactly that approach, such as confronting those who have hurt you. This is also a wonderful transit for writing, since it lends itself to deep introspection and empathy. For similar reasons, it's a good transit for therapeutic breakthroughs.

TRANSITING MERCURY IN SAGITTARIUS ♐

As transiting Mercury leaves Scorpio for Sagittarius, we still see things as they are—but it's easier to laugh about them. Mercury is considered at a bit of a disadvantage in Sagittarius, a sign that enjoys focusing on the big picture and meaning, because Mercury is strictly interested in collecting details and data. However, this is a good transit for taking a broad overview or doing long-term strategic thinking. It's an effective transit, too, for questioning your beliefs, pursuing a higher level of education, and teaching others.

TRANSITING MERCURY IN CAPRICORN ♑

Capricorn is not a bad sign for Mercury to visit; they both favor a cool and dispassionate approach. Mercury reveals the details that must be handled to climb the ambitious mountains to which Capricorn is drawn. If you need to develop practical skills to advance toward a goal, this is the transit to get started. If you tend to let emotions cloud your rational mind, this transit will help you separate thoughts from feelings so you can make practical decisions.

TRANSITING MERCURY IN AQUARIUS ♒

Mercury excels in Aquarius, a sign of scientific inquiry, technological intricacies, and long-range planning. Draft your plan for the future now. If you need to document a work process, now is the time. Mastering new technology is easier now, too. If you need to have a heart-to-heart with someone you love, however, forget it. Wait a few weeks until Mercury enters Pisces!

TRANSITING MERCURY IN PISCES ♓

After at least a month and a half of Mercury traveling through dispassionate signs, we're ready for transiting Mercury in sensitive, compassionate, imaginative Pisces. Now is the time to catch up on all the delicate talks you've been putting off, the sleep you've missed, and your art projects, music, and poetry. Pisces is a challenging sign for Mercury, because Mercury is logical and Pisces is intuitive, guided by dreams, visions, and illusions. On the plus side, if you want to express an idea poetically, or need to handle sensitive matters and conversations, this is the transit for you.

TRANSITING MERCURY IN ASPECT TO NATAL PLANETS

TRANSITING MERCURY IN ASPECT TO THE NATAL SUN

You shouldn't think and talk about yourself all the time; it's narcissistic at worst and just plain obnoxious at best. But there is a time for self-consciousness, to think about yourself and ask others for their perspective on how you're managing things, and this is one of those times. A square or opposition may mean the self-examination is a little disconcerting; a trine or sextile may bring unexpected approval your way. The conjunction is a little dangerous in that you can't see yourself objectively.

TRANSITING MERCURY IN ASPECT TO THE NATAL MOON

Question your unconscious during this transit. If you want to break habits, this is a good transit, especially the transiting square or opposition. It's easy to talk about what you're feeling without getting overwhelmed by your emotions.

TRANSITING MERCURY IN ASPECT TO NATAL MERCURY

The squares or opposition from transiting Mercury to natal Mercury challenge your way of seeing or talking about the world. Other points of view are healthy! A conjunction (Mercury return) is the beginning of a new cycle of perceiving, learning, and giving language to what you see around you. Trines and sextiles bring input that supports your worldview, and pleasant and stimulating conversation.

TRANSITING MERCURY IN ASPECT TO NATAL VENUS

We don't always get what we want, and often it's because we don't really know what we want. Transiting Mercury in aspect to natal Venus helps us figure it out, either through a process of elimination (square and opposition: "I *don't* want that!") or through showing us things, people, ideas, or situations that delight us.

TRANSITING MERCURY IN ASPECT TO NATAL MARS

Careful—even the "easy" aspects (trine and sextile) can give you a day or two of contentious, confrontational communication. This transit is a good time to speak your mind, but when you're overwhelmed, it can provoke arguments and harsh words that can't be taken back. Take these couple of days to question and learn from your anger.

TRANSITING MERCURY IN ASPECT TO NATAL JUPITER

This transit can be a lot of fun, but it can also lead you to cherry-pick facts (Mercury) that support what you already believe is true (Jupiter). This is less likely in the case of the square or opposition, however. More positively, you have an opening over these couple of days to precisely articulate your beliefs and dreams for the future—grab a pen and start writing this stuff down!

TRANSITING MERCURY IN ASPECT TO NATAL SATURN

One of Saturn's symbols is the bear, and when he is awakened by inquisitive Mercury, you'll soon see why. Saturn does not appreciate having his authority questioned, and neither will you during this transit. You may also receive communication that awakens your greatest fears or makes you feel depressed. But Mercury also gives you the opportunity to gain better perspective on your ambitions, maturity, and reputation, and to take responsibility for your actions and feelings.

TRANSITING MERCURY IN ASPECT TO NATAL URANUS

Uranus symbolizes your rebellious side. When transiting Mercury aspects Uranus, you may give voice to that rebellion, the desire to rebel may reach your conscious mind for the first time, or you may come into contact with a person, book, movie, or other catalyst that awakens your desire to be free and independent. This fleeting transit will not set you free, but it will help you understand what in your life needs to be changed.

TRANSITING MERCURY IN ASPECT TO NATAL NEPTUNE

What if you could read people's minds? It's a common fantasy often cited when people are asked what superpower they would love to possess. You can't actually read people's minds during this transit, but you are far more intuitive than usual and perceptive to nonverbal cues. This is an excellent transit for putting your dreams and intuitions into a form that others can appreciate, especially through music, photography, painting, or dance.

TRANSITING MERCURY IN ASPECT TO NATAL PLUTO

There are shadowy, nasty impulses lurking inside each of us. They are where Pluto lives. If we befriend them, we can overcome them. While transiting Mercury aspects natal Pluto, we meet one of these trolls along the road. Something we read, some conversation we have, awakens an ugly thought; it might be jealousy, or contempt, or an illicit idea on which we would never act. Don't be afraid of these thoughts. They're just Mercury's way of introducing you to one of your trolls, so you can make friends with it and it will lose its power over you.

TRANSITING MERCURY IN ASPECT TO THE NATAL NORTH NODE

There are things in life that you want very badly but that seem to be completely beyond the realm of possibility. Reaching for them makes you feel happier than you thought possible, though, even if you don't exactly get what you're reaching for. These desires are symbolized by the Moon's North Node, and when Mercury makes an aspect to this point, new information comes to light about how to attain them. A chance comment can ignite that old urge to reach for the brass ring. Act fast—you've only got a short window of opportunity, a couple of days, to take action.

TRANSITS OF VENUS: THINGS THAT YOU LIKE

Planetary Dossier: VENUS

TIME TO MAKE A FULL CYCLE AROUND THE SUN: 224½ days

TIME SPENT IN EACH ZODIAC SIGN: about 18 days

TRANSITING ASPECTS LAST FOR: about 2 days

STRONGEST SIGNS: Taurus, Libra, Pisces

HAS TO WORK HARDER IN: Scorpio, Aries, Virgo

KEYWORDS: pleasure, affection, balance, complements, compliments, partners, indulgence, senses

Nearly every evening, my husband and I have a conversation that will be familiar to most couples. "What do you want for dinner?" one of us asks. "I have no idea . . . What do *you* want for dinner?" the other responds. We usually go through a few rounds of this before settling on something.

Why is it often so difficult to figure out what we want? Generally, we know what makes us feel safe and good, and what is familiar, but that is Moon territory, and another chapter. The Moon has an unconscious quality, like an itch that needs scratching. Venus's purview is entirely optional delights, things we enjoy having without really needing them.

The Moon knows we need to eat something for dinner or we'll get cranky. But a special dinner out at a nice restaurant takes us into Venus territory. What place would you choose? What makes it special? It might not even be the food. It could be the way the staff treat you, the beautiful ambience, or the company with whom you're sharing it.

Venus delights in things that appeal to the senses, that are beautiful, delicious, or lovely to listen to, or that feel wonderful. Enormous pleasure can also be found in social interactions with people we enjoy, and this is Venus's territory as well.

When Venus transits your chart, her representatives—people, especially women; money; art or other beautiful things—show you delights that you didn't even know you wanted. Not all gifts are good for us, however delicious they may be. But that does not detract from the pleasure they give us.

HOW TO WORK WITH TRANSITS OF VENUS

Pay attention when Venus changes signs or moves into a new house of your chart (see part III). Its aspects to your natal planets will be over in a couple of days, so don't dwell on them. However, let's say that your birth chart has an aspect between Venus and Uranus. A lot could be said about such an aspect and its ramifications for your personal and financial life. Each time transiting Venus makes an aspect to natal Venus and Uranus, the exciting natal aspect between the two is activated—and if a slower-moving planet happens to be making a transiting aspect to them at the same time, watch the fireworks fly.

TRANSITING VENUS BY SIGN

Think of the zodiac as a shopping mall, with each sign representing a different store—sporting goods (Aries), a hair salon (Libra), that shop with the incense drifting out of it that parents won't let their kids wander into (Scorpio). As Venus takes her nearly yearlong lap around the mall, she becomes deeply interested in shopping at a particular store for several weeks at a time. She'll bring you amazing stuff that she finds there and then move on to the next store. Each Venus sign is particularly good at unearthing certain treasures—and social opportunities—that you will enjoy.

TRANSITING VENUS IN ARIES ♈

In our mall, Aries might be a barbershop, a sporting goods store, a car lot, a sports bar, or simply a place that always boasts the newest, fastest toys. (The last time Venus was in Aries, she took me to buy my first new car in fourteen years. I *adore* it!) Do your research in advance, because Venus in Aries favors impulsive buying.

Socially, Venus in Aries prefers fast-paced activities of short duration. Romantic connections flare up but will probably fizzle out almost as quickly. For Venus in Aries, the thrill is in the chase.

TRANSITING VENUS IN TAURUS ♉

The Taurus shop could be a jewelry store, a perfumery, a spa, a music store, or a gourmet specialty foods market. Venus can get a bit spendy here, because she prefers good-quality items that will last. Social engagements during Taurus's season will probably be centered on shopping, gardening, eating, being pampered, or relaxing in a comfortable environment.

TRANSITING VENUS IN GEMINI ♊

While in Gemini, Venus can't resist bookstores, department stores, craft stores, office supply stores, greeting card stores, or stationers. You'll buy at least two of everything that catches your eye, so stock up on goods that you use all year long.

Venus tends to be quite sociable in Gemini. If you plan only one or two parties each year, make one of them a late-spring gathering while Venus is in Gemini. Buy all the greeting cards you'll want now for an entire year of birthdays, anniversaries, weddings, and graduations.

TRANSITING VENUS IN CANCER ♋

This is the best time all year to buy items for your home. Suddenly you know the exact sofa that appeals to you, the right pots and pans, the perfect garden furniture. Try new recipes, too, especially those that use scandalously expensive ingredients.

Cancer is the sign of the homebody, so Venus's transit here is a nice time to entertain at home. Limit the guest list to very close friends and family members who don't stress you out. Feed the people you like. Buy something beautiful for your home.

TRANSITING VENUS IN LEO ♌

When Venus is in Leo, she wants glamour, luxury, and excitement. She will avoid warehouse stores; they depress her, so make your trip to Costco while Venus is still in Cancer. Venus in Leo doesn't just want to buy fabulous things, she wants to have a fabulous shopping *experience*.

This is the transit for making big, thrilling, sexy purchases. Splurge on one full-price name-brand item that makes you feel like a king or queen. Social opportunities with the most appeal this month require dressy clothing and a trip to a salon. Save up your entertainment money while Venus is in frugal Cancer, so you'll have more to spend during Venus in Leo's season. And if there just isn't enough cash in the kitty, break out the Scrabble or a deck of cards; Venus in Leo loves games!

TRANSITING VENUS IN VIRGO ♍

The simplest things delight Venus in Virgo: staples for the pantry, shelves to help you organize your closets, supplies for your home office, and unglamorous necessaries such as tube socks and underwear. Tools of all kinds are Virgo territory, along with skeins of yarn for your knitting projects or big tubs for brewing your craft beer.

Virgo's ideal social engagements are casual, possibly outdoors, potluck, and feature some kind of productive, shared activity. Hikes, picnics, knitting bees, or getting a lot of friends together to help you build something or cook a big meal could hold a bit more appeal than usual.

TRANSITING VENUS IN LIBRA ♎

If something is elegant, melodious, delectable, or graceful, Venus in Libra wants it. Buy the unessential-yet-special things that make life worth living. Artwork, fine crystal or china, a beautiful chair, tickets to an art exhibit or concert, high-end clothing and accessories—all will seem like excellent ways to spend your money while Venus is in Libra.

Libra is among the most sociable signs but has very particular ideas about what constitutes a good time. You will have little tolerance for boorish behavior, vulgar language, or coarse manners while Venus is in this sign, so choose your companions accordingly.

TRANSITING VENUS IN SCORPIO ♏

This month, you'll probably feel drawn to shops that make a certain type of person shiver a little when they walk by. Places that sell magic potions, tattoos, "adult" entertainment supplies, or piercings will seem a bit more alluring. Also, any shop devoted to your particular obsession, whether it's books, shoes, or anything else, stands to collect a lot more coin from you while Venus is in Scorpio.

Socially, Venus in Scorpio lends itself to solitude or gatherings with your very closest friends, or else people and activities that push the limits of what makes you feel comfortable. There is no in-between with Venus in Scorpio!

TRANSITING VENUS IN SAGITTARIUS ♐

Venus in Sagittarius has a voracious appetite for books, a lust for travel, and a delight in anything from another part of the world. If you don't have money to shop for books, dust off and organize your bookshelves or rediscover what you've downloaded to your e-reader. If you can't travel, this is at least a great time to decide on a destination you'd really love to visit and come up with a plan for making it happen. Take a trip to an import store or an ethnic neighborhood grocer.

Venus in Sagittarius signals a time to enjoy outdoor activities and all kinds of sports. Anything that is very different and unusual is likely to appeal now. Go to the symphony when you're normally a hip-hop fan? Sure! See the latest action-hero blockbuster when your tastes usually run toward intro-spective foreign films? Venus in Sagittarius asks, "Why not?"

TRANSITING VENUS IN CAPRICORN ♑

Venus in Capricorn is more of an investor than a shopper. You will be more likely to review your investment portfolio, refinance your mortgage, or put money into your business than to indulge in shopping sprees this month. Put your assets to work begetting other little assets. (Which is not to say you couldn't be seduced by an antiques store. Hey, antiques are investments!)

This is not a terribly sociable season overall, but it's a good time to hobnob with colleagues and fulfill family obligations. Time spent with older people or mentoring younger people will be enjoy-able and rewarding for all involved.

TRANSITING VENUS IN AQUARIUS ♒

Been wanting a new computer or smartphone? Here's your chance. Want to throw a big party and in-vite all your friends? Do it this month. Alternately, if you're trying to rein in your spending, eliminate your debt, and increase your savings so you can eventually buy your freedom (retire), this transit will help. Long-term financial planning is a good use for Venus in Aquarius energy.

TRANSITING VENUS IN PISCES ♓

Venus in Pisces finds the newest fads, trends, and toys nearly irresistible, so if you need to save money, freeze your credit card in a block of ice for a few weeks! Instead, focus on enjoying the here and now. Let the people in your life know how much you care about them. Make a donation to your fa-vorite charity. Find pleasure in nature, especially sitting near the water. Make music or catch a movie with friends. Pisces is one of the few signs for whom the best things in life truly are free.

TRANSITING VENUS IN ASPECT TO NATAL PLANETS

Transits of Venus to natal planets and angles are fleeting, lasting only for a couple of days. Venus will often appear in the form of people, especially women, who represent something that you desire or enjoy. Pay attention when you see someone enjoying him- or herself during these transits; it's a reminder that even when times are difficult, there is always something in life that's worth enjoying.

TRANSITING VENUS IN ASPECT TO THE NATAL SUN

If you've been feeling overlooked and unappreciated, this transit should comfort you with several days of soul-soothing compliments and, possibly, money.

TRANSITING VENUS IN ASPECT TO THE NATAL MOON

A neighbor brings a beautiful plant from her garden or a delicious home-baked snack, or says something really nice about your home.

TRANSITING VENUS IN ASPECT TO NATAL MERCURY

Ever have a friend who laughs at all your jokes and thinks you're incredibly bright and witty? That's what it feels like when transiting Venus aspects your natal Mercury. With the square and opposition, the friend laughs at someone else's jokes and makes you work harder to get the attention back on you.

TRANSITING VENUS IN ASPECT TO NATAL VENUS

The conjunction is a Venus return and sets the tone for the rest of the nearly one-year Venus cycle. Squares and opposition make you doubt your attractiveness; trines and sextiles make you feel adorable.

TRANSITING VENUS IN ASPECT TO NATAL MARS

Something (or someone) attractive either excites you sexually or awakens your competitive urges. Venus could take the form of money, motivating you to work harder.

TRANSITING VENUS IN ASPECT TO NATAL JUPITER

Your desire to experience something new is briefly awakened by an appealing person, social opportunity, or piece of art.

TRANSITING VENUS IN ASPECT TO NATAL SATURN

A welcome expression of praise, or perhaps a romantic interest, brightens your day and makes you feel successful, respected, and validated.

TRANSITING VENUS IN ASPECT TO NATAL URANUS

A pleasant social encounter gives you a feeling of belonging. Occasionally, something you desire could make you want to run away from home in order to have it.

TRANSITING VENUS IN ASPECT TO NATAL NEPTUNE

Something appealing or desirable may briefly capture your imagination and make you think you're in love, or a perhaps piece of art or music captures your imagination.

TRANSITING VENUS IN ASPECT TO NATAL PLUTO

This is the transit that got Persephone into trouble. Standing in a meadow looking Venus-enchanting, she caught the attention of Pluto, who pulled her into the underworld. This is a transit when something lovely awakens your least-lovely impulses.

TRANSITING VENUS IN ASPECT TO NATAL NORTH NODE

Inspired by beauty or love, you reach for an achievement that feels completely unattainable . . . and find that it isn't so unattainable after all.

TRANSITS OF MARS: FIGHT OR FLIGHT

Planetary Dossier: MARS

TIME TO MAKE A FULL CYCLE AROUND THE SUN: 22 months
TIME SPENT IN EACH ZODIAC SIGN: a little under 2 months
TRANSITING ASPECTS LAST FOR: about a week
STRONGEST SIGNS: Aries, Scorpio, Capricorn
HAS TO WORK HARDER IN: Cancer, Libra
KEYWORDS: action, initiative, energy, aggression, anger, competition, work, sexuality

The need to defend yourself takes on a much different meaning depending on who you are and where you live. I'm a middle-class woman living in a pleasant Southern California city; my need for self-defense is limited to keeping people from cutting in front of me in line at the supermarket. If I were a young man living in a less-prosperous neighborhood four blocks away, however, I might view self-defense in quite another way.

We all have our battles to fight. Some of them are truly life-or-death matters, others are internal struggles, and some are petty grievances unworthy of your time and energy.

All of these are ruled by Mars. And when transiting Mars makes contact with a part of your birth chart, you are called into battle. It could be a battle to defend yourself or somebody else, or simply to conquer some territory (such as a job) that you want for yourself.

MARS BY SIGN

Perhaps it's because I was raised in the car culture of Southern California, but I've long believed that you can tell everything about a person by the way he or she drives. Mars seems to have a kinship with automobiles, which gives an individual the autonomy to go where, when, and how he wants to go. This serves as a handy metaphor for examining how the aggressive, "me first" energy of Mars expresses itself as it transits through the zodiac at the rate of approximately one sign every two and a half months.

TRANSITING MARS IN ARIES ♈

Mars is at home in Aries, so there is no ambiguity here: This driver insists on being first, lives for going fast, and refuses to let anyone or anything get in his way. He's the guy who cuts you off on the freeway, the teenager who dings your car in the parking lot, and the customer service representative who is rude to you.

Mars in Aries makes an excellent ambulance or delivery service driver, however. When it's essential that something get someplace as quickly and directly as possible, you'll be glad you have Mars in Aries on your side.

Rules of the road: If something needs to be done fast, decisions need to be made in a hurry, or there is something you really want, this is the perfect transit.

TRANSITING MARS IN TAURUS ♉

Mars in Taurus is the guy who is driving only fifty miles an hour in the fast lane of the freeway. He's slow and stubborn and refuses to budge, and he can make you absolutely crazy.

Mars in Taurus makes a perfect limousine driver; when people want to be transported in comfort and safety, Mars in Taurus is their guy.

Rules of the road: Taurus's slow and steady approach makes this Mars transit great for starting projects that require a lot of patience and stamina to bring to completion.

TRANSITING MARS IN GEMINI ♊

Mars in Gemini is the young girl who is texting while driving, putting on her makeup, and giggling with the five other girls she's crammed into her Volkswagen Beetle. She's distracted and surprisingly volatile behind the wheel, flipping the bird and hollering at fellow motorists.

Mars in Gemini makes a fantastic tour guide, though. Put someone else in charge of driving and hand Mars in Gemini a loudspeaker, and everyone will have a good time.

Rules of the road: Gemini's restlessness and short attention span make this a good Mars transit for activities that offer variety, sociability, and fast talking.

TRANSITING MARS IN CANCER ♋

Mars in Cancer is like a harried mother piloting her SUV full of demanding children through rush-hour traffic. She usually holds it together, but look closely and you'll see a little craziness around her eyes. If one of those kids starts choking on a Lego, though, Mars in Cancer becomes a laser-focused dynamo. Protecting home, hearth, and loved ones is Mars in Cancer's greatest strength.

Rules of the road: Cancer's emotionalism makes this a very difficult transit for handling things in a dispassionate, straightforward way. But it is splendid for dealing with domestic matters that call for courage and decisive action.

TRANSITING MARS IN LEO ♌

Mars in Leo is the driver of a luxury vehicle, probably a convertible, who is wearing a $5,000 suit and talking on the phone through his Bluetooth headset. He is probably a tad distracted by his phone conversation, not to mention his dazzling reflection in the rearview mirror. Mars in Leo should really hire a professional driver to handle the tedious business of commuting. That way, he can focus on the business of being marvelous, preferably in the back of a limousine, where he can entertain his friends with champagne and a hot tub.

Rules of the road: This is an excellent transit for initiating creative projects, entertaining others, and self-promotion. It's less effective for handling the tedious, practical details of daily life.

TRANSITING MARS IN VIRGO ♍

Mars in Virgo is a cranky driver. No one is using a turn signal, everyone is incompetent, and look at that, you made her miss her exit! It's the worst thing that's happened to her—ever.

Mars in Virgo is a very conscientious driver, but a little too preoccupied with what everyone else is doing wrong. She's a terrific navigator, though, and would make a fantastic driving school instructor.

Rules of the road: If you need to improve yourself (and, with any luck at all, others), transiting Mars in Virgo is the right time to do it. It's not the best transit for projects involving collaboration or patience.

TRANSITING MARS IN LIBRA ♎

Mars in Libra cannot decide whether to turn left or right. Freeway exits marked "east" or "west" make him split the difference by driving into the sign itself. He vacillates between being passive-aggressive and aggressive-aggressive. He gets lost a lot, because he's concentrating on changing the radio station or chatting with his passenger.

Mars in Libra is not an effective driver in the sense of reaching a specific destination in a logical way. He's a great passenger, though, because he's pleasant, soothing company and chooses the perfect music for the journey.

Rules of the road: When transiting Mars is in Libra, let someone else do the driving for a while. Do your best to be a pleasant, cooperative copilot.

TRANSITING MARS IN SCORPIO ♏

In my neighborhood, there are guys who drive mean-looking cars with darkly tinted windows, their stereos pulsing with bass you can feel from four blocks away. They want you to think they are badasses. Maybe they are. But maybe they're just living by the adage that if you look menacing enough, no one will mess with you.

Mars in Scorpio certainly looks menacing. He'd like you to think he's going to mess you up if you drive too close to his bumper. Not that you would, if you value your hearing. But watch him spring into action if he comes across an accident by the side of the road. He would make an excellent EMT.

Rules of the road: While transiting Mars is in Scorpio, an appearance of strength could prevent you from real trouble. True strength could help you save others from real trouble.

TRANSITING MARS IN SAGITTARIUS ♐

There are two kinds of Mars in Sagittarius drivers. One thinks he's Mario Andretti, weaving in and out of traffic with abandon. The other is completely distracted by whatever he's listening to on satellite radio. He tends to run over parking bumpers and is a regular at the local body shop.

Mars in Sagittarius is not that interested in driving; airplanes are more his speed. As long as he's stuck behind the wheel, though, he's going to have an adventure.

Rules of the road: Transiting Mars in Sagittarius is the time to do what feels adventurous and absorbing. If you don't, you'll tend to get a little reckless or accident-prone.

TRANSITING MARS IN CAPRICORN ♑

Mars in Capricorn is an excellent driver—strategic, controlled, and professional. There is no wasted effort, no pointless lane changing, no road rage; every move is a study in efficiency.

Mars in Capricorn would rather be sitting in back of a town car making business calls with his chauffeur at the wheel. But if he must do the job of driving, he will do it like a professional, complete with black leather gloves.

Rules of the road: Transiting Mars in Capricorn is terrific for managing virtually any practical matters with maximum efficiency and professionalism.

TRANSITING MARS IN AQUARIUS ♒

Mars in Aquarius admires cars but doesn't particularly enjoy driving. He'll take exactly the same route to work every day for months, until he suddenly can't bear it anymore and switches. He finds traffic claustrophobic and hates wearing seatbelts.

Mars in Aquarius would make a pretty good bus driver or train conductor, though. He's at his best organizing groups of people all headed in the same direction.

Rules of the road: While transiting Mars is in Aquarius, change up your routine, go your own way, and don't play it safe. If you do what feels right for you, others will follow your lead.

TRANSITING MARS IN PISCES ♓

Oh, Mars in Pisces. You're very sweet. You don't mean to drive us crazy with your rush-hour left turns at busy, uncontrolled intersections and failure to notice when a light has turned green. You're just grooving to your tunes and talking on the phone without a care in the world. Even though you don't follow a straight path, or even use a map, you somehow get where you're going.

Cars aren't really her thing, but Mars in Pisces would be an excellent tour guide or cruise ship director.

Rules of the road: Transiting Mars in Pisces is best for letting life unfold the way it wants to. Don't force things to happen in a particular way or at a particular time.

TRANSITING MARS IN ASPECT TO NATAL PLANETS

Mars moves relatively quickly, but not as fast as Mercury and Venus. In fact, it takes Mars more than twice as long as Venus to circuit the zodiac. But the battles of transiting Mars are skirmishes, not full-fledged wars. Mars's transits of a sign, or a house of your birth chart (see part III), usually take no more than a couple of months. His aspects to your natal planets are finished within a week.

But he can do a lot of damage in a week if you don't keep a lid on your temper, take care on the freeway, or be cautious about walking through bad neighborhoods after dark. When Mars comes knocking on your door, he might come in the form of a neighbor who is annoyed about your barking dog, or he might be a fellow motorist battling you for a parking space. Mars is there to make you fight for your right to be who, what, and where you are, and to not let yourself get pushed around. Just don't get carried away; remember, everyone else has the same rights that you do.

TRANSITING MARS IN ASPECT TO THE NATAL SUN

For about a week, while Mars aspects your natal Sun, you may be more energetic, focused, and competitive than usual. But you may also be prone to bouts of temper, particularly if someone disrespects you.

TRANSITING MARS IN ASPECT TO THE NATAL MOON

This is one of the best weeks all year to tackle daunting projects around the house. You might also feel hurt or threatened by another person's show of temper or competitive spirit.

TRANSITING MARS IN ASPECT TO NATAL MERCURY

Your mind works overtime this week. It can be an excellent transit for digging into writing projects, studying, or anything else that requires a sharp mind. But it can also be a grouchy transit. You're not at your most tactful because your mind is focused on getting things done, and chitchat gets in the way.

TRANSITING MARS IN ASPECT TO NATAL VENUS

You are motivated this week to pursue the things you want, the things you enjoy, and the objects of your affection. But remember that the pursuit matters; you will not be able to fully enjoy your spoils if getting them requires that you treat others poorly.

TRANSITING MARS IN ASPECT TO NATAL JUPITER

Been collecting a lot of big dreams? Now is the time to take action! Even the smallest step in the direction of a wish or adventure will be rewarding this week. Irrational exuberance can backfire, though, so don't take unnecessary risks. Start with a single step—Rome, as they say, was not built in a day.

TRANSITING MARS IN ASPECT TO NATAL SATURN

Careful. While transiting Mars aspects natal Saturn, you are apt to beat up on yourself for your faults and failings, real or imagined. But it's not a productive approach to self-improvement. Instead, bring all your energy to the task of getting your life organized in a way that will move you forward from a stronger platform.

TRANSITING MARS IN ASPECT TO NATAL URANUS

Sometimes we have to get good and angry before we are willing to make a change. If that's the case for you, this week will likely be a catalyst for shaking things up. Step a little lightly, though. Once the world is shaken up, it's easy to trip over fallen debris.

TRANSITING MARS IN ASPECT TO NATAL NEPTUNE

This week, take a small action that you feel will improve someone's life. Volunteer or contribute to a cause, or stick up for someone who can't defend himself. If you have artistic intentions, initiate a new project this week. If you simply give in to anger, it may prompt self-defeating behavior.

TRANSITING MARS IN ASPECT TO NATAL PLUTO

When push comes to shove, sometimes we react by curling up in a ball—and sometimes we push back. This week, you'll get the opportunity to show what you're made of. Don't let a challenge defeat you; let it inspire you to empower yourself.

TRANSITING MARS IN ASPECT TO THE NATAL NORTH NODE

The Moon's North Node represents one of the few "can't fail" areas of your chart. If you make any step in the direction of your fondest desires this week, you will be rewarded—even if the prize takes a different form than the one you had envisioned.

TRANSITING MARS IN ASPECT TO THE NATAL ASCENDANT

This is normally a pretty quick transit. But if you've been in an angry or self-defeating mind-set, a transit such as this can trigger a temper tantrum or worse. The best strategy is to consciously channel strong emotions and energy into directed physical exercise. Drive cautiously. Handle kitchen knives carefully. Wear red. And count to ten before you tell that guy who stole your parking space what you really think of him.

TRANSITING MARS IN ASPECT TO THE NATAL MIDHEAVEN

By all means, keep a lid on your temper. Social media flame wars, meltdowns in the workplace, or angry talk about someone will probably backfire on you. This transit is quick, but it could do long-term damage to your reputation.

It's a good transit, however, for actively pursuing something that will move you closer to your goals—especially in your career. Tackle your to-do lists and initiate long-term plans.

chapter 9

TRANSITS OF THE SUN AND MOON:
THE DANCE OF LIGHT

Growing up in Los Angeles, I spent a lot of time at Disneyland. Back then, you paid admission and received a coupon book with tickets, labeled A through E, to gain entry to various attractions. Everyone knew that all the best, most exciting rides were the ones that required an E ticket.

In astrology the big, slow transits of Saturn, Uranus, Neptune, and Pluto are the E-ticket rides. They're the ones that are exciting and life-changing, and occasionally make you nauseous; they are the transits in your chart that an astrologer will usually spend the most time talking about.

In contrast, transits of the Sun and Moon would probably qualify only as A-ticket attractions. They move quickly, repeat often, and in and of themselves, they're never going to bring about important changes to your life. But their cyclical dances symbolize the development of emotional well-being (symbolized by the Moon) and a healthy ego (the Sun), both of which will help you handle the larger, life-altering transits more gracefully.

In this chapter, we'll take a look at each cycle and place these fast-moving but important transits into perspective.

TRANSITS OF THE MOON: DAILY AND MONTHLY

Planetary Dossier: MOON

TIME TO MAKE A FULL CYCLE AROUND THE SUN: 28 days

TIME SPENT IN EACH ZODIAC SIGN: about 2½ days

TRANSITING ASPECTS LAST FOR: approximately 3 hours

STRONGEST SIGNS: Cancer, Taurus

HAS TO WORK HARDER IN: Capricorn, Scorpio

KEYWORDS: home, family, comfort, security, safety, privacy, the public, the subconscious, habits, routines, diet, mother, nurturing, nourishing

You were born into a family and a community where your physical and emotional needs were (hopefully) met. Most likely, you absorbed the customs and tribal identity of this community before you were old enough to realize it; they allowed you to feel safe. You also developed particular habits, routines, and emotional attitudes as ways of comforting and protecting yourself.

The familiarity of family, hearth, and community, as well as the mostly unconscious patterns of daily habit, are represented in astrology by the Moon. Your approach to the days and months of your life is aligned with the phases, signs, and aspects of the transiting Moon. One of the most profound rewards of following lunar cycles is a better understanding of your unconscious habits so that you can choose healthier, comforting, and nurturing ones.

HOW TO FOLLOW THE MOON

Because the Moon moves quickly, whipping through a sign of the zodiac in two and a half days, tracking its aspects to the natal chart—even its location in the houses of the horoscope—is not all that useful. Yes, if you look back at crucial moments in your life and cast a horoscope for them, you'll probably see that the Moon was making interesting aspects to your birth chart. But most of us simply don't have the time to track all of those aspects daily.

What I have found helpful is keeping track of the Moon's current phase, its current sign, and the aspects it will make to other transiting planets on a given day. Taken together, these paint a picture of the day's mood and reveal the most productive way to plan your day and your month.

LUNAR PHASES

The monthly lunar cycle is as familiar as a mother's face, beginning at the dark of the New Moon, waxing toward its First Quarter, reaching its zenith with a completely illuminated Full Moon, and waning toward its Last Quarter. Each of these points in the Moon's monthly cycle offers a particular opportunity for developing self-awareness and taking action.

NEW MOON (TRANSITING SUN AND MOON IN THE SAME SIGN)

This is the quiet, dark time of the month. Something new is coming, but you can't see it yet. Energy is building, but it hasn't quite taken hold. Seeds are being planted, but evidence of their growth is weeks away.

This is one of the most powerful times of the month for performing magic. It's common practice at this time of the lunar cycle to set intentions based on the New Moon's sign and use some kind of ritual to affirm those intentions.

FIRST QUARTER (TRANSITING MOON SQUARE THE TRANSITING SUN)

At the First Quarter phase, about one week after the New Moon, a bit of the Moon is visible early in the night sky. Symbolically, the light is beginning to dawn for you, as well. The road forward becomes clearer; you're more energetic, even feisty. What was hidden from you at the New Moon is rising up now, into your consciousness. You know what needs to be done, and you have the energy and will to do it.

FULL MOON (TRANSITING MOON OPPOSED THE TRANSITING SUN)

About two weeks into the lunar cycle, the Full Moon illuminates the night sky. If you wished, you could go outside and work through the night without any other light source. You now can see exactly what has been blocking your progress in the area of life represented by the New Moon's sign and house. This is the best phase for releasing what is no longer working.

LAST QUARTER (TRANSITING MOON SQUARE THE TRANSITING SUN)

Three weeks after the New Moon, the Last Quarter Moon is visible late in the evening. Once again, as at the First Quarter, you are energized, ready to adapt, and prepared to make a final push to achieve your goals.

THE TRANSITING MOON BY SIGN

What mood is the world in today? What are people looking for? What colors, clothes, and attitudes will appeal to the public on a subconscious level?

The Transiting Moon's sign is a terrific tool for any situation that requires tuning in to others, such as interviews or social engagements. And it's a good way of figuring out which activities and endeavors will come most easily to you today.

The Moon changes signs every two and a half days, so if you don't like what's on today's menu, you won't have to wait long for a new selection!

TRANSITING MOON IN ARIES ♈

Aries is the Nike moon: "Just do it" is the motto for the day. While the Moon is in Aries, don't make excuses. Don't give in to self-doubt or fear. Be brave enough to live a life that's right for you, not one that's meant for someone else.

What to get done today: This is one of the better Moon signs for breaking old habits, standing up for yourself, and doing the things you're afraid to do.

What people want today: action, speed, courage, sass, the color red, plain talk

TRANSITING MOON IN TAURUS ♉

Immersed as we are in modern life, with its sedentary pace and wall-to-wall electronic gadgets, it's easy to become estranged from our bodies. Today, while the Moon is in Taurus, the sign representing the joy of physicality, be in your body and enjoy life's simple pleasures.

What to get done today: Taurus is determined and habit oriented, so it's essential that you use these few days to form positive and healthful routines.

What people want today: enjoyment, good food, a happy use of the physical body, the pleasures of the senses, the colors pink and baby blue

TRANSITING MOON IN GEMINI ♊

When the Moon is Gemini, your attention easily wanders—not because you don't care about others, but because you're listening to so many stories at once. From songbirds to the whisper of wind in the trees, in your email inbox and on social media, the whole world seems to be talking to you today. Like a restless bird or butterfly, you crave motion; your mind needs stimulation and variety.

What to get done today: Gather information. Gossip shamelessly. Deviate from your usual routines and habits. Socialize. Catch up on email and phone calls.

What people want today: variety, conversation, new ideas, information, bright colors, distractions

TRANSITING MOON IN CANCER ♋

Cancer the Crab doesn't let go easily; just look at those claws. Inside each of us there's a little Cancer-shaped box with a secret cache of beloved objects, people, and memories that we treasure and hold on to for dear life. They make us feel connected with someone we used to be, someplace we used to live, or loved ones who are gone. Part of a glowing, lacquered shell of familiarity and warmth, these treasures feel like home.

What to get done today: The Moon is strongest in this sign, and the pull of personal rituals and routines is strong. Don't push yourself to change these while the Moon is in Cancer. Instead, take care of yourself, eat what you like, and enjoy your home and family.

What people want today: comfort, security, tenderness, nourishment, silvery colors, old songs and movies, relaxed times with people whom we consider members of our tribe

TRANSITING MOON IN LEO ♌

So many of us—even Leos!—are embarrassed by our need to express ourselves and to be acknowledged by others. We create but refuse to share our creations for fear of rejection. Or we share our artistry but pretend that we don't care how others respond. How often do we simply stand before an audience, looking great, doing our best, sharing everything in our hearts, and trusting our audience to love us back? It takes a lot of guts and conviction to take the stage and offer up a part of one's soul. While the Moon is in Leo, take your place in the spotlight and show us what you've got.

What to get done today: These are good days to solidify habits and routines that you're hoping will last. It's also an inspiring time for creative work and one of the best times of each month for self-promotion.

What people want today: an audience, dramatic fashion, fiery colors, spicy food, glamour, fun, parties

TRANSITING MOON IN VIRGO ♍

To be of service—untangling the knots of the world, solving vexing problems, relieving pain and suffering—is a Virgo impulse. Throw the Moon into the mix, and even the psyche grows watchful. You don't need to be asked for help; today you observe need in the smallest gesture, like the faint tightening around a loved one's mouth. The physical world whispers to you, and intuitively, almost unconsciously, you respond. You add more oregano to the sauce without tasting it; somehow you know just how much it needs. You reach for precisely the right size screwdriver to fix the cupboard hinge. The computer that's been acting up for days suddenly hums in your presence. You are ready and able to fix the world's problems.

What to get done today: Offer yourself in service. Aspire to craft, to art, to empathy; show the world how well you understand it, how carefully and thoroughly you can love it.

What people want today: something to fix, a job to do, a problem to solve, useful things, practical fabrics, time outdoors

TRANSITING MOON IN LIBRA ♎

As its symbol—the scales—suggests, balance is key to understanding Libra. In any situation, Libra instinctively notes which side of the scales is too heavily weighted and then jumps to the other side to balance things out. The nastier the mood of the room, the sweeter Libra is apt to be. But when confronted with an atmosphere laden with cloying sentiment and excessive politeness, Libra won't hesitate to level it out with acerbic observations and irreverence.

While the Moon is in Libra, the sign of balance, harmony, and partnership, we instinctively temper volatile situations with diplomacy and instigate trouble if life grows tame. When we find the perfect partner to provide the harmony to our melody, the result is magical.

What to get done today: Bring situations into balance. Play music, paint a picture, or feng shui your house. Beautify yourself and your surroundings. Collaborate.

What people want today: companionship, beauty, someone who brings balance to the situation

TRANSITING MOON IN SCORPIO ♏

When the Moon moves through Scorpio, dragons need slaying. Some are outside of you, but the scariest dragons live in your heart. Today, if you don't feel equal to the task of wrestling your demons, it's not the end of the world; you'll have other chances. In the meantime, don't let your fears, or the terrible discomfort of vulnerability, provoke you into attacking others for their own frailties. Before letting loose with Scorpio's legendary sting, examine why you want to do it. Sometimes it's easier to attack others instead of our own problems—or worse still, to let our emotions ice over or give in to cynicism.

What to get done today: Be patient with others and gentle with yourself. Dig deep to get to the root of problems.

What people want today: someone trustworthy; honesty; dark, dramatic colors; emotionally challenging films, television, and music

TRANSITING MOON IN SAGITTARIUS ♐

Ask a Sagittarian anything: He or she will usually answer honestly. It's tempting to think that's because Sagittarius is more trusting than the rest of us are. But I don't think that's it, exactly; rather, Sagittarius simply sees honesty as a road to freedom. The only information that can be used against us, Sagittarius reasons, is what we try desperately to keep hidden—from other people, and from ourselves. The less Sagittarius hides, the freer, more energetic, and more creative he or she is.

What to get done today: You may never be as comfortable as Sagittarius about sharing your secrets. But today, while the Moon is in this uninhibited sign, try, at the very least, not to take yourself too seriously. Laughing first gives others the chance to laugh with you, rather than at you.

What people want today: a good laugh, optimism, a big idea, an adventure, the colors—and the spirit—of Mardi Gras

TRANSITING MOON IN CAPRICORN ♑

New Year's resolutions are tough to keep. Sometimes that's because we don't really know what we want to accomplish. Other times, we find that we're daunted by the sheer distance that lies between us and our goal.

Capricorn, symbolized by the mountain goat, knows there's only one way to close the gap between you and the summit: one hoofstep at a time. It's not important that every step be graceful, or that you smile and think positive thoughts while you're climbing—it's only vital that you keep moving forward. If you're determined to reach a goal, whether small and personal or of social significance, you can generally find success simply by showing up and doing the job—and, with dogged determination, by outlasting the competition.

What to get done today: Choose one goal you can reasonably reach in the next twenty-eight days. If you're willing to sweat, to be discouraged and exhausted, to sacrifice comfort, luxury, and afternoon naps—you can achieve that goal by the next Capricorn Moon. Practice this exercise every month, and you'll develop strength and confidence in your ability to meet your resolutions.

What people want today: respect, authority, competence, and maturity; old movies, cars, and songs; subdued colors and classic fashions; excellent quality

TRANSITING MOON IN AQUARIUS ♒

Aquarius is a sign of contradictions. It symbolizes society's oddball, the rebellious square peg who stubbornly refuses to be shoved into a round hole. The world needs its rebels, outcasts, and weirdos. Without them, nothing much ever changes.

Aquarius is also the sign of the local celebrity, the person who knows everyone in his neighborhood. In some cases, it's the sign of the master politician or superstar, someone of singular stature who nonetheless exudes human-scale warmth. An Oprah Winfrey, Ronald Reagan, or Franklin D. Roosevelt succeeds because others relate to him or her.

The mark of a leader is the ability to embrace the spirit of the collective. The mark of a great leader is the ability to elevate the discourse and move the collective out of its comfort zone—and into history.

What to get done today: Ask yourself how you can best influence the world: by shaking up the status quo, or by persuading the world to be better, braver, and more compassionate than it thinks it can be? Gather with others who share your views, interests, and goals. Walk toward the future.

What people want today: feelings of belonging; a friend; a place to fit in; exciting, unexpected experiences; socializing; a feeling that they are doing something that will matter long after they're gone; cool, electric colors

TRANSITING MOON IN PISCES ♓

A nap. You could really use a nap. For the two and a half days each month when the Moon is in Pisces, you alternate between being delightfully sociable and finding your fellow humans unendurably exhausting to be around. Suddenly you find that you absorb every feeling around you—joy, anger, jealousy, inspiration. Holding all that emotion can make you feel heavy, like a rain cloud before a storm or a sponge that needs wringing out. This is the time of the month for rest, for release, and for emptying your mind and soul to prepare for new experiences to come.

What to get done today: Like the sleek, vulnerable fish for which it's named, Pisces is a gentle creature with only a few scales for protection. No matter how tough you normally are, today you may feel helpless. Wiley escape may seem to be your only defense—and this is excellent astral weather for time spent alone in rest, reflection, and meditation.

What people want today: rest, retreat, and inspiration; shimmering ocean colors; music; positive words and thoughts

THE TRANSITING MOON IN ASPECT TO TRANSITING PLANETS

The Moon moves about 1 degree every two hours. Its orb of aspect to another transiting planet is about 1 degree approaching the exact aspect. So a lunar aspect to another transiting planet is really in effect only for a couple of hours at most. This makes it a relatively minor transit but potentially a powerful trigger for other, more important transits.

Most of all, the Moon's aspects in a given day point to the day's "flow": How easy or difficult is it to get things done? If the Moon is making a lot of squares and oppositions during the day, or conjunctions to difficult planets such as Mars, Saturn, Uranus, or Pluto, it's going to be One of Those Days—everyone seems grouchy and you can't get anything done. As I write, for instance, the Moon is in Capricorn—already a bit of a tough sign for it—and is making a conjunction to Pluto and squares to Mars/Uranus. Basically, write off everything before 11:51 a.m. Then the day gets a bit nicer, with the Moon making a trine to Venus.

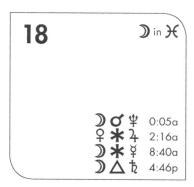

If, on the other hand, the Moon is awash with pleasant trines and opportunity-bringing sextiles, life generally chugs along in a fairly productive way.

How to Tell If It's Going to Be a . . .

TOUGH DAY:

The Moon is making mostly:

Square or opposition aspects to other planets,* or

Conjunctions to Mars, Saturn, Uranus, Neptune, or Pluto

* Venus and Jupiter are generally considered to be favorable planets, so even traditionally difficult aspects such as squares and oppositions are not so bad when Venus and Jupiter are involved.

NICE DAY:

The Moon is making mostly:

Sextile or trine aspects to other planets, or

Conjunctions with the Sun (New Moon), Mercury, Venus, or Jupiter

VOID-OF-COURSE MOON

After the Moon has finished making all of the major planetary aspects it will make in its current sign, we say that she is void of course, or VOC. Depending on the positions of the Sun and other planets, this VOC period may last anywhere from a few seconds to a day or more.

The traditional interpretation of the VOC Moon is "nothing will come of the matter." These are probably not the best times to initiate an enterprise that needs to grow and change.

Weirdly, though, there are very particular and helpful uses for the VOC Moon. My teacher swore by sending her tax returns on a VOC Moon, figuring "nothing comes of the matter" would mean she wouldn't get audited! I'll also confess to having saved certain email inquiries about things I didn't really want to do, and responding to them during the VOC Moon.

Here's an interesting bit of trivia: I started two of the longest and most satisfying relationships of my life during the VOC Moon: I bought my first new car, and I'm still driving it twenty-nine years later. And in 1991, a cute guy with a neat accent walked into my office for a reading during the VOC Moon. We recently celebrated our twenty-first wedding anniversary!

So I'm not sure I'd say, exactly, that "nothing comes of the matter" when you begin something on a VOC Moon. It seems to me what happens is that things keep on keeping on. The late astrologer Darrell Martinie, who went by the colorful moniker "The Cosmic Muffin," used to say the VOC Moon was his favorite time to begin a diet. So if you're initiating a new habit—or starting a relationship—that you hope will last, you could do much worse than to begin it when the Moon is void of course.

TRANSITS OF THE SUN: THE MAN WHO CAME TO DINNER

Planetary Dossier: SUN

TIME TO MAKE A FULL CYCLE AROUND THE SUN: 365 days

TIME SPENT IN EACH ZODIAC SIGN: 30 days

TRANSITING ASPECTS LAST FOR: approximately 3 days

STRONGEST SIGNS: Leo, Aries

HAS TO WORK HARDER IN: Aquarius, Libra

KEYWORDS: vitality, life force, confidence, creativity, charisma, playfulness, happiness

In adolescence, the security and familiarity of home are no longer quite enough. You're ready to test your mettle against the world outside those gates. You yearn to make a name for yourself and to figure out who you are apart from your family.

To locate the qualities and character of the core self, astrologers look to the Sun. It's easy to trivialize the Sun's cycle, since it moves quickly. The transiting Sun covers one house of your chart in a month or two and the entire birth chart in one year. When a slow-moving planet such as Saturn or Pluto transits an important point in your chart, it's like a hostage situation. They take over and stay for a decade. Naturally this is juicy fodder for the astrologer, and these transits tend to get the lion's share of attention in a reading.

But really, when you've got a crazy relative living in your basement for a decade at a time, you feel his presence less and less. He's a problem everyone else can see, but day to day, you might not even notice he's there.

The Sun transiting your chart, on the other hand, is like *The Man Who Came to Dinner*. In this classic film adaptation of a popular play, an overbearing, self-centered celebrity is invited to dine with the family of a prominent businessman. As he arrives, he slips on some ice outside their house, is injured, and moves in for the duration of his convalescence. In very short order he comes to dominate the lives of everyone in the household with his imperious nature and blunt comments.

The Sun can be sort of an overbearing, self-centered celebrity himself, and when he is transiting your chart, he has a way of making you feel that your furniture is a little shabby and your conversation a bit dull. At worst, he briefly dominates your life with his ego, demands, tantrums, and theatrics. But at best, he motivates you to bring your "A" game: to want a little more from life, get a better haircut, mind your posture—in short, to make your life a bit better and happier.

THE TRANSITING SUN IN ASPECT TO NATAL PLANETS

The transiting Sun's aspects to the planets in your birth chart are worth watching. The influence of these aspects is strong for several days: the day before the aspect is exact, the day of it is exact, and the day after it is exact. Several days is long enough! These aspects are uncommon enough (you only get a handful of aspects to each planet from the transiting Sun in a given year) to make an impression.

If you have a copy of your birth chart and an ephemeris (use the free online ephemeris at Astro.com or buy a used copy of the complete ephemerides for the twenty-first century online), it's extremely easy to find when these days will occur, and they'll be within the same day or so every year.

For instance, if Venus in your chart is at 9 degrees Gemini, you know the transiting Sun will make a conjunction to this point sometime after the Sun moves into Gemini in late May. Since that usually happens around May 20 and the Sun moves about 1 degree per day, you can expect this transit around May 29, give or take a day.

The transiting Sun's challenging aspects are the square, the opposition, and any aspect to a planet in your chart that's a bit difficult. If a planet in your chart has many challenging aspects, it's like having a shabby room in your house that you desperately try to keep hidden, and the Sun is a nosy guest who throws open the door and tells you how awful it looks.

The transiting Sun's more encouraging aspects are the sextile and trine. These transits usually bring with them some small measure of acclaim or praise, or pleasant events and feedback that make you feel better about yourself.

TRANSITING SUN IN ASPECT TO NATAL SUN

If the aspect is a conjunction, happy birthday/solar return!

Challenging aspects: Stand tall in defense of your authority, dignity, and right to be noticed.

Flowing aspects: Accept praise and admiration graciously and take advantage of opportunities to shine.

TRANSITING SUN IN ASPECT TO NATAL MOON

Challenging aspects: If others invade your privacy or make you feel threatened, consider how to create healthy boundaries and defend yourself.

Flowing aspects: These are days when you gain appreciation for and pride in your home, family, and heritage.

TRANSITING SUN IN ASPECT TO NATAL MERCURY

Challenging aspects: Consider whether you can frame the difficulties in your life in a more positive way; consider whether it's time to change your name or title to something more appropriate.

Flowing aspects: Your ability to express yourself creatively and charismatically soars.

TRANSITING SUN IN ASPECT TO NATAL VENUS

Challenging aspects: Treat yourself well; if you don't value yourself, no one else will.

Flowing aspects: These are some of your most magnetic and attractive days of the year! Look your best, put yourself out there, and accept compliments gracefully.

TRANSITING SUN IN ASPECT TO NATAL MARS

Challenging aspects: Someone provokes your fighting instincts, probably through a display of arrogance or authoritarianism. Take advantage of the opportunity to practice handling conflict more effectively.

Flowing aspects: Conflict is still possible under the flowing aspects, but you probably feel a lot more energized, and even creatively inspired, by it.

TRANSITING SUN IN ASPECT TO NATAL JUPITER

Challenging aspects: Your tolerance for being told what to do or to believe is very low. Take this opportunity to consider whether you're apt to be a bit bossy yourself, or too vehement in expressing your beliefs.

Flowing aspects: Mark these days on your calendar and capitalize on them. Unless your natal Jupiter has very poor aspects, these are usually times when it's much easier than usual for you to get what you want.

TRANSITING SUN IN ASPECT TO NATAL SATURN

Challenging aspects: The spotlight is shining on your deepest insecurities and wounds. Don't lash out; rather, let these days deepen your compassion for yourself.

Flowing aspects: You are likely to be acknowledged—if only by yourself—for your achievements, leadership, and maturity. Give yourself a gold star for all the obstacles you've overcome and for all the hard work you've done that no one knows about but you.

TRANSITING SUN IN ASPECT TO NATAL URANUS

Challenging aspects: These days, it can feel as though you just don't fit in anywhere. Take the opportunity to appreciate the qualities that make you unique.

Flowing aspects: You may find yourself connecting with people who make you feel like part of a group or network. You might literally join an organization that makes you feel included.

TRANSITING SUN IN ASPECT TO NATAL NEPTUNE

Challenging aspects: You may feel others are critical of you, especially pointing out your lack of practicality or focus. It's vitally important to safeguard your health now, since your sensitivity is very high and your resistance to disease (and negativity) is low.

Flowing aspects: If you are a creative or spiritual person, these extraordinarily rewarding days may leave you feeling touched by a divine and benevolent spirit. Create today.

TRANSITING SUN IN ASPECT TO NATAL PLUTO

Challenging aspects: Some of the most uncomfortable for many people, these days you tend to get the message that you just aren't very important. Take the opportunity to claim the attitude that each of us is vitally important, and that includes you.

Flowing aspects: These can be some of the most powerful days of your personal year, as long as you don't try to grab power that doesn't belong to you. Place yourself in the vicinity of powerful people; they could respond well to you.

TRANSITING SUN IN ASPECT TO NATAL NORTH NODE

Challenging aspects: You may feel as though you're not getting anywhere and will never reach your most cherished goals. The message today is to refuse to accept that belief and to recommit yourself to taking even the smallest step toward what is important to you.

Flowing aspects: Even if you don't seem to be reaching exactly the goal you set for yourself, today you recognize that you may be reaching a related goal that is even better for you, that you would never have imagined for yourself.

YOUR PERSONAL SEASONS

A Southern California girl, I never gave much thought to the seasons until I married someone from the Southern Hemisphere and listened, baffled and captivated, to his stories of spending Christmas at the beach and celebrating his October birthday in the spring.

Regardless of which hemisphere you're in, you can relate to the seasons in a way that brings them into your bones and makes them your own. Begin your personal springtime on the day that the transiting Sun moves over the Ascendant of your birth chart, and then follow the Sun's annual cycle through the wheel of your chart.

The annual solar cycle mirrors the lunar cycle, beginning with the dark of the Winter Solstice (rather like the New Moon), followed by the Spring Equinox (similar to the First Quarter Moon), Summer Solstice (day of longest light, evocative of the Full Moon), and Autumnal Equinox (like the Last Quarter Moon).

The work of this transiting solar cycle is about reclaiming different facets of the self and learning to overcome blockages to self-expression. Your own personal seasons can be defined by the Sun's annual conjunctions with the angles of your chart.

YOUR PERSONAL WINTER SOLSTICE

Sun Conjunct Midheaven (tenth house cusp)

The seasons begin with the Sun's conjunction with your Midheaven, the most elevated point in your birth chart. It is the angle associated with Capricorn, the sign the Sun enters on the shortest day of the year. The Midheaven is associated with career, calling, and ambition. (Our calendar year starts soon after the Winter Solstice; this is when we enjoy setting resolutions for health, finances, and career in the coming twelve months.)

At this time, you're determined to do more, to be more. But like the New Moon, this is a dark time, and you can't completely see yet exactly where you're going.

YOUR PERSONAL SPRING EQUINOX

Sun Conjunct Ascendant (first house cusp)

Your personal spring begins the day the transiting Sun crosses your Ascendant. Regardless of the season that the rest of the world is experiencing, this is the time of year that speaks to you of excitement, new beginnings, and the energy to make a big push forward.

YOUR PERSONAL SUMMER SOLSTICE

Transiting Sun Conjunct IC (fourth house cusp)

The indolence, relaxation, and break from everyday life that we associate with a great summer vacation begins, for you, on the day that the transiting Sun crosses your IC. Your energy is often a bit low, you don't want to be around people much, and you need a respite from your routines so that you can daydream and reflect on the year so far.

YOUR PERSONAL AUTUMN EQUINOX

Transiting Sun Conjunct Descendant (seventh house cusp)

You are beginning the third quarter of your personal year, and it's time to make a last push to achieve what you set out to do when the sun crossed your Midheaven. Because the Descendant is the relationship and partnership area of your chart, it may become clear to you now to ask others for help and support to make it to the finish line.

YOUR SOLAR AND LUNAR RETURNS

YOUR ASTROLOGICAL BIRTHDAY AND YOUR MONTHLY REBIRTH

Each year, within one day of your birthday, the Sun returns to the same degree and sign it was in at the moment of your birth. This is called your Solar Return. Similarly, every twenty-eight days, the Moon returns to the same degree and sign of the zodiac that it was in at your birth; this is your Lunar Return.

Calculate a chart for the moment of the Solar Return or Lunar Return, and you can read it as a snapshot of the year or month ahead.

How to Calculate Your Return Charts at Astro.com

1. From the navigation menu, click on "Free Horoscopes."
2. Navigate to "Horoscope Drawings & Calculations" and select "Extended Chart Selection."
3. Under "Methods > Please select the type of chart you want," from the drop-down menu select "Solar Return Chart" or "Lunar Return Chart."
4. Under "Options," select the start date to begin your search; that will calculate the next solar or lunar return chart.
5. Press the button that says "Click here to show the chart."

What to look for: The house of the chart where the Moon (Lunar Return chart) or Sun (Solar Return chart) falls shows which area of your life could benefit from a review of unconscious habits, and creation of some rituals to set intentions for the month ahead. (See part IV for delineations of each house of the horoscope.)

The house(s) of the chart with Cancer (Lunar Return chart) or Leo (Solar Return chart) on the cusp shows where in your life you are able to work out some of your emotional challenges this month.

Planets close to the angles of the chart represent external challenges and opportunities that affect your emotional nature this month and have an effect on your ability to feel safe and secure (Lunar Return) or your confidence, sense of self, and creative expression in the coming year (Solar Return).

ECLIPSES

NEW AND FULL MOONS ON STEROIDS

Eclipses involve a specific alignment of the Sun, Moon, and Earth. Although these celestial bodies align twice each month, we don't have monthly eclipses because the Moon's orbit is slightly tilted in relation to the ecliptic, the Sun's apparent path through the stars.

Eclipses are by no means unusual, though. We have at least two solar eclipses each year, six months apart, at the New Moon closest to the Lunar Nodes. Lunar eclipses usually, but not always, precede or follow a solar eclipse at the Full Moon.

SOLAR/LUNAR ECLIPSES

During a solar eclipse, the Moon passes between the Sun and the Earth, temporarily blocking our view of the Sun. Symbolically, at a solar eclipse, lunar function such as intuition and instinct temporarily overpower solar functions such as confidence, creativity, and sense of self. The result is a bit like a short-circuit of your internal wiring.

In my observation, solar eclipses are experienced most intensely in the week leading up to the event. They also seem to have more of a physical effect than lunar eclipses, making us feel drained, stressed, or overexcited.

During a lunar eclipse, the Earth casts a shadow on the Moon, preventing it from reflecting the Sun's light. Similarly, during a lunar eclipse, our ability to transmit and receive light is blocked by worldly concerns, such as the pain of earthly need or loss. In my observation, lunar eclipses are most intensely felt up to a few days before they actually happen and have less of a physical effect than do solar eclipses.

WHAT THEY MEAN

Eclipses indicate moments of crisis. Sounds scary—but it's worth noting that a crisis is not always negative. A crisis can be a difficult or dangerous situation, but sometimes it is simply a decisive moment of change. Even the happiest moment of your life—a marriage, a birth, enormous career success—can be a crisis. Much happiness is associated with big events such as these, but ask any newlywed and they'll often admit that some days, they wake up and don't know who they are, don't recognize their own life. It's exciting but disorienting.

Eclipses indicate times of crisis—some joyful, some tragic. All of them shake you out of your normal routines or way of seeing the world.

ECLIPSES TO WATCH

Not all transits are created equal, and that includes eclipses. Generally, to really get your attention, eclipses need to:
- Make a close (no more than 4 degrees of orb) . . .
- hard aspect (conjunction, square, opposition) . . .
- to an important planet or group of planets in your birth chart. An "important planet" is the Sun, the Moon, or one that's involved in a number of aspects (especially difficult aspects) with other planets, or is very close to an angle (the cusp of the first, fourth, seventh, or tenth houses).

Of course, other transits happening at the same time may color your experience of a particular eclipse cycle. Also, eclipses that occur at the Moon's North Node are thought to represent opportunities for positive change. Eclipses at the Moon's South Node are considered by some to be harbingers of loss and bad luck.

ECLIPSE CYCLES

Like everything else in astrology, eclipses have predictable patterns. Every eighteen years, an eclipse occurs as part of a Saros cycle family of eclipses. These macro cycles unfold over thousands of years. Many astrologers use the chart for the first eclipse in a Saros family to read the characteristics that will be common to all eclipses in the cycle.

In addition, every nineteen years, an eclipse falls close to the same degree of the zodiac. That means an eclipse at the same degree as one of the planets or angles in your birth chart will repeat roughly every nineteen years.

Eclipses move in cycles, the way earthquakes happen along a fault line. This year's eclipses share characteristics with the ones that happened eighteen and nineteen years ago. Those years, and the events that happened then, are relevant to your life right now; they are part of a continuing story unfolding over the entirety of your life.

Mark Twain once famously wrote, "History doesn't repeat itself, but it rhymes." Eclipses don't bring identical events over and over, but rather bring experiences having similar themes in your life, related to the most challenging planetary aspects in your chart.

part III:

TRANSITS
IN HOUSES

Lots of people were born on the same day you were, and quite a few around the same moment you were, but only a handful of those were also born in the same place that you were. The twelve houses of the horoscope, derived from the date, time, and location of your birth, are arguably the most personalized points in your birth chart. This bespoke configuration of the sky is what is missing in astrology when you don't know the exact time and place of a person's birth. Without the houses of the horoscope, an important dimension of transit work is incomplete at best.

If your life is a play and the planets are characters, the twelve houses of the horoscope represent the situations in which the characters find themselves. When transits enter a new house of the birth chart, a different area of your life is awakened and impacted. The plot thickens.

HOUSE SYSTEMS

House systems are the various methods astrologers use to cut the chart into pieces. Think of house systems as schools of architecture: A midcentury modern house tends to have a very different layout than a Victorian one.

Because house systems are arbitrary—there are no lines separating the sky into twelve parts—the topic of which one is best is fraught with controversy. In most systems, the Ascendant/Descendant (first and seventh house cusps) and Midheaven/IC (tenth and fourth house cusps) are the same. It's the secondary houses—the second and eighth, third and ninth, fifth and eleventh, and sixth and twelfth houses—that differ. In popular systems such as Placidus and Koch, pairs of houses can vary hugely in size based on the time of year and latitude at which you were born. Different degrees and sometimes different signs appear on the cusps depending on which house system is used.

Some systems simplify the issue by making all houses the same size. The Solar House system, for instance, places the degree and sign of the natal Sun on the Ascendant, then the same degree of subsequent signs on the second house, third, and so on. The Whole Sign system, probably the oldest house system, is one of the simplest and has come back into widespread use in recent years. In the Whole House system, each house is the same size. The first degree of the sign of your calculated Ascendant is placed on the first house cusp, with the first degree of all the subsequent signs following counterclockwise on each house cusp. If you have, say, 10 degrees of Sagittarius on your calculated Ascendant, then 0 degrees Sagittarius goes on the first house cusp, 0 degrees Capricorn on the second, 0 degrees Aquarius on the third, and so on, ending with 0 degrees Scorpio on the twelfth house cusp.

Personally, I'm agnostic on the subject of house systems. I inherited the Koch house system from my teacher, and it has served me well. But I have experimented with the Whole Sign system and liked it, and if a client requests a different house system I'm more than happy to comply. I picture house systems as different lenses a photographer might use on his camera. Each gives a somewhat different perspective.

I recommend you calculate your birth chart in a number of house systems, then watch what happens as fast-moving transits cross each house cusp. Most likely, one system or other will emerge as your personal favorite.

WHY I HAVE ORGANIZED THE HOUSES IN PAIRS

Most astrology books that deal with the houses of the horoscope handle them one by one and sequentially. In this book, I've chosen to group them into six pairs. Each pair represents two houses that are directly opposite each other on the horoscopic wheel. These two houses are always the same size in any house system, with the same degree of opposite signs on their cusps, and the areas of life they represent are opposite and complementary as well:

- **First and Seventh:** Self and Important Others
- **Second and Eighth:** Personal and Shared Resources
- **Third and Ninth:** Learning and Understanding
- **Fourth and Tenth:** Origin and Destination
- **Fifth and Eleventh:** Creations and Legends (Legacy)
- **Sixth and Twelfth:** This World and the Next

In my experience, transits in one house of the chart also have an impact on the opposite house. Either increased focus on one house causes imbalance as the affairs of the other are neglected, or, if the transit is especially difficult, we may choose to spend less time involved with the matters of that house and "hide out" in the opposite one. If a very slow-moving planet such as Uranus, Neptune, or Pluto is transiting a house of your chart, you might find it helpful to read the section on the opposite house as well.

HOW LONG TRANSITING PLANETS ARE IN A HOUSE

Again, this depends on the house system you're using, and possibly the time of year and place where you were born. Let's assume the houses in your chart are all roughly the same size. Typical transit periods for each planet in a single house would be:

- **The Moon:** about two and a half days out of each month
- **The Sun:** about one month out of each year
- **Mercury:** about three weeks out of each year
- **Venus:** a little under one month out of each year
- **Mars:** about one to two months out of every two and a half years
- **Jupiter:** about one year, every twelve years
- **Saturn:** about two and a half years, every twenty-nine years
- **Uranus:** about seven years, every eighty-four years
- **Neptune:** about fourteen years *(Neptune will not transit every house of your chart in your lifetime)*
- **Pluto:** varies depending on Pluto's sign, but somewhere between fourteen and thirty years *(Pluto will not transit every house of your chart in your lifetime)*
- **North Node:** about one and a half years, every eighteen years

If you were born at a latitude very far north or south of the equator, the house sizes can vary dramatically, and so can the amount of time each planet spends in them.

HOW TO FIND OUT WHEN A PLANET IS TRANSITING A HOUSE

Consult the online ephemeris at Astro.com or a print ephemeris for the coming year. If you want to find when slow-moving planets enter a new house, you may need the jumbo ephemeris for the twenty-first century.

In any ephemeris, find the year and month, as well as the planet you want to track. Scan down the column until you find the date it reaches the degree and sign that is on one of your house cusps. It will be in that house (except for retrograde periods) until the date when it reaches the degree and sign of the next house cusp.

For example, my natal Ascendant is at 1.54 Sagittarius. Soon transiting Saturn will cross my Ascendant, and while that doesn't sound like the happiest transit on earth, I'm really ready for Saturn to leave my twelfth house. To find out the date of this joyous event (I may want to order a celebratory cake), I consulted the ephemeris, found the current year and month, located the column with Saturn's glyph at the top, and kept scanning forward month by month until I saw Saturn changing signs. Finally, on January 12, 2015, I found Saturn had reached 1.55, just one minute past my Ascendant degree. Cake time!

SWISS EPHEMERIS FOR THE YEAR 2015

January 2015

00:00 UT

DAY	Sid.t	☉	☽	☿	♀	♂	♃	♄	♅	♆	♇	☊	☊	⚸	⚷
T 1	6 41 19	10♑13'50	20♉37	23♑39	26♑43	21♒ 3	21°R46	0♐52	12♈37	5♓23	13♑10	15°R26	14♎56	3♍48	13♓46
F 2	6 45 16	11°14'58	3♊44	25°14	27°58	21°50	21♌41	0°58	12°37	5°25	13°12	15♎20	14°53	3°54	13°49
S 3	6 49 13	12°16'06	16°39	26°49	29°14	22°37	21°36	1° 4	12°38	5°26	13°14	15°10	14°50	4° 1	13°51
S 4	6 53 9	13°17'14	29°24	28°23	0♒29	23°24	21°32	1°10	12°39	5°28	13°16	14°57	14°47	4° 8	13°53
M 5	6 57 6	14°18'22	11♋59	29°56	1°44	24°11	21°27	1°16	12°39	5°29	13°18	14°43	14°44	4°14	13°55
T 6	7 1 2	15°19'30	24°22	1♒27	2°59	24°58	21°21	1°22	12°40	5°31	13°20	14°28	14°40	4°21	13°57
W 7	7 4 59	16°20'38	6♌34	2°58	4°14	25°45	21°16	1°27	12°41	5°32	13°22	14°15	14°37	4°28	14° 0
T 8	7 8 55	17°21'46	18°36	4°27	5°29	26°32	21°11	1°33	12°42	5°34	13°25	14° 3	14°34	4°34	14° 2
F 9	7 12 52	18°22'54	0♍31	5°54	6°44	27°19	21° 5	1°39	12°43	5°36	13°27	13°53	14°31	4°41	14° 4
S 10	7 16 48	19°24'02	12°20	7°18	7°59	28° 6	20°59	1°44	12°44	5°37	13°29	13°47	14°28	4°48	14° 7
S 11	7 20 45	20°25'10	24° 7	8°39	9°14	28°53	20°53	1°50	12°45	5°39	13°31	13°43	14°25	4°54	14° 9
M 12	7 24 42	21°26'17	5♎58	9°57	10°30	29°40	20°47	1°55	12°46	5°41	13°33	13°42	14°21	5° 1	14°12
T 13	7 28 38	22°27'25	17°56	11°11	11°45	0♓27	20°41	2° 1	12°47	5°43	13°35	13°42	14°18	5° 8	14°15
W 14	7 32 35	23°28'33	0♏ 8	12°20	13° 0	1°14	20°35	2° 6	12°48	5°44	13°37	13°42	14°15	5°14	14°17
T 15	7 36 31	24°29'40	12°40	13°24	14°15	2° 1	20°28	2°11	12°49	5°46	13°39	13°41	14°12	5°21	14°20
F 16	7 40 28	25°30'48	25°35	14°21	15°30	2°48	20°22	2°17	12°50	5°48	13°41	13°37	14° 9	5°28	14°23
S 17	7 44 24	26°31'55	8♐58	15°11	16°45	3°35	20°15	2°22	12°52	5°50	13°43	13°31	14° 5	5°34	14°25
S 18	7 48 21	27°33'02	22°51	15°53	18° 0	4°21	20° 8	2°27	12°53	5°52	13°45	13°23	14° 2	5°41	14°28
M 19	7 52 17	28°34'09	7♑11	16°26	19°14	5° 8	20° 1	2°32	12°54	5°54	13°47	13°12	13°59	5°48	14°31
T 20	7 56 14	29°35'15	21°55	16°50	20°29	5°55	19°54	2°37	12°56	5°56	13°49	13° 1	13°56	5°54	14°34
W 21	8 0 11	0♒36'21	6♒54	17° 3	21°44	6°42	19°47	2°42	12°57	5°58	13°51	12°49	13°53	6° 1	14°37
T 22	8 4 7	1°37'26	21°59	17°R 5	22°59	7°29	19°40	2°46	12°59	5°59	13°53	12°40	13°50	6° 8	14°40
F 23	8 8 4	2°38'30	6♓59	16°55	24°14	8°16	19°33	2°51	13° 0	6° 1	13°55	12°33	13°46	6°14	14°43
S 24	8 12 0	3°39'33	21°48	16°34	25°29	9° 3	19°25	2°56	13° 2	6° 3	13°57	12°29	13°43	6°21	14°46
S 25	8 15 57	4°40'35	6♈17	16° 1	26°44	9°50	19°18	3° 0	13° 4	6° 5	13°59	12°D27	13°40	6°28	14°49
M 26	8 19 53	5°41'37	20°25	15°18	27°59	10°37	19°10	3° 5	13° 6	6° 7	14° 1	12°27	13°37	6°35	14°52
T 27	8 23 50	6°42'37	4♉12	14°25	29°13	11°23	19° 3	3° 9	13° 7	6° 9	14° 3	12°R28	13°34	6°41	14°55
W 28	8 27 46	7°43'36	17°38	13°23	0♓28	12°10	18°55	3°14	13° 9	6°12	14° 5	12°27	13°31	6°48	14°58
T 29	8 31 43	8°44'33	0♊45	12°15	1°43	12°57	18°47	3°18	13°11	6°14	14° 7	12°25	13°27	6°55	15° 1
F 30	8 35 40	9°45'30	13°38	11° 3	2°57	13°44	18°39	3°22	13°13	6°16	14° 9	12°20	13°24	7° 1	15° 4
S 31	8 39 36	10♒46'26	26♊16	9♒48	4♓12	14♓30	18♌32	3♐26	13♈15	6♓18	14♑11	12♎12	13♎21	7♍ 8	15♓ 7

Delta T = 67.90 sec.

chapter 10

HOUSES 1 AND 7:
SELF AND IMPORTANT OTHERS

People seek the advice of astrologers for any number of reasons, but the most common of these is relationships. How can they meet someone, marry someone, keep someone interested, or get someone back? Is a spouse cheating? Should they leave their spouse and run away with their boyfriend/girlfriend?

Eventually, I mostly gave up offering advice in this area, because I became convinced that my clients, however sincere and well-meaning, were asking the wrong questions. Mind you, they're a lot of the same questions I asked when I was single, and they were the wrong questions then, too. Every minute of my life, I was looking for love. It wasn't until I took a brief intermission from that search to focus on something else important to me that I finally became the person I needed to be to find love.

That's the dichotomy of the first and seventh house axis. The first house is the house of self and identity, the house of "me." The seventh house is the house of significant others, the house of "you" and of "us." When we picture being in a relationship, that picture features an idealized version of ourselves—the right weight, looking happy, with a satisfying career and the perfect haircut. Which is all well and good, except that on some level we assume that the idealized version of ourselves will be achieved simply by finding the right relationship. It's true that through the closest relationships in our lives we have the opportunity to become better versions of ourselves. But it's also the case that we have to like who we are before we can attract a relationship with someone else who likes us.

THE FIRST HOUSE: BECOMING YOURSELF

Traditional name: House of Self

Terrain: individuality, selfhood, personality, physical appearance, thresholds, emergency situations

Shares common ground with: the sign of Aries; the planet Mars

The way we go about attracting love is often wrongheaded. Instead of embracing who we are and making that the ideal, we try to mold ourselves into some creature that we imagine others will find attractive. If we succeed, we attract the partner we also think looks attractive. But unfortunately we end up with someone who is attractive, and possibly a very nice person, but who doesn't really suit who we are inside.

The only way to have good relationships is to accept yourself as you are and where you're at now, and that is first house work. If you need serious improvement (and who among us doesn't?), get to work overhauling yourself. As your teachers used to say, keep your eyes on your own work: Find the look that works for you, the career, the house, the friends, the fun. Fall in love with yourself in the first house, and the seventh house will take care of itself.

When planets transit the first house, you get to figure out who you are and who you want to become. Sometimes these lessons are benign; other times they're profound and quite painful. Most of us will encounter both, and all have something interesting to teach about the people we want to be and the people with whom we want to share our lives.

TRANSITING SUN IN THE FIRST HOUSE

A friend of mine had a very good method for deciding whether a new outfit or hairstyle was right for her. "I just look in the mirror," she said, "and ask, 'Do I look like myself?'" That's just the question to ask when the transiting Sun is in your first house. Do your outsides match your insides? Do others see you as you truly are? Do you look like yourself?

The Sun will not be satisfied this month until you are able to look yourself in the eye and smile. Yes, you look like yourself. Yes, you like what you see. And if some people don't seem to like you as you are, well, you'll just have to spend more time with the people who do instead.

This month, to the extent that you can, put yourself first. Oh, I know—you have kids, you have commitments. I get it. But I'll bet you can find fifteen minutes each day to put yourself first. Driving to work, for instance: Instead of spending that time coming up with new and more colorful ways to call someone an idiot, use it to listen to an audiobook. Use it to sing, to shout. Use it for you.

Most of all, the Sun's transit of the first house is a time to challenge yourself. Eleanor Roosevelt once said, "You must do the thing you think you cannot do." And this is the month to do it. Tackle frightening tasks this month and you'll find they probably increase not only your vitality but also your overall sense of well-being and happiness.

TRANSITING MOON IN THE FIRST HOUSE

This is a fleeting and minor transit, with the Moon moving through a house of your chart roughly every two and a half days of every month. The Moon is a changeable influence, and as it moves through the first house, your self-assurance may be a bit wobbly. On the plus side, this can be a good period to try a new look or to make small changes in the daily habits that affect your appearance and strength.

The most important lunar transit here comes each year in the month when the New Moon falls in the first house of your chart. This is a powerful New Moon for setting intentions related to your appearance, personality, physical strength, courage, and willingness to try something new.

TRANSITING MERCURY IN THE FIRST HOUSE

Mercury moves quickly and will usually transit each house of your chart in a few weeks (except when it is retrograde—then you can tack on an extra week). Mercury is the planet of the mind, perception, and communication, so when it transits the first house you'll be thinking (and probably talking) a lot about yourself: who you are, what you want, how you look, and where you want to be. You will be curious about how to improve this area of your life, interested in talking about these subjects with others, and eager to read everything you can about them.

TRANSITING VENUS IN THE FIRST HOUSE

Venus represents what we enjoy and is also associated with money and property. When Venus transits the first house, beautify and enjoy yourself.

During this month, indulge in some pampering. Take special care with your appearance; if it's within your budget, a trip to a salon or spa could be a wonderful treat. Have a professional advise you about your hairstyle or wardrobe. Also, be more gracious in your approach to others. Venus's gifts are beauty and charm, so you should be able to handle conflicts diplomatically now, disarming even your fiercest opponents.

TRANSITING MARS IN THE FIRST HOUSE

This transit is energizing, especially physically. You may feel particularly motivated and self-directed, if a little bit impulsive. But there is a caveat here: Mars can dump a heaping dose of conflict at your door when it transits the first house. If it seems everyone is picking a fight with you, there are two possibilities. One is that you have a lot of anger or frustration poking its head out, looking for a way to get engaged. The other is that you are being provoked into showing anger or standing up for yourself in a way that is absolutely legitimate but often hard for you to do. This transit is an opportunity to learn something about sticking up for yourself without sticking it to anyone else.

TRANSITING JUPITER IN THE FIRST HOUSE

The old joke among astrologers is that when Jupiter—a planet everyone calls "expansive"—transits your first house, you'll gain a bunch of weight. That isn't necessarily the case, but it is true that limits are easily adjusted and belt notches loosened when Jupiter visits this part of your chart. Jupiter loves to eat, drink, and have a great time. While Jupiter is in your first house, it's often easier than usual to project a jolly, fun-loving, generous persona. Jupiter is usually described as a "lucky" planet, but while he transits here, you truly make your own luck. A merry disposition generally attracts goodwill, and you are likely to have more than your share by the time Jupiter moves on.

TRANSITING SATURN IN THE FIRST HOUSE

When Saturn transits your first house, you may seem to age overnight. You meet each new situation with gravity and maturity, taking on more responsibility than you probably need to. If you are carrying literal extra weight, Saturn in the first house will likely help you slim down through his rigid discipline and goal setting. Your grooming and dress may become more subdued and tailored.

The biggest challenge with Saturn transiting your first house is resisting a pessimistic attitude. Saturn tends to focus on what is wrong rather than what's right. You may also have difficulty expressing your personality in a natural, unselfconscious way. Be patient with yourself and limit your self-criticism to correcting characteristics that make you less effective.

TRANSITING URANUS IN THE FIRST HOUSE

BOOM! Uranus entering the first house is like a thunderclap. If you've been living a less than authentic life, tethered to rules and restrictions and governed by fear, you will be startled awake and eager to liberate yourself. It's time for reinvention, of everything from your appearance to your career to your ethics and morality. The process will be very disruptive to the life you've built for yourself, and possibly upsetting to yourself and others, but undeniably freeing and exciting. Some days, you'll feel you no longer know yourself. The truth is, you don't. This transit can usher in one of the most dramatic overall changes of your lifetime. The work now is to let yourself change; you can get reacquainted with yourself later.

TRANSITING NEPTUNE IN THE FIRST HOUSE

Transiting Neptune can be a siren that comes to your door and calls you far from home, sometimes literally, but sometimes by taking you into the otherworldly realm of spirit, music, or metaphysics. You may find yourself in a place or circumstances that are so different as to be utterly disorienting, and that call into question everything you knew about yourself. With Neptune, there is nearly always some kind of loss or sadness, the kind a sailor feels as he sets out to sea. But in order to explore new waters, you must pull up anchor and wave good-bye to some people who will be left behind on shore.

TRANSITING PLUTO IN THE FIRST HOUSE

Transiting Pluto in the first house will change the landscape of your life just as surely as Uranus or Neptune will. But the effect of Pluto transiting this house is to strip you bare of any artifice or insincerity, like an actress caught by the paparazzi without her makeup. You won't always look or behave your best during this transit. In new and extremely challenging territory, you may struggle to find a way to cope. You are like a wall being sanded down in preparation for a new coat of paint. By the end of this transit, you'll probably be a lot less eager to please others than you were at the beginning of it. And when you look in the mirror, you'll see a stronger, truer version of yourself.

TRANSITING NORTH NODE IN THE FIRST HOUSE

As the North Node transits your first house, the road to happiness lies in putting yourself first. This is easier for some of us than for others. Putting yourself first doesn't mean you will give nothing to your loved ones. This transit comes around only once every eighteen years, so you needn't worry that it is going to make you a selfish egomaniac! In fact, as the North Node transits the first house, the South Node, representing what's easy and comfortable, is in the people-pleasing seventh house. If your instinctual response in every situation is to honor others' needs, that must be brought into balance by having more respect for your own.

THE SEVENTH HOUSE: GROWING WITH IMPORTANT OTHERS

Traditional name: House of Marriage

Terrain: partners, marriage, relationships between equals, open enemies, judgment, negotiation, arbitration, mediation

Shares common ground with: the sign of Libra; the planet Venus

Traditionally, the seventh house was called the House of Marriage. To our modern minds, this conjures visions of romantic couples. Certainly, we find committed marriage partners in this house. But we also find other relationships of great importance. This is a house of equals, so our closest peer friendships and business partnerships are found here, as well as our sworn and open enemies. If you are being sued, the plaintiff will be represented by this house.

The seventh house describes your close relationships, yes. But since it's in *your* birth chart, it also tells us about you. So the seventh house symbolizes the way others perceive you in relationships, the way you approach relating, and whom you can hope to become through close relationships.

Transits in the seventh house provide catalysts to begin or end relationships, renegotiate their terms, and learn significant lessons that you can only understand through your closest relationships.

TRANSITING SUN IN THE SEVENTH HOUSE

When the Sun moves into the seventh house, contemplate how to have happier relationships with those closest to you. The great, bright klieg light of the Sun is wheeled in so that this month you can scrutinize and evaluate your marriage, best friendships, and other seventh house connections. Is your best friend letting you initiate all the phone calls and lunch invitations? Has your marriage grown boring, or is your spouse making comments that make you feel overlooked and unappreciated? Is a rival stealing your spotlight? This month, bring these situations back into balance, so you can shine as brightly as you deserve to.

If, on the other hand, you are prone to nitpicking or criticizing your loved ones, practice showing care and acceptance this month. One of the best—and hardest—ways to do this is to listen. We fall into a habit of having the same conversations over and over with the people who know us best. Really listen and ask questions now.

TRANSITING MOON IN THE SEVENTH HOUSE

For this brief two-and-a-half-day period each month, you get the opportunity to pay attention to how the important relationships in your life make you feel. Be careful about acting on these feelings, though, because the Moon is completely irrational. You perceive offense where none was intended, for example. Do, however, pay attention to your intuition about those close to you on these days, because sometimes we notice what's really going on only when we are guided by the gut rather than the mind.

TRANSITING MERCURY IN THE SEVENTH HOUSE

Listen. Really listen. Particularly with the people closest to us, we get in the habit of not paying close attention to what others say, and even less attention to what they don't say. While Mercury, the planet of perception, is moving through your seventh house, pretend that you're a journalist, investigating the lives of the people you care about most. Pretend you're meeting them for the first time. What would you ask them?

TRANSITING VENUS IN THE SEVENTH HOUSE

Venus is right at home in the seventh house, because both are associated with harmony, balance, and partnership. If you're in a long-term relationship, this is a good time to take a minivacation with your partner, or at least schedule a special outing; you'll really enjoy each other now. If you're looking for love, you'll certainly encounter some appealing prospects during this transit. Treat your best friend to a little extra attention and affection during this transit, too. Where your rivals are concerned, remember what Abraham Lincoln said: "Do I not destroy my enemies when I make them my friends?"

TRANSITING MARS IN THE SEVENTH HOUSE

It's a familiar scenario in horror movies. The spunky heroine, alone in the house on a stormy night, is menaced by a shadowy foe. After a series of harassing phone calls, she asks the police to tap her telephone. Another particularly threatening call comes through, and the police call her immediately: "The call is coming from inside the house! Get out now!"

Brace yourself: While transiting Mars is in your seventh house, it can be nearly impossible to avoid conflict. The hardest part is, most of the attacks are coming from the people closest to you— your spouse, best friend, business partner. The seventh is the house of closest friends and open enemies; with both, the time inevitably comes for airing grievances. While Mars is transiting your seventh house, that moment has arrived. Just remember to fight fair—which means airing grievances without name calling and ad hominem attacks. Fighting fair means stating what's important to you and not backing down about that, but doing so with respect and trust.

TRANSITING JUPITER IN THE SEVENTH HOUSE

People get excited when they see this transit coming, especially if they are single and unhappy about it. When the luckiest planet in the solar system enters the house of relationships, it can only mean good things—right?

Yes, but it may not mean exactly what you expect it to mean. You will almost certainly encounter people who open your mind to new relationship possibilities, who encourage you to take risks and have adventures. If you're a good student, your relationships will certainly teach you a lot during this transit. But if you're expecting your noncommittal boyfriend to propose to you, don't hold your breath; if he's not certain he wants to be with you, this may be when he'll call it quits—and it'll be the luckiest thing that ever happened to you, because you deserve someone who will really make you happy. Jupiter may bring you the relationship you want, but it's also a planet that craves freedom.

This may be a better transit for liberating yourself from relationships that feel confining than for leaping into new commitments.

TRANSITING SATURN IN THE SEVENTH HOUSE

Saturn is serious, conservative, and respects social order. Committed relationships are, in Saturn's estimation, a cornerstone of a civilized society. So when Saturn enters your house of relationships, he is not messing around. If you are in a faltering relationship, Saturn will put it out of its misery. If you are in a relationship that requires a commitment, Saturn will push you toward the altar. If what you need is time to yourself without any relationship at all, Saturn will make that happen.

In the best interest of society, Saturn will not let you get away with any funny business. He needs you to step up to the plate, take responsibility, and either make your relationships work or let them go. While Saturn transits your seventh house, he asks, "Can you handle a relationship? Do you really want one? And do you want it badly enough to overcome a load of obstacles to get it—or to keep it?"

TRANSITING URANUS IN THE SEVENTH HOUSE

If you're in a partnership of true equals, independence is already a vital part of the equation. That will come in handy as transiting Uranus enters your seventh house for a good, long stay. Uranus demands freedom above all else, and during this transit the vitality and happiness of your relationship depends on each of you having plenty of it. Obviously the relationship must come first, for both of you, but unless you honor and nurture your independence, making time for your individual friendships and interests, your partnership may come to feel like a Saturnian obstacle course rather than a nurturing vessel. And that's when transiting Uranus begins to look like a wrecking ball, leveling your marriage and your dearest friendships.

Interestingly, if you aren't in a long-term relationship and would like to be—especially if you're a bit older and have been holding out a long time for the right person—this can be the transit that finally brings one your way. Transiting Uranus is associated with breaking old patterns, so if your relationship patterns have not served you well up to now, this is your chance to break free from them.

TRANSITING NEPTUNE IN THE SEVENTH HOUSE

As Neptune transits your seventh house, you'll learn a lot about who other people are and who they are not. Becoming disillusioned with people is painful, and unfortunately it's often part of this transit. Usually the disillusionment is most severe in the cases where you have a lot invested in your illusion of the person. In all close relationships and partnerships in the years ahead, what you thought you knew about people—and in fact, your confidence in your ability to judge character—continues to be put to the test.

The positive side of Neptune is that when you are really clear about what's going on and whom you're dealing with, you can confidently give your whole heart to a relationship. What we experience when we fall in love can be a beautiful thing—as long as we know we're choosing to believe in an illusion. Most people can't stay happily married for a long time, for instance, without believing the best about their spouse and feeling a little bit in love with him or her. The happiest couples seem to be the ones who manage to remain in love despite living with another person and their idiosyncrasies—loud chewing, leaving the toilet seat up—day in, day out.

So illusion can be a lovely thing, but it must be used sparingly in relationships. While Neptune transits your seventh house, it's particularly important to be cautious about the partners with whom you choose to work and share your life. Be prepared to see glimpses of the real person peeking through from time to time.

TRANSITING PLUTO IN THE SEVENTH HOUSE

You may find relationships difficult during this transit, but you might also just find that the people closest to you are going through some very difficult changes and challenges. A spouse who loses a parent, a friend who is diagnosed with a debilitating disease, a business partner in the throes of a midlife crisis—all are perfectly reasonable ways transiting Pluto might express itself in your seventh house. In any event, a marriage in particular may need some bolstering during this transit; in extreme cases, a complete renovation is in order.

Pluto transiting the seventh house demands that you take an honest view of your relationships and that you allow yourself to be seen as you truly are by those closest to you. Things "get real"—everyone shows who they really are. When you get right down to it, there are relatively few people in our lives who deserve every last ounce of our devotion, and they are the ones with whom we can share the best and the worst of ourselves. While Pluto transits the seventh house, you will get the chance to figure out who deserves to remain in your life and who doesn't. Relationships based on anything other than honesty will not survive this transit.

TRANSITING NORTH NODE IN THE SEVENTH HOUSE

Are your relationships fair and equal, or have you been doing more than your share of the heavy lifting? While the North Node transits your seventh house, and particularly when eclipses occur in this house, you'll increasingly feel that you can't continue with any relationship that doesn't honor both individuals equally. Relationships often end during this transit, and ones that don't will need some fine-tuning to get the scales in balance.

While the North Node is transiting your seventh house, the South Node will be transiting your first. You may be tempted to play the lone wolf, remaining alone rather than meeting others halfway. But there is another road available, one that leads to life-changing relationships, provided you have a strong enough sense of your own identity that you know how much you can afford to bend for others.

chapter 11

HOUSES 2 AND 8:
PERSONAL AND SHARED RESOURCES

The second and eighth houses are traditionally known as the houses of money. But to get to their essence, I think it helps to begin with the most essential of all resources: your body. Money comes and goes, but your physical body is the most important piece of property you'll ever own. Your relationship with the physical world is located, astrologically, in the second house. When you consider that the eighth house symbolizes other people's bodies, you begin to understand why it's the house most often associated with sex (the ultimate example of sharing what's yours with someone else).

Certainly, money matters—and more precisely, the money you earn—are found in the second house. We'll also find property here, including the clothing you use to adorn your body and the furnishings for your home (though note that land and your actual domicile belong to the fourth house of the chart).

Some of what we wish to purchase, however, is beyond the resources of all but the wealthiest individuals. To accomplish various big-ticket objectives requires access to the eighth house, traditionally the House of Other People's Money. If you need to raise the money to buy a house, you will usually need a mortgage, which gives you the use of other people's money. Should the state in which you live wish to finance an enormous public works project, it might sell bonds or collect revenue through taxes, both ways of drawing from pools of shared resources. The expense of a catastrophic accident or illness is the reason most of us own an insurance policy of some kind, which is another way of pooling individual resources for the use of all.

Finally, there is the difference between physical evidence (second house) and that which is invisible and unknowable (eighth house). This moves us from the second house certainty that you are a discrete individual and into the eighth house, where you explore the notion that all of us are actually connected in some mysterious way.

Transits in the second and eighth houses may affect you in a variety of physical, financial, or sexual ways. Depending on the transiting planet and the condition of these houses in your birth chart, you may come out ahead or experience a bit of a setback. Either way, you'll come to a better understanding about what it means to own and to share, and to live in the visible and invisible worlds.

THE SECOND HOUSE: WHAT IS YOURS

Traditional name: House of Money

Terrain: movable property, income, confidence, personal values, stability

Shares common ground with: the sign of Taurus; the planet Venus

In his delightful book *Around the House*, David Owen tells the story of a family who moved to a new house with two young girls. The younger, Marie, was tired of living in her sister Mimi's hand-me-downs. When it came time to choose bedrooms in the new house, her parents told Marie that for once, she could have first choice. She immediately proclaimed, "I want Mimi's room!"

Anyone who has shared a bedroom with a sibling growing up can tell you that we all want a room of our own. Even after we've grown up and married someone with whom we enjoy sharing as much as possible, we still hanker after our own space: our side of the bed, our own sink in the bathroom, our own home office. We want our own stuff, too, and a minor infraction such as swiping the last bagel at breakfast can tip an unsteady relationship into the red zone.

We want our own space and stuff because they confirm that we exist. They are tangible expressions of how we value ourselves and how we expect to be valued by others. Our stuff and spaces reflect our personal tastes and style, declaring to the world, "I am a person who likes this, and not that." As kids, we're encouraged to share with others. As adults, we have a lot more agency about who gets to share our stuff and our space.

The second house of the horoscope was traditionally called the House of Money. That's a succinct and not untrue way of putting it. But digging a little deeper, we might say that the second house is where you use talismans from the physical world to reinforce your identity.

Your car, for instance, says more about you than your ability to drive and your need for convenient transportation. It demonstrates whether you value speed over reliability, styling over fuel efficiency, or safety over all else. How well you treat your car once you've bought it is often a gauge of how well you take care of yourself. And astrologer Dana Gerhardt says she always asks her clients about their cars, reporting that "the ones who say they love their cars are always happy and prosperous in their careers."

The second house is also the realm of income, specifically the resources you possess that can be exchanged for money. These might be marketable skills, but also personal qualities such as confidence, self-sufficiency, and reliability.

Planets transiting the second house bring new people, events, and experiences that affect your world of personal space and possessions, and your ability to earn money. These transits may also signal times when you're asked to share. Are you cheerfully willing to do so, or do you begrudge others a taste of what's yours?

TRANSITING SUN IN THE SECOND HOUSE

The second house symbolizes your money and possessions. And while money can't necessarily buy happiness, your attitude toward it is crucial to being truly content.

However dissatisfied you are with your physical body, possessions, or income, make a conscious effort while the Sun transits your second house to count your blessings.

This month, show respect for possessions by balancing the books. Reconcile your checking account. Repay loans and return borrowed objects. Repair or recycle broken possessions.

And finally, invest in your happiness. Sometimes this means charitable giving, other times, cheering a friend with an unexpected gift. If you've been putting off making an important change in your life because you don't have the money, this is the month to start investing, however modestly. Find a big jar and empty your loose change into it each night; something is better than nothing.

The Sun wants you to be happy. This month, what will make you happiest is gratitude and appreciation for all that you have.

TRANSITING MOON IN THE SECOND HOUSE

This is a fleeting and minor transit, with the Moon moving through a house of your chart roughly every two and a half days of every month. The Moon is a changeable influence, and during this transit your finances, self-confidence, and willpower may be a bit unstable.

Mostly, you won't pay a lot of attention to this transit, except for the month each year when the New Moon occurs in the second house of your chart—usually the same month when the Sun is transiting your second house. This is a powerful New Moon for setting intentions related to your finances, your body image, and your sense of security.

TRANSITING MERCURY IN THE SECOND HOUSE

Mercury is the planet of the mind, perception, and communication, so when it transits the second house, your focus will be on money, your body, and the other possessions you value. You will be curious about how to improve this area of your life, interested in talking about these subjects with others, and eager to read everything you can about them. Mercury is always game to learn and develop skills, so this is the time to master technology that can be used to handle your finances or monitor your fitness goals.

TRANSITING VENUS IN THE SECOND HOUSE

Venus represents what we enjoy and is also associated with money and property, so it's right at home in the second house.

This month, spend your money and use your resources in ways that you enjoy. You needn't overspend to get maximum enjoyment, either. Simply giving your house a thorough cleaning and rearranging your furniture in a more pleasing way can do the trick. All things being equal, you probably feel pretty flush this month; if you have a little extra spending money, use it to beautify your appearance or your home. Venus represents femininity, so females in your life can have an effect on your finances or property during this month.

TRANSITING MARS IN THE SECOND HOUSE

When the god of war comes to visit, expect passions to be stirred up and conflicts to emerge. In the second house, the subject of these conflicts may be your assets. Your sister may accuse you of having too much of the ancestral china, for instance, or someone at work may compete with you for a lucrative promotion or client account.

Mars also brings energy and initiative to the areas of the chart that he transits. When Mars is in the second house, it's an excellent time to start a fitness program or a diet. Trim your budget and curb your spending; in particular, avoid impulse spending (Mars tends to act before thinking). If you've been trying to summon the courage to tackle a new money-making project, ask for a raise, or increase the prices you charge for products and services, Mars transiting your second house is on your side.

TRANSITING JUPITER IN THE SECOND HOUSE

Transiting Jupiter will spend roughly one year in each house of your birth chart. What happens when the planet of higher learning, adventure, and "long journeys over water" visits your chart's equivalent of the Federal Reserve?

While Jupiter is in your second house, you tend to believe in yourself a bit more than usual. Perhaps others show their faith in you, too—maybe even the people who make decisions about your salary. Generally, while Jupiter is in the second house, you will see an increase in your income or a windfall that makes you feel more upbeat about your financial security. Sometimes a more positive attitude encourages you to take risks and make social connections that eventually pay off—literally.

On the other hand, if all this confidence and optimism gets out of hand, you may be prone to overspending. This isn't usually a transit that brings excessive debt into your life (look to the eighth house for that), but rather a lack of prudence about economizing or saving.

TRANSITING SATURN IN THE SECOND HOUSE

First, the good news: This could well be the transit that helps you identify the career that would be most meaningful to you. And while Saturn transits your second house, you will be eager to invest in your long-term goals and implement practical, long-range plans to improve your finances.

Wherever Saturn transits, however, your chickens come home to roost. If you have been saving diligently since the day you got your first job, this could be a phenomenal transit that moves you up to the next rung of the financial ladder. However, if you haven't handled your finances wisely in the past, you will likely begin this transit feeling as though you don't have enough resources to invest. If you've been taking care of your body, you should look and feel great, but if you haven't, you will probably be seeing and feeling those effects as well. Learn from past mistakes. In time, and with patience, you can still build the physical strength and financial health that you want and need.

TRANSITING URANUS IN THE SECOND HOUSE

While Uranus transits the second house, you will probably feel a strong urge to liberate yourself financially. That sounds like some glib marketing come-on, but it's actually true. Uranus transiting your second house doesn't guarantee that you will have everything you want or that your fortunes will change overnight. What it does guarantee is that by the time the transit finishes, you will be free on some level from financial constraints. If you've always been a person who has worried about money, you will be less so. If you've always worked for a paycheck, you may end up in the tenuous but autonomous position of being self-employed.

While Uranus is transiting your second house, you are growing to appreciate freedom, perhaps as a result of meeting someone whose life does not emphasize money and possessions. You may move into a place of your own, rent an office or workspace, or otherwise carve out some bit of real estate that you can have all to yourself. More valuable than any amount of money, you yearn to live life on your own terms.

TRANSITING NEPTUNE IN THE SECOND HOUSE

During this transit, your values and attitude toward the material world might be increasingly influenced by compassion and spiritual yearning. Under such an influence one might, for instance, give up all his earthly belongings to join the Peace Corps or the priesthood. It's a wonderful opportunity to bring your values about money and possessions into a closer alignment with your convictions.

On the other hand, you may need to confront illusions about materialism. Have you been an idealist who insists that money and possessions are meaningless? You may be compelled to reevaluate that notion during this transit. One possible consequence of underestimating the power of money is the refusal to acknowledge the link between one's most limited natural resource—life—and the acquisition of money and possessions. When you don't see the connection between the two, you don't see that trivializing money and possessions is the same as trivializing the effort that it took someone to obtain them, or the possible good this money can do in the world.

Astrology teaches us that valuing what you have is, in a very real sense, valuing who you are. Refusing to pay attention to money, "forgetting" to pay your bills, refusing to acknowledge the reality of your financial situation, hiding your financial affairs from important people in your life—these are what astrologer Steven Forrest might call "low-energy," or less than enlightened, responses to Neptune transiting your second house.

The moral of the story: Money doesn't mean everything, but that's not to say it doesn't mean anything.

TRANSITING PLUTO IN THE SECOND HOUSE

Pluto was the wealthiest of the gods—hence the term *plutocrat*. While Pluto makes his long, slow transit through your second house, it's reasonable to expect that you have the ability to make yourself wealthier. That may be true, especially to the extent that you have direct control over your earning ability (as a contractor, for instance).

But where Pluto transits, he strips away everything that isn't serving the highest good. He takes things we don't want to get rid of so we can figure out what we actually need. So while Pluto transits your second house, you may have both great windfalls and disappointing losses. You will likely go through long periods when you yearn to get rid of all the stuff that is using up space and cluttering your life, and live a more Spartan existence. And at the end of this long transit—possibly as long as three decades!—you will know what you truly need and be prepared to do without the rest.

TRANSITING NORTH NODE IN THE SECOND HOUSE

The gift of this transit is a deep and hopefully lasting sense of your importance. The confidence of the second house has nothing to do with being more significant than other people. It's simply the confidence that comes from knowing you have a place in the world and that you are valuable.

While the North Node transits the second house, the South Node is transiting the eighth house, the house of support from others. It's a common mistake during this transit to imagine that you need others to validate you and that confidence is a gift bestowed on you by others. Real friends will support you by encouraging your self-reliance, not your reliance on them.

During this transit, and particularly when eclipses fall in this house, you may confront financial challenges. There is usually a change in direction between relying on others and gaining confidence by proving you can take care of yourself.

THE EIGHTH HOUSE: WHAT'S YOURS IS YOURS AND COULD BE OURS

Traditional name: House of Other People's Money

Terrain: collective resources, insurance, investments, banks, sex, mortality

Shares common ground with: the sign of Scorpio; the planet Pluto

Ask someone if she feels she has received the support she deserves in life, and you're talking to her eighth house. Someone with difficult planets in this house will usually say that no, she's done everything for herself because no one else will help out. Someone with nice planets here, on the other hand—say, Venus or Jupiter—has often had a lot of help from others and may even feel a little guilty about it, or somewhat insecure about her ability to provide for herself.

Opposite the second house of personal possessions, the eighth house symbolizes what other people bring to the table. Specifically, this house symbolizes your partner's money. Difficult planets in the eighth house suggest a spouse with a complicated or diminished financial situation, or who may not be thrilled about sharing. Nice planets in the eighth house suggest the opposite.

The eighth house also represents pools of other people's resources. Insurance, for instance, is an eighth house matter, because many contribute but not all benefit directly. Taxes are ruled by the eighth house for similar reasons. Banks are ruled by the eighth house, because they're full of other people's money. If you're applying for a loan, you go to the eighth house to do it, whether to a bank or a shady-looking underworld figure lurking in a nearby alley; both have money you need.

The adage goes that sex, death, and taxes are the three things no one can avoid. Along with taxes, sex and death have also traditionally been associated with the eighth house. Sexual activity ended up here because it's where one person's . . . er, assets are comingled with another person's assets. And while the French refer to an orgasm as *la petite mort* (the little death), there is a more direct connection between death and the eighth house. It may or may not refer to actual, physical death. (I think that is more likely the purview of the fourth house, but I confess that I deliberately skipped that lesson in astrology school, as I'd prefer my own death to come as a surprise.) But it certainly challenges our notions of mortality and the mystery of what comes after life. The eighth house is where you'll find all manner of experiences that transform you from one person into another.

TRANSITING SUN IN THE EIGHTH HOUSE

The transiting Sun spends just about one month of each year in your eighth house. Probably it won't be your favorite month. Most likely, the dark and dusty recesses of your psyche will be thrown open and the gremlins therein will recoil from the light. This is the month each year when you grapple with your demons; for that reason, it can actually be a pretty good month for replacing toxic habits with healthier ones, such as exercise or meditation.

The eighth house is complicated, but above all I think of it as one of the houses of passion. In the eighth house, we can become so engrossed in a pastime that we completely forget who, where, and what we are.

Sometimes our passions become compulsions. And I'm going to offer a piece of advice that may sound odd: While the Sun is transiting your eighth house, honor your compulsions! Compulsions are signs of a passion that are trying to be expressed. So become aware of them. Acknowledge them. Then you can understand where this unexpressed fervor is trying to lead you.

This month, make room for your passions. Taking time to listen to yourself can be as difficult as taking time to listen to your partner and friends. There are many demands on all our time, and of course it's always necessary to prioritize. But just this month, make it a priority to give some time to something you're passionate about.

It doesn't matter whether time spent with your passions is productive. Forget about results! Passions may lead you to interesting places, but that's not the only reason to follow them. The best reason is that they help you feel alive and happy.

TRANSITING MOON IN THE EIGHTH HOUSE

Second only to the Moon transiting the twelfth house, this can be a low-energy time of the month. You're particularly vulnerable to absorbing others' emotions now, so insist on carving out time for yourself, alone in your cave. Your intuition is at a peak, though, and it's a very good time for writing, painting, counseling, or doing any other work that requires empathy and the ability to get into other people's heads and hearts.

TRANSITING MERCURY IN THE EIGHTH HOUSE

Mercury is the planet of perception, thoughts, and communication. This is the moment in Mercury's cycle when it's time to ask some hard questions, both of yourself and of others. Natally, this is an excellent Mercury placement for research or detective work; it describes the ability to read extremely subtle signals and clues. These are also the benefits of Mercury's transit here. On a practical level, there are few better transits for reviewing your investments and insurance policies, and for decluttering your house. Any task that requires a keen eye and a healthy sense of skepticism is well suited to this transit!

TRANSITING VENUS IN THE EIGHTH HOUSE

While Venus transits here, you'll usually receive more support and affection than you're used to getting. If you need to apply for a loan or ask for favors, this is a favorable time to do it. Partnerships, in particular, can feel supportive, encouraging, and enjoyable now. Physical relationships are especially satisfying, and this could be a transit that marks the moment when a close relationship turns intimate.

It may sound like a downer, but this can be a good time for estate planning. Use this transit to ensure that your wishes are documented and that your earthly possessions (including your body) will find their way to the appropriate people and places when you are no longer here to look after them.

TRANSITING MARS IN THE EIGHTH HOUSE

Mars is the planet of conflict, and the eighth house is the one of shared resources and intimacy. Think you'll have a dust-up or two with the people closest to you during this two-and-a-half-month period? Yeah. So do I.

Mars symbolizes the impulse to take what's yours and to make things happen the way you want them to. Mars transiting your eighth house can be healthy and beneficial if you've given too much power, too many decisions, and too many resources to other people; this will be a period of correcting any imbalances and reclaiming what's yours.

But usually they won't just hand you a check or say, "Yes, you're right, these are your decisions to make." So there will be conflict. It might be about handling the money or property you share with others, or fighting for an insurance settlement or inheritance that is owed to you. It could be about renegotiating a relationship that has grown codependent. It could be about problems with physical intimacy.

It can be exhilarating to cut through the often hazy territory of intimacy to say, "This is what's really going on, this is how I see it, and this is what I want from you." Exhilarating, and kind of scary. You can let this window of opportunity close without doing anything, but these conflicts are not going away—merely going underground. Better to resolve them now, while Mars is on your side.

TRANSITING JUPITER IN THE EIGHTH HOUSE

When Jupiter transits the eighth house for approximately one year, should you expect other people to shower you with their riches?

Well . . . maybe. If you're in a position to gain control of your trust fund or inherit a huge amount of wealth, or if you marry a person who has a lot more money than you do, this transit might do nice things for your bank balance.

But it's also likely that you may assume a large amount of debt, even something large such as a mortgage or a car loan. Remember that banks are ruled by the eighth house, too. So while you may be in possession of other people's money, it doesn't necessarily mean that there are no strings attached.

With Jupiter in the eighth, you probably feel optimistic enough about your ability to repay a loan that you are more likely to make long-delayed, big-ticket purchases. You'll have to buy insurance (also ruled by the eighth house) to cover those purchases. And to some extent, taking on debt can make you less free—Jupiter's least favorite feeling.

So Jupiter's transits of the eighth house aren't necessarily the part of its cycle that will make you feel the wealthiest. But this yearlong period *can* expand your access to other people's resources—for better or for worse.

TRANSITING SATURN IN THE EIGHTH HOUSE

Saturn is a planet of constriction, rules, and deprivation. But he also symbolizes the strength and maturity that come from overcoming daunting obstacles. During the roughly two and a half years Saturn transits your eighth house, you have some work to do in shoring up your self-sufficiency.

It is all the fashion today for well-meaning parents to try to shield their children from disappointment and hardship to protect their self-esteem. Ironically, though, overcoming disappointment and hardship is precisely the formula for building self-esteem. When you have proven that you can take care of yourself, you feel much more confident.

The eighth house is where we find support from others—financial, emotional, intimate support. When Saturn transits this house, you may find that your accustomed sources of support dry up. You may spend a couple of years scrambling to build up emotional and financial self-sufficiency. The frightened child in you may holler, "Won't anybody help me? How can I buy a house/eat dinner in a restaurant/raise a child on my own?"

But by the time Saturn is finished with your eighth house, you will have proven to yourself that you can do these things on your own, or that you can't, or maybe that in the end, they really weren't all that important to you after all.

TRANSITING URANUS IN THE EIGHTH HOUSE

During Uranus's long transit of your eighth house, you will almost certainly find yourself at some point suddenly alone. The person you trusted to hold on to the ladder while you climbed to the top abruptly disappears. Someone you thought you could trust lets you down, perhaps, or other people's money—maybe an inheritance, maybe alimony or child support, or simply a personal loan—complicates your life.

When Uranus transits a house of your chart, unexpected developments force you to deal with the matters you keep there. Some houses are filled with creepier stuff than others. In the eighth house, we keep sex and death, wills and trusts, taxes, and all the terrifying things that we most fear will happen to us. Sudden, unanticipated occurrences are not what we hope for in this area of our lives, but sometimes they're the only way to make ourselves deal with this stuff. Sometimes they are absolutely the only way to make yourself truly free.

TRANSITING NEPTUNE IN THE EIGHTH HOUSE

More often than not, reality is hard to deal with. It would be terrific if we were always able to face up to whatever horrors life throws at us, turn weaknesses into strength, and grow more compassionate and empathetic toward others as the result of our experiences. For some lucky souls, a deep and abiding spiritual belief system makes this possible.

But sometimes pain doesn't improve your character; it just wears you down. So you seek solace or anesthesia. For instance, you wouldn't want to have a root canal without a very strong local anesthetic. In the days after a death in the family, you would probably prefer to hide out in a safe place with the people who won't make you cry. If you have lost your job, a couple of margaritas with a good friend might be just the medicine you need.

Neptune is the great anesthetic. Its transit through the eighth house can be welcome, because this house is full of some crazy, often painful stuff. It's where we are vulnerable to all kinds of hurt and betrayal and abuse, things we'd rather not think about. Having Neptune transiting there can make it all easier to bear.

Unfortunately, it can also make it much harder to deal with whatever is really going on, so you can heal the source of the hurt and perhaps even grow closer to the important people in your life. This is why some kind of spiritual or psychological guidance can be truly helpful during this transit—it reduces the chances of giving in to unhealthy avoidance, denial, and self-destructive habits.

TRANSITING PLUTO IN THE EIGHTH HOUSE

This can be an important transit for making peace with the interdependent nature of life, love, and relationships. It is the house of inheritance, and I do know one woman who came into a sizable inheritance during this transit, including a home that needed a complete transformation. But the inheritance came from her father, and their relationship had been acrimonious and painful. Remaking the house has been a kind of healing exercise.

Where Pluto transits, he may bring wealth and power . . . but there is always a catch. In the house of other people's resources, we may see the lottery winner who loses his friends and becomes estranged from all that has been familiar to him; a man who inherits a great fortune when his partner dies of AIDS; a woman who receives a huge insurance settlement because she was profoundly injured while doing her job.

As the old saying goes, be careful what you wish for. What you want is not necessarily what will make you happy. Transiting Pluto in the eighth house teaches that wealth and gain for their own sake are mere vanities. The best course of action is to appreciate whatever comes our way and try to use it for the greatest possible good, while remembering that we ultimately have little control over what the universe will send our way.

TRANSITING NORTH NODE IN THE EIGHTH HOUSE

Can you trust the people closest to you? Are they there for you when you need them? Do they show you the respect that you deserve?

What about your possessions—do they serve you? Are you spending too much of your energy fixing things that are broken, nursing plants back to health, keeping your ancient jalopy limping along?

While the Moon's North Node transits your eighth house, the path forward in your life depends on ridding yourself of the dead weight. If someone you've been calling a friend hasn't phoned you in ten years, what you have on your hands is less a friendship than a friendly habit. If you've been giving your energy and money to a cause that is important to you, but others are not showing the same commitment, you may need to let it go. When the transiting North Node is in the eighth house, the South Node is transiting the second house. The comfortable approach to this transit is to maintain the status quo and hold on to what you've got. But if you're living in a house that is too large, too small, too old, or too packed with junk to move around, you need to get some boxes, rent a moving truck, and take a trip to the dump.

chapter 12

HOUSES 3 AND 9:
LEARNING AND UNDERSTANDING

On a popular *Saturday Night Live* skit from the 1970s, Don Novello in character as Father Guido Sarducci proposed his idea for the Five-Minute University. As he explained the concept: "In five minutes, you'll learn what the average college graduate remembers five years after he or she is out of school."

The third and ninth houses of the horoscope represent the polarity of knowledge. In the third house we learn remedial and necessary skills, gather random data, and collect perceptions and impressions about the world. In the ninth house, the level of difficulty is raised to encompass teaching, thinking critically, and gleaning meaning from perceptions and impressions. That's the stuff we're supposed to learn in college, tools for making sense of and finding meaning in the world. But as Father Guido Sarducci suggests, the mind can be a hard, rocky place where knowledge is not easily absorbed or retained, let alone converted into real understanding.

For most of us in the modern world, the third house works overtime. There are new ideas, more facts and figures, and never-ending distractions hurtling our way. The danger is that it can be difficult to slow down and digest all this brain food. Without context and critical thinking, the shiny objects that distract us become mental junk food. This is why higher learning, travel, and religion have traditionally been associated with the ninth house: They provide context and encourage analysis.

But without third house curiosity, without the persistent inner toddler and its maddening "Why?" the mind becomes convinced it knows everything. Spend a few minutes at a cocktail party chatting with a self-infatuated professor or a political or religious fanatic and note how many of her sentences would, if written down, require a question mark at the end of them. You won't find many. When you know everything, the world has nothing to teach you.

When planets transit the third and ninth houses, you are called to explore the landscape of your mind, to learn new things, and to share what you know. Even a fast-moving transit in these houses can introduce an idea that has a long-lasting impact on the way you see the world.

THE THIRD HOUSE: PERCEPTION AND COMMUNICATION

Traditional name: House of Communications

Terrain: communication, memory, the mind, ideas and perception, basic education, practical skills, your neighborhood, siblings, short trips, land transportation

Shares common ground with: the sign of Gemini; the planets Mercury and the Moon (traditionally, the Moon is in its "joy" in the third house)

Traditional astrologers referred to the third house as the House of Communications. It's a great deal more than that, but communication provides a helpful metaphor for understanding what happens here.

When we think of communication, we often think first of conversation. A conversation requires a speaker and a listener. So the third house describes where and how we speak or write and how adept we are at listening and perceiving.

Communication is more than conversation, though. It's all the ways we express what's in our minds, how we feed our minds with ideas and perceptions, and how we notice details, label them, and remember them.

If you have siblings, you developed your communication style directly through your interactions with them. They knocked you down to size when you got too full of yourself, taught you verbal sparring, and helped you figure out how to be heard when other voices threatened to drown yours out. Not surprisingly, siblings are also associated with the third house.

Traditional astrologers specifically assigned "early learning" to this house, and it's usually associated also with mastering basic skills. If you need to acquire practical skills or improve the ones you have, transits in your third house will provide the impetus or, at least, the opportunity.

TRANSITING SUN IN THE THIRD HOUSE

In his book *Man's Search for Meaning*, Viktor Frankl explored the psychological reactions he observed among fellow prisoners during his time in a Nazi concentration camp. His conclusion was that a prisoner's psychological reactions are not solely the result of external circumstances, but also result from his freedom to choose how he will react to those circumstances.

Make no mistake: The one thing that can't be taken away from you is how you choose to frame your life. Mind-set is destiny.

When the transiting Sun moves into the third house of your chart, pay attention and be mindful. For some of us, this can mean meditation or other techniques that train the mind in a particular direction.

The third house is the house of documentation, so it can be an interesting time to track how resources are used. Experiment with recording every penny you spend for a month, or how many calories you're consuming, or your pulse rate. Start keeping a journal to record your thoughts.

And this month, make resolutions and affirmations. Affirmations—especially written ones—are ways of focusing the awesome power of the mind. That's the first step in creating a happier life.

TRANSITING MOON IN THE THIRD HOUSE

Each month as the Moon transits your third house, speak or write about your feelings and pay attention to the way others' words affect you emotionally. Traditionally, astrologers consider the Moon to be in its "joy" in the third house, meaning this is territory that the Moon very much likes visiting. Therefore, it is one of the better times of the month to write, since your intuition, powers of perception, and ability to express your feelings in words are very strong now. However, it's not necessarily the best time to have sensitive conversations, as your emotions may actually be a bit too close to the surface.

TRANSITING MERCURY IN THE THIRD HOUSE

Mercury should be pretty happy transiting your third house, since the two have much in common. This transit will give you an excellent few weeks for brainstorming, transmitting your message in an effective way, mastering a new skill, or beginning your novel. Unless Mercury is retrograde, you should be firing on all intellectual cylinders. If you need to take an important exam, now could be a good time, since your memory will probably be sharp and your critical skills at a peak.

TRANSITING VENUS IN THE THIRD HOUSE

If you wish to persuade or charm someone, this is a very good transit for it. Something about the way you speak, write, and otherwise communicate with others is especially seductive during this transit. Likewise, you will be particularly susceptible to the way others communicate, being turned off by coarse or impolite language and utterly charmed by someone with a lyrical speaking voice. Do a little singing. Ask for a raise.

TRANSITING MARS IN THE THIRD HOUSE

You will tend to take the direct approach while Mars transits your third house. This is very effective for dealing with situations that require courage and strength, but usually disastrous for situations requiring diplomacy (unless there is a Libra influence to your third house). That's okay; there will be other times to charm people. Now is the time for clearing the air, telling it like it is, and setting the record straight. Mars and the third house both have some connection with automobiles; keep your temper in check and your road rage under control while Mars is transiting your third house! Siblings and neighbors are also found in the third house, so settle differences with them—but be careful about saying things that can't be taken back.

TRANSITING JUPITER IN THE THIRD HOUSE

You and your big ideas! Stuffing Jupiter into the third house can be like trying to fit an elephant into your car's glove compartment. Your mind can only handle so many ideas at one time, and with Jupiter in your third house, you've got more than your share. Keep a notebook handy for recording any and all random ideas that come your way during this transit; you can always pull them out later, one at a time, during those periods when ideas are few and far between.

This can be a year for travel, usually longer trips within your own country, or especially short trips abroad. Jupiter has an expansive influence, and the third house includes the neighborhood you live in, so you might move to a bigger or more ethnically diverse neighborhood or simply develop new relationships with your existing neighbors. This is also a good transit for having adventures with your siblings or mending fences with them.

TRANSITING SATURN IN THE THIRD HOUSE

There is a time to learn from books and example and a time to learn by doing, and this is the latter. Whatever work you do, Saturn transiting your third house marks a period of apprenticeship. Like an English literature graduate student who teaches basic composition to college freshmen, you may be called on to teach others in the basic skills and techniques of your field.

You will learn the hard way how important it is to choose your words carefully. Others are paying close attention to what you say and look up to you as an authority or mentor—at precisely the time you're reaching the stage where you doubt your knowledge and competence. Part of Saturn's lesson in this house is the need to balance intellectual rigor with practical know-how and how to handle your communications with others in an ethical, responsible way.

TRANSITING URANUS IN THE THIRD HOUSE

Wherever Uranus transits, an awakening is under way. To the third house, Uranus brings a subject or focus that makes you want to study hard. Keep your mind open during this transit and you will probably find the path that makes sense to you, that in many ways has been in front of you for your entire life but that you were unable to recognize as the path with heart.

Like all Uranus transits, this begins with an ending. We're made up of so many old stories that we tell ourselves—"I'm not good at math, not physically coordinated, not likable." When Uranus transits the third house, it's time for some new stories. That means a declaration of independence in one form or another. One woman I know impulsively left her job as this transit was beginning. Her boss had yelled at her, and then she calmly grabbed a cardboard box, filled it with her personal belongings, and simply walked out, never to return. Soon after, she enrolled in college to pursue her long-delayed degree and discovered a field of study that she loved.

We're not all in a position to make such a drastic move. But while Uranus transits your third house, something has to change about the way you think of yourself. Sometimes that begins with refusing to let anyone—including yourself—speak to you disrespectfully.

TRANSITING NEPTUNE IN THE THIRD HOUSE

The mind is an amazing mystery. The ability to communicate with our fellow humans is a wondrous gift. But as Neptune transits your third house, you'll learn something about the limits of intellectual understanding.

The traditional interpretation of this transit would be that your mind will be cloudy and distracted, your communications with others rife with misunderstandings. But this can be a very, very long transit. Personally, I've been living with it for sixteen years as I write this, with four more years to go! In that time I've already earned a degree in communications and launched a writing career. While I won't say I've always been the sharpest crayon in the box, I've at least managed the fundamentals of scheduling and organization.

But I have learned, as well, the importance of speaking not just from the head but from the heart. I've learned that communication is not just a function of finding the right words, but also of using them to express what others have a hard time finding language for. Siblings are also found in the third house, and mine have suffered profound losses, joys, and travails during this transit.

When Neptune transits the third house, the mind must be opened to the ineffable. Expressing yourself poetically, with music, art, or simply great empathy, and teaching yourself to read between the lines to better intuit what others are trying to say, even when they say nothing at all—these are the great lessons of transiting Neptune in the third house.

TRANSITING PLUTO IN THE THIRD HOUSE

Back in the days of my youth, comic books boasted an advertisement for X-ray Specs. These marvelous glasses would allegedly give you the ability to see through pesky obstructions such as clothing to see what was really going on underneath the surface.

Pluto transiting your third house is a little bit like being gifted with a pair of these spectacles. Instead of seeing through people's clothing, however, you are given a much more complicated gift—the ability to see through artifice and dishonesty.

You will not abide being lied to with Pluto transiting the third house, and you will become far more astute about recognizing when it's happening. In the movie *Fearless*, Jeff Bridges plays a man who survives a horrible airplane crash. Subsequently, he finds himself completely unable to tolerate the slightest hint of dishonesty or manipulation, occasionally yelling loudly or, in one instance, slapping the perpetrator. That's what it's like when Pluto transits the third house.

Pluto usually brings some kind of dramatic circumstances that help you probe the structure of your life for weakness. With Pluto transiting the third house, you will stand for nothing less than the truth, from yourself and others. If others lie to you, how can you trust them? If you lie to yourself, who are you? Like a TV detective, you will stop at nothing to get to the truth, will speak your truth without a lot of delicacy, and will see the world in much sharper focus than you ever have before.

TRANSITING NORTH NODE IN THE THIRD HOUSE

Time to bring your focus and skills to bear on a long-contemplated goal. To go after your dreams, you need to fill in some gaps in knowledge, credentials, or skills. This transit will bring eclipses to your third house, and the need to improve your résumé will reach a critical point. Problems may arise with neighbors or siblings, but that will be a blessing meant to move you to a more nourishing location or improve your family relationships.

When the transiting North Node is in the third house, the transiting South Node is in the ninth. The safest action is to stick with what you know. But the road to growth is to remain curious about everything the world has to teach you.

THE NINTH HOUSE: THE QUEST

Traditional name: House of Long Journeys over Water

Terrain: beliefs, higher education, philosophy, the quest for meaning, foreign countries, overseas travel, teaching, religion, airplanes, ships, books, publishers, large animals, theaters and performance spaces

Shares common ground with: the sign of Sagittarius; the planet Jupiter and the Sun (traditionally, the Sun is in its "joy" in the ninth house)

This was known by traditional astrologers as the House of Long Journeys over Water or the House of Philosophy. In some cases, transits in the ninth house will literally carry you to faraway lands. In others, the journeys are metaphorical. Let's say you're invited to dinner at the home of a new friend whose family comes from a country halfway around the world and doesn't share your language or background. Strange food might be served; you may not understand their customs and etiquette. In all ways, you are being challenged to stretch and adapt to a very new experience, nearly as much so as if you had literally flown to a remote land.

There are many ways of exploring different worlds of experience and of the mind. When planets transit the ninth house, something unfamiliar will come your way, bringing with it the opportunity to see the world through a larger and more inclusive lens.

TRANSITING SUN IN THE NINTH HOUSE

If you're a little uncomfortable during the month that the Sun moves through your ninth house, then you're on the right track! This is the time of year to stretch, to experience unfamiliar ideas, sights, smells, tastes, and sounds. Contemplate the heavens, figuratively speaking, by thinking deep thoughts and having important conversations. By the end of the month, you may find you've developed a taste for new things.

It might also be a good month to *literally* contemplate the heavens. A few years ago I was in New Zealand during the month that the Sun moves through my ninth house. One night I stepped outside into a cool, clear evening and looked up at the sky. I became almost dizzy—not only was there a thick blanket of stars, but the stars were different from the ones I was used to seeing! As an urban dweller, I had no idea that I'd become accustomed to the night sky until I saw one that was utterly foreign.

Make yourself uncomfortable this month. Ponder the big questions. Look at a new sky. Happiness lies in unfamiliar constellations.

TRANSITING MOON IN THE NINTH HOUSE

During this time of the month, your intuition and gut reactions have a strong influence over what you believe. If something doesn't *feel* right, you can't be convinced that it *is* right. It's not always the best strategy to base all your beliefs on gut instinct instead of exposing them to logic and rationale, but every now and then it's healthy to subject your religious, cultural, and political attitudes to your intuition. The ninth house is associated with foreign places and long-distance travel, so if you have a big trip coming up, this can be an excellent time to do a little planning. Your instincts will guide you more strongly than usual in choosing sites to visit and finding good deals on airfare, lodging, and other travel-related services.

TRANSITING MERCURY IN THE NINTH HOUSE

When Mercury transits the ninth house, a new piece of information comes your way that leads you to question how you look at things. You may read an article, hear a lecture, or catch a snippet on a radio or television program that introduces an entirely different line of thinking. It could be as simple as someone asking you a question and you realizing that you don't have an answer. It's not the most comfortable sensation; our beliefs are our beliefs for a reason, and we generally feel we've given them careful consideration. But it's essential to keep growing, stay flexible, and maintain an open mind, and this brief transit of Mercury through your ninth house will help you do all those things.

TRANSITING VENUS IN THE NINTH HOUSE

Have you ever heard someone say that hearing a piece of music or seeing a piece of art for the first time changed his or her life? It may sound hyperbolic, but it does happen. At its best, art has a transformative effect, elevating your mind and opening up an entirely new way of looking at the world.

During Venus's transit of your ninth house, make an effort to broaden your exposure to beauty, art, and social events. These will provide the catalyst for opening your mind to new concepts and may even inspire you to broaden your life experience through travel, foreign cultures, or simply taking a risk.

TRANSITING MARS IN THE NINTH HOUSE

There are times to fight for what you believe in, and one could argue that Mars's transit of your ninth house is one of those times. As anyone who has spent a contentious Thanksgiving meal arguing about politics with their relatives knows, forcing your beliefs on others rarely wins hearts and minds. Instead, consider how you can put your energy, initiative, and courage to practical use on behalf of the people and causes that are important to you.

This is an excellent transit for embarking on a course of study, particularly one that will lead to an advanced degree. Where Mars is transiting we find the motivation to tackle tasks that may seem daunting at other times, so if education is important to you but has been difficult to pursue, now is a good time to try again.

TRANSITING JUPITER IN THE NINTH HOUSE

Jupiter is in his wheelhouse as he transits the ninth house, and this is generally a time to think about how you could be living bigger. Long to travel? Book a ticket, or at least apply for your passport so you'll be ready when the opportunity for travel arises. Want to be a published author? Write your book this year. If you've written it already, it's time to look for a publisher or begin the process of self-publishing. Finishing college? Consider graduate school!

If you lack inspiration and a sense of adventure as this transit begins, it's a sign that your Jupiter is undernourished. Feed it books, foreign films, ethnic cuisine, train trips, and suitcases. You can't think big if you keep your world too small.

TRANSITING SATURN IN THE NINTH HOUSE

It used to be that if one attended college, graduation marked the beginning of professional life. You'd land an entry-level position in your chosen field and begin the long, arduous climb through the ranks toward mastery and accomplishment.

When transiting Saturn is moving through your ninth house, you're in a similar situation, regardless of whether or when you graduated. You've proven that you have achieved a basic competency in some field of study or professional development. Now it's time to share what you know with others by accepting your first important professional challenge. It will be one that stretches you to the limit of your capabilities, but meeting the challenge will give you unshakable confidence in your abilities moving forward.

TRANSITING URANUS IN THE NINTH HOUSE

A friend described the reaction of his staunchly conservative family when he revealed he was gay. "They felt they had to either turn their back on me or turn their back on God," he said. "In the end they chose me, but the decision was so difficult that my mother says she's still mad at God!"

Wherever Uranus transits, liberation is sure to follow. The problem is, freedom is scary. When Uranus transits the ninth house, you're being unmoored from your belief system. For some, this may mean leaving an established religion; for others, this may be a time of trading one ideology for its exact opposite. Perhaps, like my friend's mother, you're confronted with a case of cognitive dissonance so extreme that it shakes you loose from everything you've ever believed was true or right. Uranus is a lot like lightning, and it's never easy to predict exactly where it will strike. But one thing's for sure: By the time Uranus leaves your ninth house, you will look at the world in a very different way.

TRANSITING NEPTUNE IN THE NINTH HOUSE

Like Uranus transiting the ninth house, Neptune's transit here makes you reconsider what you believe about the world. But Neptune's approach to bringing about change is generally quite different. What often happens when Neptune transits the ninth house is a softening of beliefs and a deepening of compassion, usually based on experience. Sometimes we have to go through hardship or have direct contact with others who are experiencing setbacks before we can really open up to others who are suffering.

Neptune always insists that you let go of what is no longer viable; its journey through the ninth house will open your eyes to what you have believed is untrue, unkind, or unhelpful. Let those parts go and replace them with kindness, love, and compassion.

TRANSITING PLUTO IN THE NINTH HOUSE

What needs to happen as Pluto transits your ninth house is for you to come to terms with the fact that life is inherently beyond your control. So many of the belief systems we embrace are the result of trying to feel we have some ability to influence the course of our lives and even the lives of others. But as Pluto moves through your ninth house, various important events, usually including power struggles involving institutions of all types, eventually bring you to the realization that, ultimately, nothing is really within your control. The view of Pluto in the ninth house is that nothing has any inherent meaning, just the meaning we choose to ascribe to it.

TRANSITING NORTH NODE IN THE NINTH HOUSE

As the North Node transits the ninth house, and in particular during the months when eclipses fall in this house, it's common to experience a crisis of faith. As the North Node transited your tenth house, you had a chance to review your standing in your career and your community, your status and reputation. Based on that review, you now feel the urge to take a leap of faith into something new. You may not feel you're ready, but the universe sees it differently, insisting that it's time you made a big change.

The South Node is transiting the third house as the North Node is in the ninth. The third house is where we are eternal students, asking questions, collecting endless pieces of data, convinced that if we just have enough facts we'll know everything. But the North Node's ninth house message is, "You've been a student long enough. You have all the skills and information that you need. Now, it's time to throw yourself off a cliff and learn to fly."

chapter 13

HOUSES 4 AND 10:
ORIGIN AND DESTINATION

don't recall where I first heard it, but there is an old joke about a lost tourist who asked an Irishman for directions to Dublin. The Irishman thought for a moment, then replied, "Well, I wouldn't start from here."

You can only start from where you are, of course. Your starting point is certain and unchanging—your true north. Symbolized by the astrological fourth house, your origin determines how you move forward into the world and, to a great extent, what you perceive to be possible for you. The opposite point in your birth chart, the tenth house, symbolizes where you are headed. There, we find not only hints about your ultimate destination but also, to some extent, what you'll have to overcome in order to reach it.

If a self-educated young lawyer, born to dirt-poor and uneducated parents, came to you and asked, "How do I become the president of the United States?" you might very well be tempted to answer, "Well, honey, I wouldn't start from here." But where else could Abraham Lincoln have started from?

We don't always know exactly where we're going, but we do know we can't stay where we began, in swaddling clothes and safe in a cradle. When planets transit the fourth house, they indicate a journey of leaving home, finding home, or perhaps yearning for home. Transits in the tenth house compel us to define our destination; it may defy every expectation the world holds for us, or it may be exactly the path we'd be expected to take.

Like the North and South Poles, the latitudes of our lives constrict at the fourth and tenth houses. The terrain of home and work can make us feel safe and offer a sense of belonging, to a tribe and in community. But they can also be places where we feel constricted, confined by expectations, and limited in a way that begs for escape. Transits to the fourth and tenth house axis of the chart invite us to explore the balance between origin and destination, and to negotiate a healthier balance between safety and certainty at home and the satisfaction of worldly achievement.

THE FOURTH HOUSE: WHERE YOU'RE PLANTED

Traditional name: House of Home and Family

Terrain: home, family, history, ancestors, one parent, real estate, genealogy

Shares common ground with: the sign of Cancer; the Moon

Why is genealogy so fascinating? It could be a way of getting to know the ancestors who lurk in your DNA. Where were they from? What did they do for work? What part of them lives on in you? In the most primitive sense, these are the building blocks of the astrological fourth house, like a big old, dusty hope chest filled with your backstory. Your biology, your biography, one of your parents (astrologers debate which one), the place where you first drew breath—all are contained in the fourth house. Mostly, the fourth describes the anchor that keeps you rooted inside your existence.

When planets transit your fourth house, the hope chest is thrown open. The dust goes flying. Old, creased, yellowing photographs flutter out, along with memories: an afternoon at the beach when you were very small; the longing in your mother's face when she told you, soon after your grandfather's death, that you had his eyes. A bit of an old song. Your high school locker combination.

There is yearning in the fourth house, nostalgia, safety—the safety of knowing who your people are and where you come from. This is sacred territory, but it has an expiration date. You can't stay here forever. The world has other things in mind for you. Planets transiting here summon you to sort through everything you have been and decide what to leave behind and what to carry forward with you into your future.

TRANSITING SUN IN THE FOURTH HOUSE

Think of the people you know whose natal Sun falls within the degrees of your fourth and fifth house cusps. The ones I know make me feel happy. They feel like family. They also make me a little bit crazy sometimes; they seem a little *too* cheerful, a tad *too* upbeat and positive. They lift my spirits, but they also make me feel a little dark in comparison, as they shine a light into the shameful, jealous, mean-spirited parts of me that I'd prefer to keep hidden—even from myself.

And so it is during the month each year when the Sun transits your fourth house. There is a glimpse of what things could be like if you let your heart grow sunnier. But it means you'll have to open up and air out the mustier bits of yourself. This is the work of the Sun's annual transit through the fourth house: to brighten the spaces where you live, including your heart, and to enjoy the creatures that share those spaces with you.

You have an opportunity this month, however modest, to rewrite history. So much of how we react to the present and envision the future has to do with the stories we tell ourselves about the past. Rewrite your history, with yourself as the protagonist; find sympathy for yourself and forgiveness for those who haven't always made your story a happy one.

Lastly, brighten your actual, physical home while the Sun is transiting your fourth house. This might mean doing a thorough housecleaning, hanging a piece of artwork, or tending to some long-delayed home repairs. Let the Sun's transit of your fourth house bring light to the place where you live, inside and out.

TRANSITING MOON IN THE FOURTH HOUSE

During the precious hours each month when the transiting Moon speeds through your fourth house, hang out the "closed for refurbishing" sign and take care of some things that are important to you alone. Sort through old photos and put them into albums or scan them. Scratch the cat behind the ears (okay, maybe that's important to the cat, too). Cook something special. Paint your bedroom. This is a time each month that should be devoted to a bit of self-care, and you alone get to decide what will make you feel nourished and cherished.

TRANSITING MERCURY IN THE FOURTH HOUSE

The past may well be on your mind while transiting Mercury is in your fourth house. Memories and perceptions are vivid and emotionally compelling; it's a splendid couple of weeks for creative writing or for catching up on correspondence with loved ones, because you're likely to want to share your thoughts without the pressure of face-to-face interaction.

Allow Mercury to be of practical help at home, too. Mercury is a curious critter, so let him loose in your cabinets and closets with a trash bag and a label maker. When he emerges, everything will be nicely organized, complete with a written inventory and some lost objects that he found.

TRANSITING VENUS IN THE FOURTH HOUSE

When Venus transits your fourth house, you'll particularly love being at home. Buy beautiful gifts for your house, like new guest towels or a fantastic coffeemaker. Invite friends over to fill the place with affection and laughter. This is one of the best transits all year for making your space more gorgeous and inviting. Fill it with lovely things and with the people you enjoy. Your home is a reflection of your inner wellspring of contentment and tranquility, so making it more pleasant will have a similar effect on your mood.

TRANSITING MARS IN THE FOURTH HOUSE

Imagine living in a house where people are at each other's throats constantly, where workers are jackhammering the foundations, or where a bored kid spends a long summer's day repetitively bouncing his ball against your office wall. This is more or less what it's like when Mars transits your fourth house. In precisely the place that you most need a haven of sanity and rest, there is discord, noise, or disruption.

There is an upside, though. If there are projects around your house that you've been putting off for a long time, this transit will usually galvanize you into getting them started. And if you need courage to confront people and events from your past, now is the time to let Mars slay those dragons for you.

TRANSITING JUPITER IN THE FOURTH HOUSE

Sometimes retreat is the best course of action. For instance, when you've found your life moving in a direction that is as far as possible from where you had hoped to end up, it's time to take a step back and regroup. The fourth is the house of home, family, and the quiet place within, so that's where you need to go for transiting Jupiter's fourth house timeout. Home might not necessarily be the place where you currently live, by the way. You may find yourself traveling to a place that feels like, or even eventually becomes, home.

Wherever you go, the personal growth and epic adventure that Jupiter craves is directed inward now. Take the leap into your deepest self to discover all that you are, understand where you came from, and remember where you were headed before your life brought you to where you are now.

TRANSITING SATURN IN THE FOURTH HOUSE

Home may be bliss or it may be dreadful, but it is something most of us can at least take for granted. When Saturn is transiting your fourth house, though, you don't necessarily have that luxury. You will probably have a roof over your head, but you will have to struggle and sacrifice and work fairly hard to carve out a place that *feels* like home to you. You may well move to a new place during this transit. Yet the fourth house experience is not confined to the actual house that you live in or the people related to you by blood; it's also about feeling at home on the planet and in your own skin.

Wherever Saturn is transiting, you're asked to examine the container you've built for some part of your life, to figure out whether you have outgrown it or need to make it stronger. What is your definition of *home*? What does that container look like? Who are the people you would like to share it with? What is the foundation that your life is built on, and how does it strengthen or undermine you? Examining your connection to your family is key to this transit. You may find that your family grows smaller during this transit, through relocation or divorce, or as grown children leave the nest.

TRANSITING URANUS IN THE FOURTH HOUSE

You may not realize it, especially if you still have parents, but the person in the world you most rely on is you—that is, the person you are when you're completely alone. That's the one person who is always there, looking back at you from the mirror when you brush your teeth. That's the only person in the world who knows all of your secrets. And when transiting Uranus is in your fourth house, that person is going through a quiet, private, but titanic shift.

The urge is to break free of the way you normally feel and seek comfort and nourishment in new things. You're probably a little tired of who you are and of your usual tics, games, and obsessions. There is a profound restlessness in you now. You may want to run away from your home, your career, or your family—but what you really want to run away from is the person you are when you're alone.

TRANSITING NEPTUNE IN THE FOURTH HOUSE

Every kid who ever visits the beach—a good number of adults, too—immediately builds a sand castle. Most of them also walk down to the waterline and trace their names in the wave-slicked sand. They stand and watch while the waves wash ashore, erasing their names and demolishing their castles. If the person is very young, he might cry about it. If he's older, he may allow himself a rueful chuckle at this elegant metaphor for the impermanence of all things.

While Neptune transits your fourth house, you can build all the castles you like and write your name large for all to see. But this is a hard time to build things that last. When this transit is finished, you will no longer even call yourself the name that you have always given your most private self, let alone write it in the sand. So let go of the need to build, the need to make yourself permanent. You are being baptized into a new identity; you are being given a chance to be more loving and whole, to lie on the sand and let the waves tickle your toes. It's a long transit, this one. But then, it can take a long time to wash the slate clean.

TRANSITING PLUTO IN THE FOURTH HOUSE

A friend of mine who was having this transit said it felt like entering the government's Witness Protection Program. It began with her finding she no longer had the capacity to be dishonest about anything, which estranged many people close to her. By the end of this long, long transit, she no longer felt she could live in the same place, and she literally left home to start fresh somewhere new.

Wherever Pluto transits, it reflects a complete inability to bear any falsehood. In the fourth house, Pluto makes you unable to fool yourself about who you are or where you come from. You become the family whistle-blower. Living with Pluto's honesty means living without a place that feels completely safe and comfortable. At the end of this transit, though, you'll know where you really belong, how you really want to live, and who your true family members are.

TRANSITING NORTH NODE IN THE FOURTH HOUSE

This transit evokes the moment near the end of *The Wizard of Oz* when Dorothy wishes aloud that she could return to Kansas. Glenda the Good Witch points out to Dorothy that she's had the power to go home all along.

This is the transit when you truly realize that whatever fond wish your natal North Node holds for you is well within your grasp, and that, indeed, the power to achieve it has been within you all along. Sometimes this transit involves literally sitting in your home and working on something that will eventually lead you farther along your evolutionary path. And sometimes you simply need to look within yourself to find the answers you've been looking for. The South Node transits the tenth while the North Node is in the fourth, and it's tempting to use work and status to hide from these tasks.

The North Node transiting your fourth house means there will be an eclipse or two in this house, as well. Eclipses in the fourth house can bring changes in residence, often connected to your career, and changes in personnel at home. Most of all, they bring a sudden, surprising awareness of feelings you didn't even know you had.

THE TENTH HOUSE: BREAKING AWAY

Traditional name: House of Career and Social Status

Terrain: reputation, career, calling, ambitions, one parent, mentor, bosses and authority figures

Shares common ground with: the sign of Capricorn; the planet Saturn

The tenth house, according to traditional astrologers, was the House of Career and Social Status. Reputation is an interesting thing; it's the inherited part of the tenth house, the part that is yours by virtue of being born into a family, with a particular name, gender, race, nationality, and religion. It is heritage made visible. If you aren't careful, your heritage becomes your entire future instead of simply guiding you to it.

Make conscious decisions about how you will be seen by the world. How are you like the family you were born into and the people who shared your early years, and how are you different? Do you want to live the life that's expected for you? Some people do; they love it, they're happy, and that's wonderful. You may have something very different in mind.

The tenth house symbolizes the world's expectations for you, but the challenge is to claim it as your own and to create your own tenth house destiny. If you can glimpse the mountain's summit, then you can reach it, even if you started in the depths of the valley below, and even if no one else thinks you are equal to the task. Planets transiting the tenth house aim to see you get to the top of your personal mountain. Sometimes these transits bring people and situations designed to assist and inspire you. And sometimes they help by letting you see what's standing in your way—even if it's you.

TRANSITING SUN IN THE TENTH HOUSE

While the Sun transits your tenth house, ask yourself how your work, your calling, and your legacy can make you happier. The tenth house, and ambition generally, tends to have the opposite effect, making us feel we're forever lacking.

The trick to enjoying the Sun in the tenth house is to imagine not that you're in an inferior position that must be escaped at all costs, but rather that you're in the perfect position to get where you're going. Part of that journey begins with a plan—for your career or even for your whole life. If you already have a plan, revisit and revise it. If you don't know where you're going, you won't recognize it when you arrive.

Also, since you probably work plenty hard already, work smarter—and learn to delegate. Even if you can do anything, you don't have to do *everything*. Partner with others who like to do the things you don't care for, and vice versa. You'll go much further with help from others than you can alone.

TRANSITING MOON IN THE TENTH HOUSE

The promise of the tenth house is not achieved in a couple of days, and that's as long as the transiting Moon gets to spend there each month. What you can do during this monthly transit, though, is examine your to-do lists, affirmations, and ambitions and give them a gut check. When you imagine having accomplished your goals, how does your gut feel? When you review the steps you've taken so far toward achieving them, and as you think about your treatment of others along the way, are you completely satisfied with the means by which you are approaching the ends? While the Moon transits your tenth house, make sure you are proud not just of *what* you're achieving, but *how* you're achieving it.

TRANSITING MERCURY IN THE TENTH HOUSE

When I was young, I spent hours lying on my bed filling notebooks with lists and doodles about the amazing future I envisioned for myself. What is a little surprising to me is how many of those visions eventually came true. I didn't realize that what I was doing was a form of visualization and affirmation; I just enjoyed imagining the cool things that might happen to me someday and writing those thoughts down.

Whether you write affirmations at every New Moon or never write them down at all, use the energy of Mercury transiting your tenth house to create precisely the future you want, even if it's only on paper. Describe your future self and life in grand, rich detail. Write a press release about your imaginary book, album, company launch, or illustrious reward. Mercury's magic lies in words, so use them to visualize your tenth house future and commit it to the reality of pen and paper.

TRANSITING VENUS IN THE TENTH HOUSE

What is your calling? A calling may strike the modern reader as a very old-fashioned notion, or as something singularly religious, such as a calling to join the priesthood or to serve the world as a missionary.

But the tenth house, while we generally think of it as a house of career, can more precisely be thought of as describing your calling, what you feel you were born to do, even if it's not something that you can reasonably expect will earn much money. As Venus transits your tenth house, expect something pleasurable to lead you to a better understanding of your calling, or perhaps some unexpected bit of money to allow you to pursue something you love. Keep your eyes open for examples of people who are doing what they love, or simply loving what they do. They are showing you what it looks like to make love your calling.

TRANSITING MARS IN THE TENTH HOUSE

Ready for a challenge? When Mars transits your tenth house, the Universe throws down a gauntlet and dares you to pick it up. Usually it's related to your career and comes in the form of a truly audacious challenge that you would have to be a little crazy to accept. Go ahead and pick it up!

A friend of mine once said that she will never turn down an amazing opportunity to do something just because she's never done it before. She says yes, and then she figures out how to do it. That's exactly what the world wants from you when Mars is transiting your tenth house. Blaze a trail. Show us how it's done. Do the audacious, impossible thing.

TRANSITING JUPITER IN THE TENTH HOUSE

An astrologer shouldn't play favorites, but this is one of my very favorite transits. Who doesn't love to achieve a goal and win accolades? This is the equivalent of graduating from university with honors in your field, so celebrate what you've accomplished. It's not exactly all downhill from here, but it's pretty hard to top a great Jupiter transit. Not only do you win a prize that has been coming your way for twelve years but you also get to begin dreaming up where you want to be in another twelve years. Aim high. Think big. Expand your idea of what you think is possible for you in the world. The only limit is your imagination!

TRANSITING SATURN IN THE TENTH HOUSE

As transiting Saturn reaches the apex of your chart, you've reached the end of one twenty-nine-year journey and the beginning of another. It's a voyage that will ultimately determine how the world sees you, and to a great extent, the way it will remember you after you're gone.

As always at the beginning of a new adventure, the road forward is not clear. You are probably at a career crossroads, or otherwise coming to grips with what it means to be a grown-up, in charge of your own life. What do you want? Where are you going? These are important questions, and it will take you the next few decades to answer them properly.

For now, it's not important to have answers. Your questions don't have to be all that specific, either. You just need to find the grit and tenacity to get up each day, set one foot in front of the other, and move forward. In time—even by the time Saturn moves out of your tenth house—you will begin to see the way more clearly.

TRANSITING URANUS IN THE TENTH HOUSE

If you're not fully committed to your career path, it will not hold up against Uranus's transit of your tenth house. And it probably shouldn't. Uranus is like a natural disaster that you would never have hoped for, but that ends up being a blessing in disguise because it allows you to start over, from scratch.

Having a fixed career path is likely to feel a bit itchy and uncomfortable to you at this point in your life. If you're close to retirement age, you'll be chomping at the bit to leave the world of nine-to-five employment. If you must work, a career that allows maximum flexibility and autonomy is the only one with any chance of longevity. Working as a contractor, for instance, with the freedom to set your own schedule, is an example of a situation that would probably feel ideal during this transit.

Your life has taken a permanent turn in a different direction. This can be a very long transit, and there's no telling exactly where you'll be at the end of it. All that's certain is that you'll be doing a lot of improvisation along the way, and that your life will look a lot different by the time this transit is over.

TRANSITING NEPTUNE IN THE TENTH HOUSE

We live in a world that is fond of certainty. In the West, our prevailing narrative is one of free will and the ability to make what we want of our lives.

But what happens when you no longer know what you want your life to look like? What happens when your career no longer seems to mean anything, or the kids have flown the coop and left a black hole where the center of your life used to be?

As Neptune transits your tenth house, your vision of the future grows splotchy, like when old movie film breaks and leaves melty projections on the screen. It's as though you've been on a huge ship, happily cruising along with a capable crew at the helm, and suddenly ran into an iceberg. You've leaped into a lifeboat, and all you have to rely on are the other passengers for company and the stars in the night sky for navigation. There are no computers, no cell phone signals, no magazines, no paper and pen. Your job is to drift along while you learn to let your heart and mind be fully present in each moment, instead of racing toward the future.

TRANSITING PLUTO IN THE TENTH HOUSE

Transiting Pluto moving through the tenth house of your chart tells us two things: The profession you once had is fundamentally changing. You can't get it back, because it is, at a very real level, gone. That's not to say you won't be able to support yourself, but it does tell us that even if you got your old job back, it wouldn't be the same, and it wouldn't offer security.

The other thing it tells us is that you no longer feel happy about taking orders from anybody else. You must feel in control of your destiny, and of your career path; if you fail to take control, you will likely find yourself, over and over, in workplace situations that are toxic. Pluto must be expressed—if not as empowerment, it will be expressed as powerlessness.

Where Pluto transits, there is no room for dishonest or self-serving behavior. If you are trying to keep secrets from the world, Pluto in the most public house of the chart will usually expose them.

TRANSITING NORTH NODE IN THE TENTH HOUSE

The natal position of the Moon's North Node hints at the sorts of dreams that, if realized, could lead you to great happiness. As the North Node transits the tenth house every eighteen years or so, you don't necessarily achieve these dreams, but you absolutely find the determination to put a plan into action to help you achieve them down the road. Often this means a change in career or your living situation, which is likely to come about during the months that eclipses fall in your tenth house.

As the North Node transits your tenth house, the South Node is simultaneously transiting your fourth house. Since the South Node shows where old patterns and habits need to be released, this is a transit when it's especially important to become aware of how the past may be holding you back from success, and to be willing to make the changes necessary to change that pattern.

chapter 14

HOUSES 5 AND 11:
CREATIONS AND LEGENDS

I don't have children, and I used to be perplexed by those minivans with a bumper sticker that reads something like, "My child is an honor student at XYZ School." But when it eventually occurred to me that these are a sort of appeal to the gods of both the fifth and eleventh houses, they suddenly made a lot more sense.

Having a child is the ultimate act of creative self-expression, with the added bonus of perpetuating the species. Children and creativity are both part of the fifth house terrain, and having a child is as pure a fifth house experience as you'll ever have. But the desire to have your child's achievements acknowledged by fellow motorists takes us into the heart of eleventh house territory, where we wish for our creative efforts to inspire a larger audience and live on after us as a legacy.

Likewise, writing a book is a fifth house experience for me. But if I simply printed it out, wiped my computer hard drive clean, and tossed the manuscript into the fireplace, it would remain a fifth house experience. It's not until it's picked up and read by others (thank you!) that my eleventh house springs to life.

Without an audience, the circle of creative self-expression is incomplete. If you doubt it, ask a writer if she gives as much attention to her personal journal as she does to a piece of work that will be read by others. I give approximately a thousand times more attention and care to my writing when I know someone else will be reading it. It's the imagined other, the critic as well as the fan, who spurs me on.

The eleventh house doesn't represent only audiences—it's also your creative collaborators who reside here. You don't have to be close friends with the people in your local astrology group or beer-brewing club, your community theater troupe or your weekend softball league. It's enough that you share an interest in creating something that can only be brought to life by a team. The eleventh house is known as the House of Friendship, but these are less friendships of the heart than friendships of shared interests. This is where you'll find groups and organizations to which you're yoked by the communal projects and creations you help bring to life.

THE FIFTH HOUSE: A PIECE OF YOUR HEART

Traditional name: House of Children and Creativity

Terrain: children, creative self-expression, hobbies, recreation, games, entertainment, fun, love affairs

Shares common ground with: the sign of Leo; the Sun

Let's pretend you've run away from home and gone to Europe for the summer. In Paris, you meet someone whom you immediately recognize as your soul mate. No one has ever made you feel so special, as though his life began at the moment he set eyes on you. And you feel exactly the same way in return. It's kismet!

Eventually summer ends and it's time for you to go your separate ways. There are tears, promises to reunite as soon as you can disentangle yourselves from your regular lives and commitments to all those people who don't really understand you.

Back home, in familiar surroundings, time passes. Breathless memories of Paris begin to fade. Skype sessions grow further apart. You get busy at work. You can't think how to break things off with the person you've been seeing at home. And eventually, it becomes clear that while this brief love affair was one of the most heart-opening experiences of your life, it was not meant to last.

Heart-opening experiences are the purview of the fifth house. A brief love affair in a foreign city, the exhilaration of sharing your true self through a creative project, the exquisite delirium of welcoming your first child into the world—are all fifth house experiences. Fifth house experiences make you grateful beyond measure that you are you, and no one else. Sometimes they turn into long-lasting relationships, careers, or interests. But often they exist simply for a brief moment in time, for the sole purpose of introducing you to your own heart.

The real world happens between these fireworks displays. When we're not in love, when the toddler is screaming, when the painting lies unfinished in a corner of the living room, we still have the fifth house in our charts. When we lack time, energy, or inspiration, we feed ourselves with lesser fifth house food such as video games, television, gambling, and spending too many dollars and calories on eating and drinking.

To keep the fifth house healthy means making an effort, every single day, to contribute some vital part of your unique self to the world. To do something only you can do. To show us part of your heart.

TRANSITING SUN IN THE FIFTH HOUSE

In the film *State and Main*, a big-city writer visiting a small town chats with a local woman about the community theater group and its upcoming production. "I suppose in a small town, you have to make your own fun," the writer observes. "Everyone makes their own fun," replies the woman. "If you don't make it yourself, it ain't fun—it's entertainment."

In the horoscope, the fifth house is where you make your own fun. Sometimes, too, it's where you entertain others. And it's also where you take time out from the obligations of daily life to indulge in play, creativity, and leisure.

The truth is, you can't be productive or creative all the time. That's what recreation is for: to refill the well that you draw from. Every now and again, even a workaholic needs to take an afternoon off.

In the two or three months before the Sun enters this part of your chart, save up ideas of fun things to do. Perhaps there's an attraction in your city that you've never explored, a few books you want to read, or a weekend trip with your best friend that you've been putting off. Try to save enough of them to do a couple each week that the Sun is in your fifth house.

The Sun's transit of your fifth house is also your chance to be an inspiration to others. Even if you don't feel as though you're leading the most exciting life, I'm willing to bet there's at least one person who looks up to you. This month, get out of your own way—give happiness to others and let them find their inspiration in you.

TRANSITING MOON IN THE FIFTH HOUSE

This is one of the most creative times of each month, a rich opportunity to transform vulnerability and emotional chaos into art. If you have the luxury of taking to the typewriter, studio, kitchen, or workshop to express yourself through a bit of wild creativity, this transit could be the most fun you'll have all month long.

Children may try your patience a bit while the Moon is in your fifth house. If you have kids, schedule playdates and other activities that give you a break from one another. Alternately, toss out your normal routine for a couple of days and try to enjoy an artistic project together. The key is to find a way to appreciate each other, sometimes together, sometimes apart.

TRANSITING MERCURY IN THE FIFTH HOUSE

In the fifth house, transiting Mercury looks for new ideas, skills, or strategies related to having a good time. Mercury's innate curiosity and love of variety will lead you to find ways of having more fun, finding love, and generally enjoying yourself during this transit. Make it a priority to read a new book, visit with friends, and add at least one new skill or piece to your creative repertoire. You'll find it delightful to use your brain during this transit—that's Mercury's idea of a good time. And if you've thought about joining a dating website, this could be a very good time to do it—your ability to sell yourself and to navigate inscrutable technology is better than usual now!

TRANSITING VENUS IN THE FIFTH HOUSE

The world does not always look upon us fondly and with benign indulgence when we decide to strut our stuff. That's the tricky part of fifth house transits, which can be so much fun as long as you don't care what people think of your creations or your idea of merriment and play. This is a fairly quick transit, so it may not bring the love of your life to you, but it will likely provide appreciation for your fun-loving side, creative efforts, or children.

You'll probably receive creative support and favorable reviews when Venus transits your fifth house, but hopefully you'll be too preoccupied with having fun or enjoying an influx of cash to care what others think about what you wear, what you do, or whom you love. Money might emerge as a motivation for a new creative project or might be offered for something you've already created.

TRANSITING MARS IN THE FIFTH HOUSE

Play hard while Mars is transiting your fifth house. Pursue the object of your affection, and let no one else take your prize. Creative and romantic energy and drive are at their peak, so make joy, play, romance, and creativity a top priority. Competition comes more easily to Mars than collaboration, so if you're working with others on a creative project, expect some squabbles; you'll want to do everything your own way, so it's best to focus on individual projects during this transit.

If you have children, they'll be a handful during this transit. Be sure to guide them toward high-energy activities to burn off some steam, although you may need to offer some lessons about patience and sportsmanship along the way.

TRANSITING JUPITER IN THE FIFTH HOUSE

Are you willing to take the risk of showing the world who you really are? Many of us say we'd like to have more love and creativity in our lives, and Jupiter in the fifth house evokes visions of bodice-ripping romance and many happy hours spent dabbling with finger paints.

But there is a risky side to giving your heart in love or in creativity: the chance of falling short of your own expectations, and perhaps most of all, the possibility of rejection. Jupiter's transits urge you to take that risk. Jupiter in the house of creativity will settle for nothing less than your most daring and heartfelt effort. Try a new hobby, take a new approach in your creative work, or simply share yourself in a way that is scary but a little bit thrilling. Embrace your inner adventurer. Express what you truly believe, and do it with style.

TRANSITING SATURN IN THE FIFTH HOUSE

Saturn transiting your fifth house insists that you create something that will last. It will require some of your hardest work; at times you will despair that you will never reach your goal. This is a transit often associated with literally having a child, and no creative work has a more profound effect on the direction of your life or demands more from you.

Romantic relationships that arise during this transit tend to have a quality of mentorship, with one partner older and more experienced than the other. Some sort of impediment, such as geographical distance or another person in the picture, is likely in the relationship.

Where Saturn transits he also brings a change in status, which in the fifth house could range from becoming a parent to changing careers. This change in status won't necessarily bring immediate and unconditional joy. Even a happy new parent becomes intimately familiar with the exhaustion and self-sacrifice that comes with providing a strong foundation for a new creation to prosper. If you launch a creative enterprise or commit to fulfilling some beloved dream during this transit, expect a lot of initial toil and disillusionment—but don't let that discourage you! Saturn will not prevent you from having what you really want and are willing to work for, but he often presents roadblocks along your path to test your commitment. Prove that you're ready and worthy. Persevere.

TRANSITING URANUS IN THE FIFTH HOUSE

This transit begins with dissatisfaction. Your life lacks creative opportunities or love; your heart has been sleeping, but it will awaken as Uranus inches its way through your fifth house. Uranus's influence is not subtle, and it delights in the element of surprise. Love affairs, creative opportunities, sometimes even children appear and shake you awake. Occasionally, their impact on your life will be as inconvenient as it is thrilling.

If you have spent years toiling in a creative field, this could be the transit that brings an important breakthrough—but at first, it may seem more like a breakdown! If your imagination and passion for particular activities has grown stale, bid them farewell. You can't move ahead to the activities that make you feel alive until you are freed from the things that don't.

TRANSITING NEPTUNE IN THE FIFTH HOUSE

There's a fine line between faith and delusion, and transits of Neptune are always devoted to exploring that line. As Neptune transits the fifth house, that line runs right through the heart of your creative self. Are you hanging on to the dream of writing a novel, working as an actor, or having children, holding on long past the point when friends, family, society, and even your own inner voice tell you it's hopeless? Some would call that faith; others would call it delusion. You probably won't know for a long time which is true. But if it's time to let go of the dream, Neptune will give you a signal. Once the dream brings more pain than joy, it's probably a clue that it needs to leave your life.

Romantic relationships in particular can be alluringly star-crossed during this transit, often involving attraction from across race, class, or cultural lines. Often one partner is expected to play the role of savior for the other. The characters portrayed by Leonardo DiCaprio and Kate Winslet in the film *Titanic* are a perfect example, right down to the whole relationship taking place at sea (ruled by Neptune). Rose is from an aristocratic background, and Jack is poor but self-reliant. About to wed a cad in a marriage of financial convenience, she despairs, to the point of attempted suicide. Luckily, Jack appears at the right moment to rescue her.

It's a lovely and romantic story despite its tragic ending. But it's worth noting that part of the reason the love story works is that this unlikely couple never faces the reality of living together in the world. Relationships between people from different worlds can absolutely work, but in reality such unions require more than just romantic attraction. Relationships that begin while Neptune transits the fifth house can be rapturous but may not survive the practical realities of daily life.

TRANSITING PLUTO IN THE FIFTH HOUSE

It's sometimes hard to say exactly how Pluto transits will play out. Will Pluto flay you and leave you in tatters? Will it align you with powerful forces that catapult you to wealth and celebrity? I've seen both happen. Mostly, as Pluto transits the house of creative self-expression, love affairs, and children, my clients report difficulty with love and tremendous struggles with creative projects. Hobbies and pastimes meant to bring enjoyment and recreation become fraught with power struggles and betrayal. Romantic relationships end badly, often with one or the other partner holding on in an unhealthy and even obsessive way.

Pluto's transits here help rid you of false expectations about relationships and help you align yourself with creative pursuits better suited to your authentic self. If you're a parent, it can be a trying period in your relationship with your children. You may experience issues of control, or your children may develop characteristics or make major decisions that trouble you. One of a parent's most difficult tasks is to know when to intercede and when to leave a child alone, and that is the nature of many of the challenges you'll face during this transit.

TRANSITING NORTH NODE IN THE FIFTH HOUSE

Whatever the dream of your natal North Node, the transiting North Node in the fifth house asks you to examine whether you are pursuing that dream with your whole, true heart. Are you going after it in a way that makes you completely happy, regardless of how others react?

As the North Node transits the fifth house, the South Node will be in the eleventh house. The urge will be strong to fit in, be part of a group, and blend in rather than standing apart. This is the comfortable path, but not the one that will lead to growth and happiness. This transit will bring an eclipse or two to the fifth house, signaling a moment of truth: Will you give birth to a dream created in your true image or settle for giving the world what it expects from you?

THE ELEVENTH HOUSE: LET'S PUT ON A SHOW IN THE BARN!

Traditional name: House of Friendship

Terrain: groups, societies, and networks; friends, money from career, investment, broadcasting, hopes and wishes, helpful people

Shares common ground with: the sign of Aquarius; the planets Saturn, Uranus, and Jupiter (traditional astrologers place Jupiter in its "joy" in the eleventh house)

I've never been much of a group person. They require so much democracy, so much equality. Born a Leo, I'm astrologically incapable of blending in with a crowd.

But even the most determinedly individualistic and creative person eventually comes up with some scheme that can only be pulled off by group effort. Some enterprising kid writes a play, and the next thing you know he's rallying his pals, Mickey Rooney–style, with the cry, "Hey kids, let's put on a show in the barn!"

Movie directors are known as tyrants and, occasionally, megalomaniacs. But even they need a huge crew of people to help them realize their vision. Someone has to write the story, come up with the money, manage the lights and cameras and other technical details, act, stock the food services table, and make sure people look fabulous on camera.

This is eleventh house creativity at work. A group of people who share an interest pool their individual creative talents to make something that is beyond a single person's ability. This is the house of clubs, societies, fraternities and sororities, and politics. And it's the house where creative ideas are, hopefully, conveyed into the future, where they can become the stuff of legends.

TRANSITING SUN IN THE ELEVENTH HOUSE

When the Sun moves into the eleventh house, embrace your friendships. Be generous with your praise, your possessions, and your time—this is the mortar that holds social contracts together. Remember that a friendship is life's only completely optional relationship: You are together only because you like and care about each other!

So show up. Be there when your friend is singing at a café, acting in a community theater production, or having a party. Show up when it's your friend's birthday, even if it's just a phone call to let them know you're thinking of them.

Cultivate new friendships, too. Maybe there's someone hanging around on the periphery of your life who you think you'd enjoy befriending. Stop putting it off; begin cultivating the friendship. Commit to one coffee date. Or when you accept that next Facebook friend invitation, write a quick note to say hi. Treat yourself to the completely optional happiness of friendship.

TRANSITING MOON IN THE ELEVENTH HOUSE

The Moon is a sensitive, intuitive influence, and in the eleventh house you are more in tune than usual with friends and associates. Take this into account when planning social engagements that tend to trigger strong emotions in you; you will be vulnerable to your friends' words, tone of voice, and body language and may be apt to take offense where none was intended.

Take note of the month each year when the New Moon falls in the eleventh house of your chart. This is a powerful time for setting intentions related to your friendships, receiving rewards from your career, and finding helpful associates who can aid you in your goals.

TRANSITING MERCURY IN THE ELEVENTH HOUSE

The house position of transiting Mercury tells you, above all, what's on your mind. For the several weeks Mercury is transiting your eleventh house, your friendships and your future occupy your thoughts. Formulate a long-range plan for your life and your legacy. Get in touch with friends whom you haven't spoken with in a while (if Mercury will be retrograde while in your eleventh house, these might be friends you haven't spoken with in a very long time).

The eleventh house has some association with technology. Mercury's transit here is usually a good one for acquiring skills, contacts, equipment, and implementing systems to improve your relationship with the gadgets in your life.

TRANSITING VENUS IN THE ELEVENTH HOUSE

Your idea of happiness this month will probably involve spending more time than usual with friends. Social gatherings of all kinds tend to be more rewarding during this transit, and overtures of friendship are also well received. It's the right moment to cultivate social media relationships or purchase new gizmos (as long as Venus is not retrograde).

The eleventh house represents rewards from your profession, so you can reasonably expect additional money, praise, or opportunities to come your way through your career or related to involvement in social organizations. It's generally an excellent transit for socializing, including professional conferences and networking functions.

TRANSITING MARS IN THE ELEVENTH HOUSE

Transiting Mars is devoted to making you fight for what is yours, and this can be an awkward element to introduce into your eleventh house relationships. Ideally, groups cooperate to achieve shared goals. In a perfect world, friends are always mutually supportive. But of course, we don't live in a perfect, ideal world, and sometimes these relationships grow stale or are proven false. Mars transiting the eleventh house can bring conflict with friends and associates, but it also clears the air and lets everyone know where they stand.

Mars can indicate leadership opportunities, so you may find yourself involved in group activities or serving on a committee—even if that's not normally your style. The eleventh house is also associated with the future, so this can be an excellent transit for initiating a long-term project that requires courage and motivation.

TRANSITING JUPITER IN THE ELEVENTH HOUSE

If you've ever hoped that a friendship would become "something more," this could be the transit you've been waiting for: I fell in love with and married my best friend while Jupiter was transiting my eleventh house! I won't say that's a common occurrence, but it's a good metaphor for the essential meaning of the transit. Jupiter transiting the eleventh house invites you to broaden the scope of your friendships and other associations. It may be time to befriend people from a different country or background; you might find lifelong bonds in college, while traveling, or through your church. Jupiter is considered the most fortunate of planets, and this can be a wonderful transit if you're willing to open your mind and look for friendship in new places—or, perhaps, to find something new in an existing friendship.

TRANSITING SATURN IN THE ELEVENTH HOUSE

Saturn is often said to be associated with the notion of karma, which asserts that what you have put out into the world returns to you in kind. It does seem true that when you have worked hard and earnestly, making sacrifices for many years, Saturn's transits will often bring your reward. You'll find that you've earned a certain status and respect as an authority in your profession or among your friends; you have arrived, professionally speaking. If you're very young or new to your profession, the rewards may not be as great—you've still got dues to pay—but there should still be an improvement in your professional prospects.

Professional networks and the sorts of friendships that take place mostly in groups will present challenges during this transit. Part of reaching a higher level in your profession is that you're expected to give more back to your community. Participation on boards of directors or other leadership roles are likely during this transit and are usually fraught with struggle. But remember that all the activities that have brought you to this point had their difficult and thankless sides, as well. Saturn is keeping track and will reward you in the future for doing your best now.

TRANSITING URANUS IN THE ELEVENTH HOUSE

I'm a sucker for a fish-out-of-water story. Television shows such as *Northern Exposure* or *Doc Martin*, which feature big-city protagonists dealing with the vagaries of rural life, are among my favorites. It's fun to watch someone come into a completely unfamiliar situation, where everyone else has already formed community bonds, and watch them interact with one another.

The situation can be somewhat less entertaining in real life, however. This transit might find you a bit out of water yourself. Perhaps after many years in the same place, you move to a new city or job and have to start all over finding new friends. To a great extent, we're defined by the people with whom we keep company. While any major move is difficult, especially at the beginning, it can also be an incomparable opportunity to redefine yourself. In a new place, you can be anyone you want to be. That freedom is a bit disorienting at first, but it can be very exciting and liberating as well.

TRANSITING NEPTUNE IN THE ELEVENTH HOUSE

Do you know who your friends are? You will by the time Neptune is finished transiting your eleventh house. Sometimes friends are revealed to be something quite different than you had imagined them to be. More often, though, we grow apart from friends without realizing it. Increasingly, you're drawn to friends and networks who share your ideals or spiritual concerns. Those who don't will be washed away by Neptune's tide.

A certain sadness and yearning for the sense of belonging you used to feel with friends is common during this transit. You may also have to come to terms with the reality that your future is not going to look exactly as you thought it would. This can be a very long transit, so you will have plenty of time to get used to the idea and to envision a new future for yourself.

TRANSITING PLUTO IN THE ELEVENTH HOUSE

It's safe to say that you can never find true friends until you are able to accept yourself as you really are and recognize when others are being false. This is the implication of Pluto's transit through the eleventh house. It's no longer enough to have a pack of people to run around with so that you don't feel alone. You want *real* friends, the kind with whom you can share your less-than-admirable qualities.

If you have a habit of showing people just what they want to see instead of what you really are, this transit will cure you of that. If the habit is deeply ingrained, you may unconsciously enlist polarizing comrades such as an obnoxious friend or a really objectionable boyfriend or girlfriend to act as stand-ins for your own dark side. "Love me, love my Obnoxious Other!" you declare to the world, and when some decide they can do without you both, you get to develop the strength that comes from standing apart from the pack.

TRANSITING NORTH NODE IN THE ELEVENTH HOUSE

Even if you are a lone wolf by nature, there is some truth to the adage that "it takes a village to raise a child." Children, or creative projects that are like our children, are found in the fifth house, but the eleventh house is where we all raise the children or collaborate on artistic visions together. During this transit of the North Node, reach out, however tentatively, to groups of people who share your creative passions.

As the North Node transits the eleventh house, the South Node, representing the easy path, is in the fifth house of individual self-expression. If you prefer doing things on your own, that's okay; you don't have to change who you are, and you don't have to work with groups the rest of your life. But explore them as a possibility now, instead of retreating into your solitary, creative cave. This transit will bring an eclipse or two to your eleventh house, and you might find you've reached a turning point in the hunt for a group of compatriots you can call your own. Sometimes this means letting go of associations that no longer enrich your life.

chapter 15

HOUSES 6 AND 12:
THIS WORLD AND THE NEXT

t's easy to see how the idea of heaven came about. Living as a human, trapped in an inconvenient, demanding body in an imperfect world, often feels like Purgatory. How could God reside in a house with unmade beds, overflowing laundry, and people hollering at each other about which bills haven't been paid? Or in a cubicle, performing rote, soul-sucking duties for forty hours each week—let alone in a prison, or a hospital?

We don't all have chaotic, miserable lives, at least not all the time. And mostly, we bear our duties and limitations cheerfully. But to bring an uplifting sense of meaning and order to our days, we often feel we have to reach toward a heaven that is remote, unknowable, and utterly separate from our earthly messes.

In the horoscope, the search for transcendence of our earthly drudgery is symbolized by the axis of the sixth and twelfth houses. Connected at opposite ends of an invisible pole, these two houses suggest that earth and not-earth are connected, and that we can only know one by also knowing the other. In the sixth house, we attend to earthly affairs. We work, clean, and brush our teeth. In the twelfth house, our minds cast us as a solitary monk, poring over sacred texts, and in the sixth house we are the servant who brings the monk his tea.

I've never cared for this way of viewing these houses. It seems to exalt the twelfth house while denigrating the sixth. Rather, I see the matters related to the sixth house as the surest way to access the spiritual transcendence of the twelfth house. Through our sixth house rituals of purification, reverence, and humility, we transform drudgery into divinity. Far from being the unloved stepchild of the twelfth house, the sixth is actually its threshold.

When transiting planets awaken this axis of your chart, your habits and rituals, your sense of life's meaning and purpose, are challenged, enlarged, and illuminated. If you were born with planets in these two houses, transits here have a special significance and resonance. If not, these transits give you a special opportunity to explore this rich territory of your chart.

THE SIXTH HOUSE: PUTTING YOUR HOUSE IN ORDER

Traditional name: House of Health

Terrain: health, work, service, servants, coworkers, duties, habits, routines, chores, caretaking, pets and small animals, skills

Shares common ground with: the sign of Virgo; the planets Mercury, Mars (traditional astrologers place Mars in its "joy" in the sixth house)

Each evening after dinner, I launch into a flurry of practical activities. I put away leftovers and wash dishes, sweep the kitchen floor, transfer laundry from the washer to the dryer, clean the cats' litter box, and give our little feline diabetic her shot of insulin. In your household, I imagine it's much the same, with some variations.

Most of us wouldn't say we necessarily enjoy these chores. We probably listen to the radio or television to ignore the fact that we're even doing them. But if they don't get done, these dozens of small tasks, life begins to falter, grinding to a halt like an engine without oil. Neglect the minutiae of daily life and you'll soon find that you're running on empty.

While planets transit your sixth house, they awaken your craving for order. Your life has, to some extent, become a mess; it's time to clean it up and sort it out.

TRANSITING SUN IN THE SIXTH HOUSE

The chores of daily life can be drudgery or ritual—the difference is one of attitude. The sixth house is our most accessible path to enlightenment, because its matters are the ones that occupy most of our daily hours. So the path to happiness during this transit is not just to wash the dishes, but to make dishwashing into a prayer for order, dignity, and sanity.

Be helpful while the Sun is in the sixth house. Sometimes you'll find yourself waiting on others hand and foot. But serving others is an important component of spiritual teaching. Through service, we have the opportunity to experience humility.

Finally, when the Sun is moving through the sixth house, it's important to give others their due. In this day and age, we're quick to criticize. Are we as quick to tell others, in great detail, just how much they're appreciated? Virgo is the sign associated with the sixth house, and one Virgo lady I know once said that she believes in being completely honest, but to her that means being very complimentary when she appreciates something about a person. Appreciation is key to happiness—both receiving it and giving it.

TRANSITING MOON IN THE SIXTH HOUSE

This is a fleeting and minor transit, with the Moon moving through a house of your chart roughly two and a half days of every month. The Moon is a changeable influence, so this is one of the best times of the month to change habits and routines related to your health, work, and service.

During this transit, you may be a little irritable and easily overwhelmed by ordinary responsibilities such as housework. The day-to-day world can suddenly seem utterly unmanageable. Hang in there—this is a quick transit!

Each year, the New Moon in your sixth house is a powerful time to set intentions related to your health and work and to find reliable helpers in your life.

TRANSITING MERCURY IN THE SIXTH HOUSE

Transiting Mercury brings with him the gift of curiosity. When your mind is intrigued by a problem, it will usually get solved. When your curiosity is aroused by creating more efficient ways to use your resources, schedules, systems, and timetables get put in place.

For a few weeks, while Mercury transits your sixth house, you're finally interested in sorting out the messes in your life. Hand it all over to Mercury as you would give a restless child a toy to keep him occupied. Make a full audit of your household, habits, and life goals; how might you streamline your routines and refine your objectives? What could you be doing, or doing better, to improve your health?

TRANSITING VENUS IN THE SIXTH HOUSE

How can you make your daily life more pleasurable, more harmonious and balanced? While Venus transits your sixth house, no one has to tell you to eat a more balanced diet, bring home a bouquet of flowers, or buy beautiful file folders and binders for your office. Venus's sixth house grace is the understanding that practicality doesn't have to be ugly and joyless. There's no reason you can't celebrate both form *and* function. Making each moment, place, and routine a little more lovely than it has to be is the assignment and the gift of this transit.

Venus is the relationship planet, so this transit may bring agreeable new people into your everyday life. A gracious new coworker, a happier coffee barista, or a smiling new hairstylist can go far to alleviate the tedium of familiar routines.

TRANSITING MARS IN THE SIXTH HOUSE

Fire can be dangerous—but in nature it also purifies, removing deadwood and enriching soil for new growth. The same is true when transiting Mars moves through your sixth house. Your home, work, and habits need to be cleaned out and reorganized periodically to make room for the things that are useful or bring you joy. Your closets and pantry need to be purged. It's time to finally shred and file that stubborn stack of papers in your office. It's easy to let things pile up and to fall into unproductive habits, and Mars's transit of the sixth house every two and a half years will motivate you to clear the decks to allow for new growth.

The sixth house is connected to the routines and habits that contribute to good health. If you've had a hard time getting motivated in this area, Mars in the sixth house is a good transit to overcome your inertia and form better, more healthful habits. Exercise, in particular, is Mars's bailiwick, so let this transit act as a no-nonsense coach and get yourself moving!

TRANSITING JUPITER IN THE SIXTH HOUSE

When Jupiter visits the house of work, health, and habit, the transit often begins with the uncomfortable feeling that your life is too small. Your job doesn't challenge you or pay well enough. Your house is a mess. You don't get to travel as much as you'd like. Jupiter brings the gift of dissatisfaction and, ultimately, the impetus to break out of your rut.

Jupiter transiting your sixth house opens up your small world to bigger opportunities than you had ever dreamed possible. That's a little overwhelming, but undeniably exciting! If you work for yourself, Jupiter will push you to try new methods, launch new products or services, or expand your business. You'll really enjoy your work this year—and if you don't, you'll almost certainly take steps to liberate yourself and move on to a more satisfying situation.

Jupiter generally ensures good health in the sixth house, probably because you have a good attitude. Overindulgence of all kinds will need to be kept in check, though. Overeating or drinking too much are obviously problematic, but indulging in extreme fad diets and pushing your body too far, too fast with exercise can be just as damaging in the long run.

TRANSITING SATURN IN THE SIXTH HOUSE

Anything worthwhile takes effort, patience, and perseverance. As Saturn transits your sixth house, these tools are available to you. What is the thing you have wanted to achieve your entire life, and what practical considerations are holding you back? Saturn in the sixth house will force you to buckle down and work your hardest to eliminate those barriers. The work you do now, the habits you form, and the grit that you demonstrate will directly influence your future success.

This is not necessarily an easy transit. You may struggle with health issues, feel underemployed, or suffer from low self-esteem about your current status relative to where you had hoped to be in your life. Saturn rewards sacrifice, hard work, and commitment, however, so just keep your eye on your long-term goal and refuse to be discouraged from working toward it. Show up, put yourself in the situations that you know could lead to success, and commit to the hard work necessary to make that happen. In time, you'll look at this as the period in your life when you planted the seeds of your most satisfying achievements.

TRANSITING URANUS IN THE SIXTH HOUSE

Has your life been getting a bit stale? Working at the same place year after year, living in the same house, socializing with the same friends, having the same arguments with your partner?

Once transiting Uranus enters your sixth house, that's all over. You'll find yourself doing things you never dreamed you'd do. Maybe your health routine needs shaking up; Uranus can do that. Your work might be boring you; Uranus flat-out refuses to be bored, so he'll see to it that you're not.

When Uranus makes his long transit of your sixth house, your daily life as you know it needs to change. And if you won't do it yourself, Uranus will be more than willing to do it himself. But you might not like his methods. He acts suddenly, unpredictably. You never know what's coming next. Sometimes you'll wonder whether anything will be left after you break it all down. It's like that moment when you've taken everything out of your closet to clean it and now wonder whether you've got the energy to put it back. Maybe you don't—but it doesn't matter, because Uranus does.

TRANSITING NEPTUNE IN THE SIXTH HOUSE

It used to be that making a long journey meant getting on a ship and traveling for months at a time. It must have been so peaceful, out in the middle of the ocean, cut off from the rest of the world. Rocking back and forth, reading, fishing, writing, contemplating; watching the sun rise and set; living in each moment, with no distractions to pull you into the past or the future.

As Neptune transits your sixth house, it's as though you are climbing onto a big ship and embarking on a long journey, a hiatus from the daily life you've known for so long. If your age is right, you might retire from professional life; if you're too young for that, your work must now conform to your sense of spiritual purpose. Everything that happens to you during this transit has meaning and is designed to move you a bit farther along your spiritual path. All that is required of you is to board the ship and surrender to the journey.

TRANSITING PLUTO IN THE SIXTH HOUSE

Where Pluto transits, we become aware of our individual insignificance and are called to align ourselves with something larger. Pluto transiting the sixth house brings you face to face with life-or-death circumstances that consume your attention and daily routine. Perhaps you take a job that requires you to respond to urgent and dramatic situations. It could be that someone very close to you struggles with a serious problem that requires your constant help and support. You might simply move to a place where, every day, you are reminded of the fragility of life and the challenge of surviving in extreme environments.

Pluto's transits are the longest, and the changes they describe are the sort of major transformations that take many years to complete. By the time Pluto moves out of your sixth house, your daily life will look absolutely different than it did at the beginning of this transit. To make sure you will like the finished product, do your best to be of optimal service to those around you and to the causes that mean the most to you. Perform good works without any expectation of reward. Be humble. Be honest. Be kind to others. Live a life that makes you proud.

TRANSITING NORTH NODE IN THE SIXTH HOUSE

Your greatest spiritual growth during this transit will come from offering support and service to others through your work, sacrifice, and acts of compassion. It's often a transit that brings a change in the workplace, or perhaps even a new career. You may also find yourself in a position of needing to support a partner or some other important person in your life. This can require great compassion, both for the person you're supporting and for yourself, should feelings of resentment arise. It can be a very challenging transit, especially during the months when eclipses fall in the sixth house, because it is not particularly fashionable in this day and age to put others' needs and desires above our own.

While the North Node transits the sixth house, the South Node is in the twelfth house. It would be the easiest thing in the world for you to retreat into self-pity and self-destructive behavior now, or to give in to the feeling of being overwhelmed by your responsibilities. But this is the time to acknowledge things for what they are and to take practical steps to improve them.

THE TWELFTH HOUSE: SANCTUARY

Traditional name: House of Self-Undoing

Terrain: hidden enemies, self-defeating behavior or attitudes, hospitals, prisons, willing retreat, secret matters, privacy, the unconscious, dreams, faith

Shares common ground with: the sign of Pisces; the planets Jupiter, Neptune, Saturn (traditional astrologers place Saturn in its "joy" in the sixth house)

In the summers, my family would often take long drives across the country, to visit relatives in California. The very best time of the day was sunrise. We'd wake up in some town such as Gallup, New Mexico, bundle ourselves into the station wagon, and take off across Interstate 40, watching the sky turn from inky black to soft blue, pink, and purple, until the sun was up and we'd stop for pancakes at a roadside diner. Everyone sat quietly at the booth, sleepy-headed and soft, without our daytime armor, eating our breakfast and gazing out at the morning. No one had to speak.

The two hours just after sunup are the twelfth house time of day, the moments when the Sun is transiting this part of the sky, low above the eastern horizon. It's a soft and hazy time for many of us, but by definition, it is not the dark, impenetrable, and fearful stuff of astrological legend, either. We hear it described as a penitentiary, a dungeon, a sanitarium, a hospital, a convent—and yes, I suppose those relate the nature of the twelfth house, these places where we are left alone with our thoughts, to do penance, to heal, to pray.

But I like to think these places represent a process of experience, not the totality of it. In the twelfth house, we seek healing. We seek benediction. We seek inspiration. If we think of the traditional twelfth house places as areas of intention rather than imprisonment, they take on quite a different dimension.

The twelfth house is, like the first hours of the day, the part of life where we are softest, most fluid, still attached a bit to the dream state. And because we aren't set in stone, it's a place of imagination—of what we can be, instead of merely what we are. It's the house where you get to *imagine* your life, to be in the world but at the same time to have at least one foot in another. It is a softly lit house of intuition and of the muse. At your best moments in meditation or prayer, you are in the twelfth house. When you're reading a novel and lost in the world of the imagination, you are in the twelfth house. When you stop to behold your newly organized desk, you are in the twelfth house. Anyplace where your mind and spirit are united in stillness becomes a twelfth house temple.

TRANSITING SUN IN THE TWELFTH HOUSE

There are two months out of each year when you need to schedule a personal retreat. One is the month before your birthday. This is the other one.

The month that the transiting Sun is in your twelfth house is like the dark phase of the Moon. There is little light shining inside you. You're tired or uninspired, give up easily, and may feel a little grumpy.

So if you can, take some time off this month. At the very least, minimize your social commitments. Spend time alone daydreaming, reading a book, listening to music. Walk on the beach, in the woods, on a mountain. Commune with nature. Commune with yourself. This is meditation time, so don't overthink it. Just leave some empty space in your life this month to recharge your batteries.

TRANSITING MOON IN THE TWELFTH HOUSE

Each month, take this opportunity to practice self-care. The skills you develop—not overscheduling yourself, learning to say no, carving out time for yourself, getting enough rest—will be absolutely invaluable when you are faced with much longer twelfth house transits by slower-moving planets. Make a standing date with yourself for "mental health days" featuring a quiet hike, a favorite old movie, or a weekend with no social engagements.

TRANSITING MERCURY IN THE TWELFTH HOUSE

When Mercury transits your twelfth house, you will probably not sleep well. Your internal mind-monkey will be nearly impossible to silence. You won't be able to stop thinking about all kinds of stuff you'd rather not think about. And even when nothing particular is bothering you, you will find yourself wishing you could turn down the volume on your own mind for a while.

Instead, indulge in daily power naps and a lot of journaling. Mercury is just going through and taking an inventory of everything stored in your unconscious, ensuring there isn't anything hidden there that would be better brought into the open and discussed. This is a fertile time for writing, sharing private thoughts with your journal or readers or in conversation with people you really trust. But by the time Mercury leaves your twelfth house, you'll be ready for some sleep.

TRANSITING VENUS IN THE TWELFTH HOUSE

Here is a simple ritual for Venus's transit of your twelfth house: Clean out your bedroom closet. Get rid of all the broken, ugly, plastic clothes hangers and all the clothes that haven't fit in twenty years. Vacuum that sucker. If you're feeling particularly whimsical, paint the inside a lovely color. Organize your clothes and shoes. Make it beautiful.

If you're not hung up on your closets, tackle some other ugly, cluttered part of your house or garage in a similar fashion. Get rid of things that are unsightly or broken, or things you hate. Make this part of your house so nice to look at that you find yourself wanting to show it off to visitors.

The truth is, the state of your closets, or other places in your life that only you see, is a pretty good barometer of how well you treat yourself when no one is looking. And that is usually based on how you feel inside. So for a few weeks, while Venus is in your twelfth house, show that part of your house—and yourself—a little love.

TRANSITING MARS IN THE TWELFTH HOUSE

Mars's transits of the twelfth house can be revealing, energizing, and helpful, but only if you're really ready for them. Mars transiting the twelfth house is like bringing a drill sergeant into an infirmary—so shouty! He stomps around the place, lecturing you about all the fear that's holding you back from having what you want. He yells. He badgers. And it's all going on inside of you.

Picking on yourself is not the best use of this transit. Instead, roll up your sleeves and get to work. What *is* holding you back? The sooner you know, the sooner you can push it aside. What *are* you afraid of? Just facing your weaknesses and foibles is more courageous than you give yourself credit for. While Mars is in your twelfth house, fight your demons. When you find yourself engaging in negative or even cruel self-talk, stop it. Beating up on yourself is not the object here; developing strength and courage is.

TRANSITING JUPITER IN THE TWELFTH HOUSE

Jupiter means well. He bounces happily into the House of Self-Undoing (as the ancients called it) and urges you to lighten up. Then, after he's spent part of the year hanging out in your personal dungeon, he begins to see your point. "It *is* awfully dark in here," he muses. "If there were just a window or something, so you could see the terrific view outside. Oh well. At least I can catch up on my reading." Then a few months go past, and our normally jovial friend is really starting to get bummed out. "I just want to *go* somewhere," he groans. "You can only read so many books, write so much haiku, take so many naps!"

By the end of Jupiter's transit through your twelfth house, you're both ready for him to be gone. You want your peaceful, quiet sanctuary back, without Jupiter's big, hearty, booming internal voice nagging at you to go outside and play. And Jupiter will be happier in the brighter, more active pastures of your first house.

TRANSITING SATURN IN THE TWELFTH HOUSE

The year before transiting Saturn entered my twelfth house, several good friends regaled me with stories of their own experiences with that transit. They faced health problems, family crises, and work challenges. Mostly, they were slowed down from their usual energetic pace by the physical necessity of taking it easy.

I believed them and took heed. But that didn't stop me from coming down with my first serious health problem within a couple of weeks of Saturn entering my twelfth house.

In modern astrology, we try to avoid the more terrifying language of ancient astrologers, who had some particularly harsh things to say about the twelfth house. It was a house of illness and confinement, they warned. It isn't always—not literally. I first had this transit in my early twenties when I was hale and hearty; I got to experience it in more psychological ways (no picnic).

But it makes absolute sense that if you're over fifty and haven't been taking care of yourself, you will eventually hit a wall. You are mortal; you have limits. And regardless of your age, this is what Saturn transiting your twelfth house is meant to make you understand. *You have limits.* Draft more sensible boundaries. Say no more often. Take care of yourself—or Saturn will find ingenious and unpleasant ways to make you do it.

TRANSITING URANUS IN THE TWELFTH HOUSE

Uranus spends a long time in each house of your chart, and I can tell you this: He is not about to spend those years in your twelfth house sitting in quiet contemplation. He's even more restless than Mercury and stays so much longer. Within weeks of moving in, he'll have rewired the place and set up a huge sound system. He'll be inviting people over constantly, and frankly, most of them are a bit weird. Always hyped up on caffeine or other stimulants, Uranus doesn't get a lot of sleep and sees to it that you don't, either.

Seven years on average is a long time to live with a loud, weird, hyper roommate hanging out in your unconscious. Deprived of quiet and rest for so long, with no gentle refuge, you may begin to get a little buggy yourself. Practice training your unconscious with meditation or even hypnosis. Really fascinating artistic or intellectual breakthroughs are entirely possible during this transit, but you've got to find a way to keep from burning yourself out.

TRANSITING NEPTUNE IN THE TWELFTH HOUSE

There are plenty of things about ourselves that we hide, including from ourselves. Our secret fears, shame, and obsessions live in the twelfth house; transiting Neptune here is a chance to let go of these toxic secrets. The process of letting go, however, is a little bit terrifying, and because the transit is so long, a bit wearying as well.

When Neptune's ocean is at high tide, everything seems okay, even better than usual. But when the tide goes out, everything is left on the beach, exposed, including stuff we didn't even know was lying around in our unconscious! Among the things we have to let go during Neptune's twelfth house transit are our convictions about how the world works, and any cherished concepts of ourselves as victims. We don't let these things go without a fight, which is why Neptune has to stay here for so long to get the job done, washing away, day after day, until we're as worn as a stone. Until all that is left is faith.

TRANSITING PLUTO IN THE TWELFTH HOUSE

Pluto prides himself on having things under control. He likes transiting your twelfth house; there is all kinds of interesting stuff in there that you try to ignore, and that lets him take over the whole show. He delights in digging up old pain, shame, and embarrassment and making you look at it. You won't get much peace of mind while Pluto transits here. What you will get, though, is an invaluable opportunity to examine and discard old psychological hang-ups and find out what is really true about you. You will need the strength of being a whole, integrated person once Pluto moves into your first house.

TRANSITING NORTH NODE IN THE TWELFTH HOUSE

Usually the North Node's transit through the first house puts you in a position of dealing with rapidly changing circumstances. You may have to move or deal with issues in a relationship, and you find yourself feeling constantly under siege. But once the North Node moves into the twelfth house, things generally calm down a bit. This is when many of us collapse for a while, retreating from the demands of the world as much as we can. Don't resist; this is the right time for you to get some rest and spiritual rejuvenation.

While the North Node is transiting the twelfth house, the South Node is in the sixth house of work and daily routines. The temptation will be strong to escape into overwork, exercise, and other behaviors that, while healthy on the surface, can actually be counterproductive. The twelfth house beckons you to spend time with your inner self. Use the sixth house gift for organization to engineer a daily routine that has plenty of room for downtime.

chapter 16

TRANSITS IN ACTION

A friend and I have been professional astrologers since the early 1990s. We often laugh together about how, even after all these years, we can sit down with a new birth chart to prepare for a reading and have absolutely no idea what any of it means. Especially when you begin adding things such as transits, all those symbols begin to swim together into one, big celestial blob.

You may feel the same way, especially if you've just waded through fifteen whole chapters of this book, covering every possible combination of transits. Luckily, after years of doing this kind of thing, astrologers develop strategies for sorting it all out. I've simplified my own process a lot over the years, and that's what I'd like to share with you in this chapter.

THE FANTASTIC MR. FOX

As an example, I offer the birth chart for actor and activist Michael J. Fox. Fox has enjoyed widespread fame since starring in the 1980s sitcom *Family Ties*, including starring roles in the blockbuster *Back to the Future* movie franchise. In 1998, at the age of thirty-seven, Fox announced that he had been diagnosed with early-onset Parkinson's disease. Now in his fifties, the eternally youthful-looking Fox works occasionally in television but devotes most of his time to his wife, four children, and his advocacy for Parkinson's disease research.

THE BIRTH CHART

We'll take a look at the transits for a couple of key events in Fox's life. First, though, let's get to know the birth chart. The aspects between natal planets and their house placements identify a chart's "funny bones," those very sensitive regions that react most strongly to additional pressure from transits.

Michael J. Fox was born on June 9, 1961, at 12:15 a.m., in Edmonton, Alberta. His Sun in Gemini is at the very beginning of the fourth house, the traditional house of home, family, history, and soulful contemplation. Without the Sun's strong aspects to the Ascendant and Midheaven, it's possible Fox would have been content to live a quiet, private life instead of moving away from home at the age of eighteen to seek a career in show business. Someone born with the Sun in the fourth house is on a lifelong journey to develop deep confidence and a sense of being at home in the world. The fourth house Sun person has emotional authenticity that gives others a deep sense of connection with them.

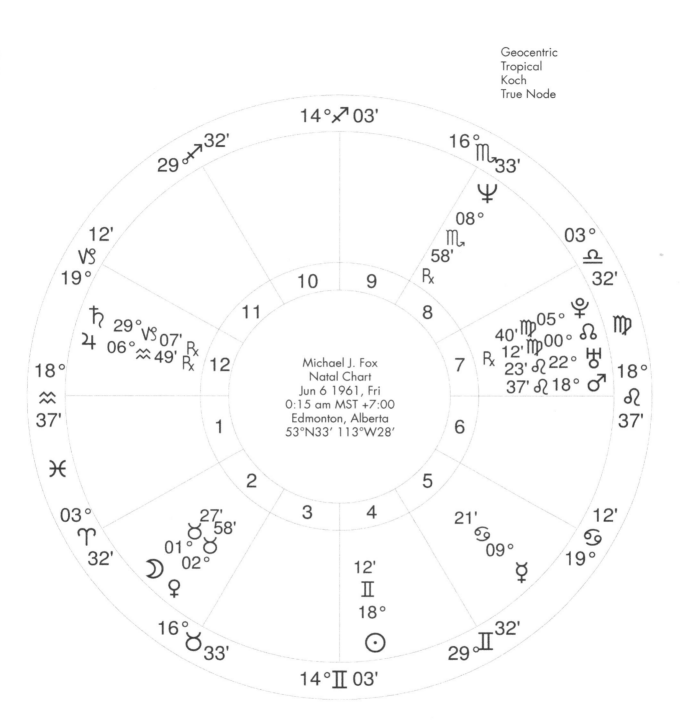

Fox's natal Sun is in a near-perfect trine to the natal Ascendant in Aquarius. The Ascendant symbolizes the persona, the techniques and traits that we consciously cultivate in response to our early environment to help us deal with the world. An Aquarius Ascendant personality is a bit cool but also has the enviable ability to put others at ease and make even complete strangers feel that they know you. When the natal Sun is in good aspect to the Ascendant, what you see is what you get; this is a person who finds it relatively easy to "be himself." The Sun/Ascendant person is generally charismatic, appears confident, and has a friendly, upbeat personality.

Fox's natal Sun is also in close opposition aspect to his Midheaven, the angle of career and reputation. I enjoyed the title of Fox's autobiography, *Lucky Man*; he has Sagittarius, the "lucky" sign, on the Midheaven. Of course, with Sagittarius's ruling planet Jupiter in a conjunction with hardworking Saturn, Fox is an example of luck being what happens when preparation meets opportunity.

Fox's Sun is in a sextile aspect to a powerful Mars/Uranus conjunction in Leo in the seventh house. Those who achieve great fame often have the Sun, Moon, Venus, or Mars in close aspect to Uranus. Uranus symbolizes that bolt of lightning, the little extra "something" that makes someone interesting to watch. Mars conjunct Uranus can suggest working in broadcasting-related fields, and it suggests that person has what we might call animal magnetism. Fox is not generally considered a sex symbol, but he has enormous popular appeal to both sexes.

The seventh house is the house of partnership, and Fox has enjoyed a long, happy marriage to actress Tracy Pollan. Fox is close in age to President Barack Obama, who has exactly the same degree of Aquarius on the Ascendant. The two share this formidable Mars, Uranus, North Node, and Pluto combination in the seventh house, and both have powerful, supportive spouses.

Mercury is in Cancer in the fifth house, an extraordinarily creative placement. If you have Mercury in the fifth house, you're probably good at lots of things, and in fact probably pretty good at most everything you decide to try. Mercury is trine Neptune and sextile the Moon, Venus, and Pluto; this is a smart guy with many different outlets for his intellect.

Fox's Moon and Venus are conjunct in Taurus, which is a strong sign for both planets. Despite past problems with drugs and alcohol (suggested by Moon and Venus opposed escapist Neptune and trine compulsive Pluto) and having at one time been one of the most famous men in America, Fox has managed to maintain both his sanity and a reputation for being down-to-earth and unpretentious.

The Moon and Venus are in the second house, the house of money, and square Jupiter and Saturn. Fox grew up in a military family that struggled to make ends meet, and in his autobiography he recounts his early days in Hollywood when he was literally starving. He eventually became enormously wealthy through a combination of luck (Jupiter) and hard work (Saturn). His autobiography also describes the punishing schedule he maintained while shooting his hit TV series at the same time he was filming *Back to the Future*. He's a hardworking, uncomplaining guy.

CHART HOT SPOTS

Every nook and cranny of a birth chart is important, and every bit of it can yield fascinating insights. But in working with clients, I've found they almost never come to me because everything's going great and they just want a consultation to do some fine-tuning. Most come because they are in crisis, major things are happening, and they're freaked out about it.

In each individual birth chart there are high-tension spots that are particularly sensitive. Find transits to those spots, and you find the source of the problem.

To find them, I first look for natal planets that are close to the angles (the cusps of the first, fourth, seventh, and tenth houses). In Fox's birth chart, for example, the Sun is conjunct the IC (fourth house cusp) and sextile Mars and Uranus, which are both conjunct the Descendant (seventh house cusp). Planets close to any angle are high-tension points, as resonant as a tightly stretched drumhead. Anytime a transit touches these planets, the chart will wake up and take notice.

Next I look for tense combinations involving the Sun or Moon. In Fox's chart, the Moon and Venus are opposed Neptune and square Jupiter/Saturn. When two or more planets in opposition to each other also make a square to another planet, the configuration is called a T-square, and it's a dynamic planetary network in the chart.

The conjunction of Jupiter and Saturn is a generational one, happening every twenty years and landing in the charts of everyone born within the same couple of years. It's a difficult combination that feels a bit like trying to drive with one foot on the accelerator and the other on the brakes. People born with this aspect in their birth charts are incredibly ambitious and hardworking. They often have the feeling that they're starting out with a disadvantage and have to work extra hard to get where they want to go.

In the twelfth house, this combination can suggest poor sleep, self-defeating habits, and even chronic health problems. Add a square from the Moon and Venus, and the struggles become very personal and even painful on a daily level. The opposition from the Moon/Venus to Neptune, and the squares to the twelfth house planets, are real danger signals for addiction, especially with the trine to Pluto. (Note: *Good* aspects, such as sextiles and trines, are not always a good thing when difficult planets are involved! *Good* can simply mean that things flow without interruption, and sometimes it's helpful to have a system of planetary checks and balances to keep planets such as Pluto in line.)

I would pay attention when planets such as Saturn, Uranus, Neptune, and Pluto, as well as the Lunar Nodes (and eclipses), are transiting through the fixed signs—Taurus, Leo, Scorpio, and Aquarius. Transits in these signs will activate this Moon/Venus, Jupiter/Saturn, and Neptune T-square and trigger any self-defeating behaviors that may be associated with them.

WHAT IT LOOKS LIKE WHEN SOMEONE BECOMES WILDLY FAMOUS

INNER WHEEL
Michael J. Fox
Natal Chart
Jun 6 1961, Fri
0:15 am MST +7:00
Edmonton, Alberta
53°N33' 113°W28'
Geocentric
Tropical
Koch
True Node

OUTER WHEEL
Back to the Future release
Natal Chart
Jul 3 1985, Wed
12:00 p.m. EDT +4:00
New York, NY
40°N42'51"
074°W00'23"
Geocentric
Tropical
Koch
True Node

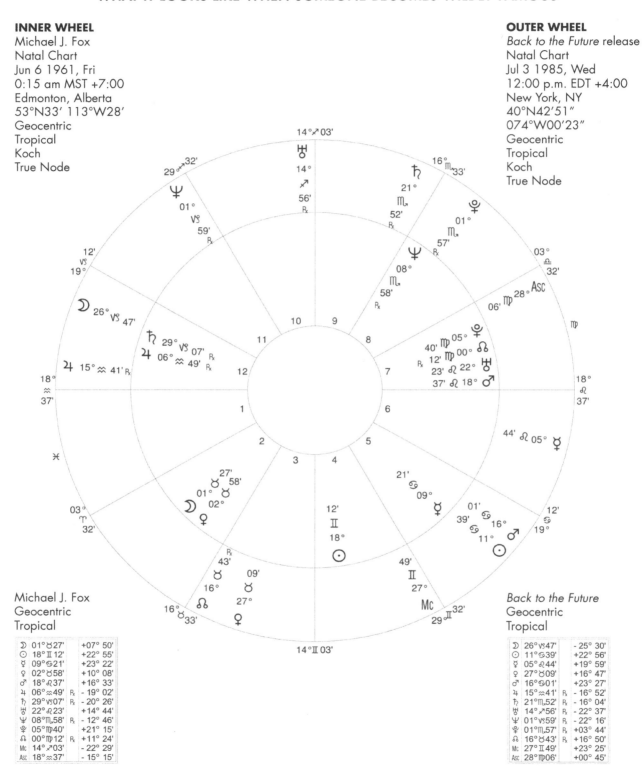

Michael J. Fox
Geocentric
Tropical

☽	01°♉27'	+07° 50'
☉	18°♊12'	+22° 55'
☿	09°♋21'	+23° 22'
♀	02°♉58'	+10° 08'
♂	18°♌37'	+16° 33'
♃	06°♒49' ℞	- 19° 02'
♄	29°♑07' ℞	- 20° 26'
♅	22°♌23'	+14° 44'
♆	08°♏58' ℞	- 12° 46'
♇	05°♍40'	+21° 15'
☊	00°♍12' ℞	+11° 24'
Mc	14°♐03'	- 22° 29'
Asc	18°♒37'	- 15° 15'

Back to the Future
Geocentric
Tropical

☽	26°♑47'	- 25° 30'
☉	11°♋39'	+22° 56'
☿	05°♌44'	+19° 59'
♀	27°♉09'	+16° 47'
♂	16°♋01'	+23° 27'
♃	15°♒41' ℞	- 16° 52'
♄	21°♏52' ℞	- 16° 04'
♅	14°♐56' ℞	- 22° 37'
♆	01°♑59' ℞	- 22° 16'
♇	01°♏57' ℞	+03° 44'
☊	16°♉43' ℞	+16° 50'
Mc	27°♊49'	+23° 25'
Asc	28°♍06'	+00° 45'

Let's pretend that it's summer 1985, and Michael J. Fox has come to you for a reading. His burning question: Will his new film, *Back to the Future*, be a success and boost his career?

Apart from his birth chart, which we already know describes a charismatic, hardworking, likeable, lucky guy, let's look at his transits for the date of the film's release and see what we find.

ASTROLOGICALLY CRITICAL AGE

First, I consider the client's age. Certain ages are an astrological traffic jam for everyone. The ages of fourteen, twenty-one, twenty-eight/twenty-nine, thirty-five through forty-two, and fifty-five through sixty, for instance, tend to be very hectic periods, as the outer planets form critical angles to their position in the birth chart. Fox was twenty-four in 1985, an age when everyone experiences a Jupiter return. Otherwise, it's a pleasant lull between the crazy rebellion of age twenty-one (transiting Uranus square natal Uranus, transiting Saturn square natal Saturn) and the age of about twenty-nine, when Saturn returns to its natal position.

TRANSITING PLANETS CONJUNCT THE ANGLES

Next, are any of the *outer* planets—Jupiter, Saturn, Uranus, Neptune, or Pluto—making a conjunction to the angles of the chart? On this day, transiting Jupiter is just a few degrees from Fox's natal Ascendant, a transit that occurs only once every twelve years. Jupiter crossing the Ascendant is like UPS delivering a very nice package to your door. And remember, Fox has just had his second Jupiter return, so he's beginning a new twelve-year cycle of personal growth and exploration; this is an energized Jupiter.

More dramatically, transiting Uranus, the planet of sudden and explosive change, has just moved over the Midheaven of Fox's chart. Anyone who lives to age eighty-four has a chance to enjoy this transit at least once, though few will achieve Fox's level of fame. Remember, Uranus is very prominent in Fox's birth chart. It's close to an angle, conjunct Mars, and sextile the Sun. It's also in a trine aspect to the natal Midheaven. When two points that are in strong natal aspect to each other also come together by transit, the significance of the transit is much greater.

Armed only with these two pieces of information, we could safely say that big things were about to happen for the charming Canadian actor.

TRANSITING PLANETS IN ASPECT TO THE NATAL SUN OR MOON

Next we'll look to see whether the transiting outer planets are making close aspects to the natal Sun or Moon. On this date, transiting Jupiter is trine the natal Sun, an aspect that generally indicates beneficial growth and popularity (and makes you a little full of yourself if you're not careful). Saturn is making a quincunx aspect to the Sun, which could suggest that some growing up is in order, and that it will not be comfortable. Uranus is opposed the natal Sun, bringing sudden attention on a level that might be a little scary to a person with the Sun in the fourth house. And transiting Pluto, newly in Scorpio, is in a tight opposition to his sensitive Moon/Venus combination. Pluto will often bring tremendous wealth when it connects with Venus or planets in the second house, and this film quickly promoted the already-successful Fox into a rarefied income bracket.

If I were chatting with him at this time, I would probably say something such as, "You know your life is never going to be the same, right?" I'd suggest making sure he really trusts his financial advisors and has a plan in place to take care of himself emotionally and physically during what promises to be a very exciting but potentially exhausting ride.

JUPITER RETURN

We mentioned the Jupiter return before, but let's take a closer look. Jupiter doesn't move as slowly as his outer-planet brethren, but a twelve-year cycle is nothing to sneeze at. You will only have a handful of Jupiter returns in your lifetime, about eight at the most. It's worth remembering, too, that Jupiter is a huge, swaggering, king-size planet, and his transits are far from subtle.

When Jupiter returns to its position in your birth chart, you're beginning an important new cycle of growth. In particular, career and education are subject to exciting developments during this time. Jupiter's return is a fortunate transit overall, but it's also like a big, powerful car: Unless you're a very cautious and experienced driver, you could run off the road.

OUTER PLANETS IN ASPECT TO PLANETS OTHER THAN SUN AND MOON

On this date, there is a lot of transiting outer-planet activity involving Mars, which as we know is a crucial planet in Fox's birth chart. Transiting Jupiter is opposed Mars, transiting Saturn is square Mars, and transiting Uranus is trine Mars. If that sounds like a lot of mixed messages, I'm sure that's the way it felt, too. On one hand, the sky is the limit (Jupiter), but on the other hand there is a lot of brutally hard work on the horizon (Saturn), and oh by the way, you will no longer recognize your own life (Uranus).

I'd be keeping an eye on transiting Neptune and Pluto, both making aspects to natal Mercury and Venus. Mental exhaustion and multiple opportunities for self-indulgence could set up a perfect storm for overdoing it with alcohol or drugs. But when Neptune connects with Venus, there is also the whisper of a possible love affair on the horizon. It was during this time that Fox worked with actress Tracy Pollan, who played his girlfriend on *Family Ties*. They later reconnected, fell in love, and were married in 1988.

ECLIPSES

The Moon's North Node is in Taurus on this date. This tells us that this year's eclipses, around May and November (when the transiting Sun conjuncts the Lunar Nodes), will probably make close aspects to the most high-tension configurations in Fox's chart: the Moon/Venus, Jupiter/Saturn, Neptune T-square, and the Ascendant opposed Mars and Uranus in Leo. I would look to the period 1975–1976, when eclipses previously aspected these same points, for more detailed insights about what to expect from the current eclipses.

In his autobiography, Fox wrote that during that period he had his first and only "real" office job. Obsessed with music, he used the money he earned that summer to buy a guitar. By the next summer, he had landed his first television acting job, earning as much in a single week as his "real" job had paid all summer. This marked a crucial turning point in his perspective about work, earnings, and the determination to make a career doing something he enjoyed.

MARS

It's helpful when talking about career to look at transiting Mars's position relative to its birth placement. On this date, transiting Mars was one full sign behind his natal Mars. He would have a Mars return in about a month and a half. My usual counsel to someone in this phase of the Mars cycle would be to rest up, ride the crest of the existing wave, and conserve your energy for a new cycle of projects that begins in a couple of months. Beginning new things at the wrong phase in the Mars cycle can lead to burnout and aborted efforts. Especially when, like Fox, you'd just spent an exhausting year filming a big-budget movie while simultaneously taping your hit television series.

MINOR TRANSITS

I wouldn't normally pay a lot of attention to the transits of a particular day, but for Fox, this was no ordinary day. I would look for some kind of connection between the inner planets, particularly the Sun, Moon, or Mercury, and the birth chart. On this day, the transiting Sun at 11 Cancer was conjunct Fox's fifth house Mercury, transiting Mercury was opposed his natal Jupiter (and square Moon/Venus and Neptune), and the transiting Moon in Capricorn was conjunct his natal Saturn. These are minor "timing" transits that tell us that, within the span of a few days, the major transiting aspects from Jupiter, Uranus, Neptune, and Pluto would be triggered, and their energy set free into the world.

And that's when *Back to the Future* was released, and made Michael J. Fox one of the biggest stars in the world.

HOW IT LOOKS WHEN SOMEONE HITS ROCK BOTTOM

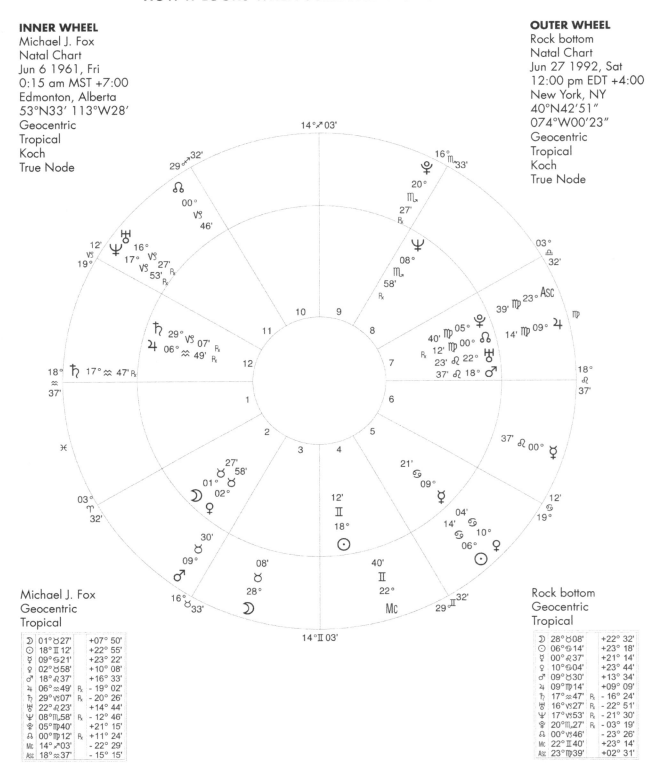

INNER WHEEL
Michael J. Fox
Natal Chart
Jun 6 1961, Fri
0:15 am MST +7:00
Edmonton, Alberta
53°N33' 113°W28'
Geocentric
Tropical
Koch
True Node

OUTER WHEEL
Rock bottom
Natal Chart
Jun 27 1992, Sat
12:00 pm EDT +4:00
New York, NY
40°N42'51"
074°W00'23"
Geocentric
Tropical
Koch
True Node

Michael J. Fox
Geocentric
Tropical

☽	01°♉27'		+07° 50'
☉	18°♊12'		+22° 55'
☿	09°♊21'		+23° 22'
♀	02°♉58'		+10° 08'
♂	18°♌37'		+16° 33'
♃	06°♒49'	℞	- 19° 02'
♄	29°♑07'	℞	- 20° 26'
♅	22°♌23'		+14° 44'
♆	08°♏58'	℞	- 12° 46'
♇	05°♍40'		+21° 15'
☊	00°♍12'	℞	+11° 24'
Mc	14°♐03'		- 22° 29'
Asc	18°♒37'		- 15° 15'

Rock bottom
Geocentric
Tropical

☽	28°♉08'		+22° 32'
☉	06°♋14'		+23° 18'
☿	00°♌37'		+21° 14'
♀	10°♋04'		+23° 44'
♂	09°♉30'		+13° 34'
♃	09°♍14'		+09° 09'
♄	17°♒47'	℞	- 16° 24'
♅	16°♑27'	℞	- 22° 51'
♆	17°♑53'	℞	- 21° 30'
♇	20°♏27'	℞	- 03° 19'
☊	00°♑46'		- 23° 26'
Mc	22°♊40'		+23° 14'
Asc	23°♍39'		+02° 31'

In the summer of 1992, Michael J. Fox, fresh off a string of box office failures, was living with a terrible secret: The previous October, he had been diagnosed with Parkinson's disease. In self-described denial, he had turned to alcohol to cope. In his autobiography he identifies June 27, 1992, as the day when he hit his personal "rock bottom."

ASTROLOGICALLY CRITICAL AGE

Fox had just turned thirty-one and had experienced his first Saturn return the previous year, just about the time he received his Parkinson's diagnosis. If he were a client and I didn't know the details, I would talk about the Saturn return as a difficult time, emphasizing the need to take authority over his life in some important way, and ask whether he'd experienced a spiritual or health crisis (Saturn in the twelfth house). This was a highly significant Saturn return, representing an ongoing process of maturation that extends well beyond the actual transit.

TRANSITING PLANETS CONJUNCT THE ANGLES

There is only one transiting planet conjunct an angle of the chart on this day, but it's a doozy: Transiting Saturn is within 1 degree of a conjunction with his natal Ascendant.

Saturn transiting the twelfth house can be awful. It's a time to sort through and take responsibility for the various skeletons in your psychological closet. This can be a difficult and often demoralizing process, especially for someone born with Saturn in this house (and particularly spooky skeletons in their closet).

Saturn finally crossing the Ascendant is an absolutely critical, once-every-twenty-nine-years transit. I've seen it reward, punish, and (literally, in the case of President Franklin Roosevelt, who contracted polio under this transit) paralyze people. Much depends on how you attended to the work of transiting Saturn in the twelfth house.

For Fox, Saturn's transit of his twelfth house was one of the most difficult periods of his life, beginning with the death of his father in January 1990. In October 1991 he received a diagnosis of Parkinson's disease. It took another year of hard drinking and denial before he was ready to accept the challenge of transiting Saturn at his Ascendant, step up to the plate, and deal with the new reality of his life.

TRANSITING PLANETS IN ASPECT TO THE NATAL SUN OR MOON

On this date, Jupiter was transiting the seventh house and preparing to square the natal Sun. It was Fox's wife Tracy (seventh house) who called him out (square) on his hubris (Sun). Transiting Saturn, besides conjoining the Ascendant, was trine Fox's Sun. Fortunately, he decided to assume personal responsibility (Sun) and accept the reality (Saturn) of the situation.

Uranus/Neptune and Pluto were all forming quincunx aspects to the Sun. When two or more planets are forming sextiles to each other while simultaneously forming a quincunx to another planet, the configuration is called a *yod*, or "the finger of God." The planet that is the focus of the two quincunxes, in this case the Sun, the symbol of pride and essential selfhood, is the planet that's being "pointed at." There could have been no more perfect expression of this symbolism than Tracy Pollan confronting her husband that morning with the question, "Is this who you want to be?" The Sun is the symbol of who we want to be, and Fox decided that the drunken mess he had become was not that person.

OUTER PLANETS IN ASPECT TO OTHER PLANETS

Transiting Jupiter trine natal Moon/Venus on this date is a kind of grace note, symbolizing a partner who is not afraid to confront you when you're wrong (in Virgo, conjunct natal Pluto), but who does it out of genuine love. Plenty of people have hit a personal rock bottom without having anyone left in their life who loves and supports them. Even at his lowest point, Fox was a lucky man.

Transiting Saturn was opposed Mars/Uranus on this date. Fifteen years before, in 1977, transiting Saturn was on the opposite side of his chart, conjunct natal Mars and Uranus. Then, Fox was an excited young kid working on his first television series, setting out on a career path that led him here, to this moment in time.

ECLIPSES

The transiting Lunar Nodes on this date are in the first degrees of Capricorn and Cancer. Ten years before, on June 21, 1982, a solar eclipse hit this same spot. Three months later, *Family Ties* debuted. In June 1992, life was again getting ready to change irrevocably for Fox. It would be another six years before he would disclose his disease to the public, but this was the moment when he began to take control and figure out how to proceed with life—and deal with his diagnosis—in a much more effective way.

MINOR TRANSITS

Interestingly, the Sun on this date was within 5 degrees of its position on the day *Back to the Future* was released: 6 degrees of Cancer, very close to a conjunction with natal Mercury. The Moon was in the last degrees of Taurus, trine his natal Saturn. And Mercury, newly in Leo, had just finished opposing Saturn. The view had gotten as dark as it could be; now it was time to turn the corner and let in the light.

• ● •

And that, my friends, is one astrologer's example of how to sort through and decipher transits of key events. My method isn't the only one, or even the "right" one; there are as many ways of decoding transits as there are astrologers reading charts. I hope you will be able to use my example, as well as the other tools in this book, to practice and eventually devise your own strategies.

Each of us, famous or not, lives a life that is a series of rich and fascinating stories. My love for following the narratives of people's lives is why I became interested in astrology. Perhaps you picked up this book for similar reasons. Learning to analyze transits is one of many tools astrology offers for better understanding your own story and the stories of the people you love. Transits define the chapters, provide the subheadings, and all in all provide a tidy outline to understand and anticipate life's highest and lowest moments.

I've written this book one hot, slow summer, with transiting Pluto making a slow, lazy trine to my natal Midheaven. It suggests a transformative journey, and that's what this has been for me. You never really know what you know until you try to share it with someone else.

I thank you for being one of those someones and wish you a lifetime of fascinating transits!

APPENDICES

TABLE 1: PLANETS IN SIGNS, 2015–2025, JUPITER–PLUTO

Jupiter enters Virgo	Aug. 11, 2015
Jupiter enters Libra	Sept. 9, 2016
Jupiter enters Scorpio	Oct. 10, 2017
Jupiter enters Sagittarius	Nov. 8, 2018
Jupiter enters Capricorn	Dec. 2, 2019
Jupiter enters Aquarius	Dec. 19, 2020
Jupiter enters Pisces	May 13, 2021
Jupiter enters Aquarius	July 28, 2021
Jupiter enters Pisces	Dec. 29, 2021
Jupiter enters Aries	May 10, 2022
Jupiter enters Pisces	Oct. 28, 2022
Jupiter enters Aries	Dec. 20, 2022
Jupiter enters Taurus	May 16, 2023
Jupiter enters Gemini	May 25, 2024
Jupiter enters Cancer	June 9, 2025
Saturn enters Sagittarius	Dec. 23, 2014
Saturn enters Scorpio	June 15, 2015
Saturn enters Sagittarius	Sept. 18, 2015
Saturn enters Capricorn	Dec. 20, 2017
Saturn enters Aquarius	Mar. 22, 2020
Saturn enters Capricorn	July 2, 2020
Saturn enters Aquarius	Dec. 17, 2020
Saturn enters Pisces	Mar. 7, 2023
Saturn enters Aries	May 25, 2025
Saturn enters Pisces	Sept. 1, 2025
Uranus enters Taurus	May 15, 2018
Uranus enters Aries	Nov. 6, 2018
Uranus enters Taurus	Mar. 6, 2019
Uranus enters Gemini	July 7, 2025
Uranus enters Taurus	Nov. 8, 2025
Neptune enters Aries	Mar. 30, 2025
Neptune enters Pisces	Oct. 22, 2025
Pluto enters Aquarius	Mar. 23, 2023
Pluto enters Capricorn	June 11, 2023
Pluto enters Aquarius	Jan. 21, 2024
Pluto enters Capricorn	Sept. 2, 2024
Pluto enters Aquarius	Nov. 19, 2024

TABLE 2: PLANETARY RETROGRADE PERIODS, 2015–2025

MERCURY RETROGRADE	VENUS RETROGRADE
Jan. 21, 2015–Feb. 11, 2015	July 25, 2015–Sept. 6, 2015
May 19, 2015–June 11, 2015	Mar. 4, 2017–Apr. 15, 2017
Sept. 17, 2015–Oct. 9, 2015	Oct. 5, 2018–Nov. 16, 2018
Jan. 5, 2016–Jan. 25, 2016	May 13, 2020–June 25, 2020
Apr. 28, 2016–May 22, 2016	Dec. 19, 2021–Jan. 29, 2022
Aug. 30, 2016–Sept. 22, 2016	July 23, 2023–Sept. 4, 2023
Dec. 19, 2016–Jan. 8, 2017	Mar. 2, 2025–Apr. 13, 2025
Apr. 10, 2017–May 3, 2017	
Aug. 13, 2017–Sept. 5, 2017	**MARS RETROGRADE**
Dec. 3, 2017–Dec. 23, 2017	Apr. 17, 2016–June 30, 2016
Mar. 23, 2018–Apr. 15, 2018	June 26, 2018–Aug. 27, 2018
July 26, 2018–Aug. 19, 2018	Sept. 9, 2020–Nov. 14, 2020
Nov. 17, 2018–Dec. 6, 2018	Oct. 30, 2022–Jan. 12, 2023
Mar. 5, 2019–Mar. 28, 2019	Dec. 6, 2024–Feb. 24, 2025
July 8, 2019–Aug. 1, 2019	
Oct. 31, 2019–Nov. 20, 2019	**JUPITER RETROGRADE**
Feb. 17, 2020–Mar. 10, 2020	Dec. 8, 2014–Apr. 8, 2015
June 18, 2020–July 12, 2020	Jan. 8, 2016–May 9, 2016
Oct. 14, 2020–Nov. 3, 2020	Feb. 6, 2017–June 9, 2017
Jan. 30, 2021–Feb. 21, 2021	Mar. 9, 2018–July 10, 2018
May 29, 2021–June 22, 2021	Apr. 10, 2019–Aug. 11, 2019
Sept. 27, 2021–Oct. 18, 2021	May 14, 2020–Sept. 13, 2020
Jan. 14, 2022–Feb. 4, 2022	June 20, 2021–Oct. 18, 2021
May 10, 2022–June 3, 2022	July 28, 2022–Nov. 23, 2022
Sept. 10, 2022–Oct. 2, 2022	Sept. 4, 2023–Dec. 31, 2023
Dec. 29, 2022–Jan. 18, 2023	Oct. 9, 2024–Feb. 4, 2025
Apr. 21, 2023–May 15, 2023	Nov. 11, 2025–Mar. 11, 2026
Aug. 23, 2023–Sept. 15, 2023	
Dec. 13, 2023–Jan. 2, 2024	
Apr. 1, 2024–Apr. 25, 2024	
Aug. 5, 2024–Aug. 28, 2024	
Nov. 26, 2024–Dec. 15, 2024	
Mar. 15, 2025–Apr. 7, 2025	
July 18, 2025–Aug. 11, 2025	
Nov. 9, 2025–Nov. 29, 2025	

TABLE 2: PLANETARY RETROGRADE PERIODS, 2015–2025 (CONTINUED)

SATURN RETROGRADE	PLUTO RETROGRADE
Mar. 14, 2015–Aug. 2, 2015	Apr. 17, 2015–Sept. 25, 2015
Mar. 25, 2016–Aug. 13, 2016	Apr. 18, 2016–Sept. 26, 2016
Apr. 6, 2017–Aug. 25, 2017	Apr. 20, 2017–Sept. 2, 2017
Apr. 18, 2018–Sept. 6, 2018	Apr. 22, 2018–Oct. 1, 2018
Apr. 30, 2019–Sept. 18, 2019	Apr. 24, 2019–Oct. 3, 2019
May 11, 2020–Sept. 29, 2020	Apr. 25, 2020–Oct. 4, 2020
May 23, 2021–Oct. 11, 2021	Apr. 27, 2021–Oct. 6, 2021
June 4, 2022–Oct. 23, 2022	Apr. 29, 2022–Oct. 8, 2022
June 17, 2023–Nov. 4, 2023	May 1, 2023–Oct. 11, 2023
June 29, 2024–Nov. 15, 2024	May 2, 2024–Oct. 12, 2024
July 13, 2025–Nov. 28, 2025	May 4, 2025–Oct. 14, 2025

URANUS RETROGRADE	
July 26, 2015–Dec. 26, 2015	
July 29, 2016–Dec. 29, 2016	
Aug. 3, 2017–Jan. 2, 2018	
Aug. 7, 2018–Jan. 6, 2019	
Aug. 12, 2019–Jan. 11, 2020	
Aug. 15, 2020–Jan. 14, 2021	
Aug. 20, 2021–Jan. 18, 2022	
Aug. 24, 2022–Jan. 22, 2023	
Aug. 29, 2023–Jan. 27, 2024	
Sept. 1, 2024–Jan. 30, 2025	
Sept. 6, 2025–Feb. 4, 2026	

NEPTUNE RETROGRADE	
June 12, 2015–Nov. 18, 2015	
June 13, 2016–Nov. 20, 2016	
June 16, 2017–Nov. 22, 2017	
June 19, 2018–Nov. 25, 2018	
June 21, 2019–Nov. 27, 2019	
June 23, 200–Nov. 29, 2020	
June 25, 2021–Dec. 1, 2021	
June 28, 2022–Dec. 4, 2022	
June 30, 2023–Dec. 6, 2023	
July 2, 2024–Dec. 7, 2024	
July 4, 2025–Dec. 10, 2025	

TABLE 3: NEW MOON TABLE, 2015–2025
(Calculated for Greenwich Mean Time)

Jan. 20, 2015	00° Aquarius 08'
Feb. 18, 2015	29° Aquarius 59'
Mar. 20, 2015	29° Pisces 27'
Apr. 18, 2015	28° Aries 25'
May 18, 2015	26° Taurus 55'
June 16, 2015	25° Gemini 07'
July 16, 2015	23° Cancer 14'
Aug. 14, 2015	21° Leo 30'
Sept. 13, 2015	20° Virgo 10'
Oct. 13, 2015	19° Libra 20'
Nov. 11, 2015	19° Scorpio 00'
Dec. 11, 2015	19° Sagittarius 02'
Jan. 10, 2016	19° Capricorn 13'
Feb. 8, 2016	19° Aquarius 15'
Mar. 9, 2016	18° Pisces 55'
Apr. 7, 2016	18° Aries 04'
May 6, 2016	16° Taurus 41'
June 5, 2016	14° Gemini 53'
July 4, 2016	12° Cancer 53'
Aug. 2, 2016	10° Leo 57'
Sept. 1, 2016	09° Virgo 21'
Oct. 1, 2016	08° Libra 15'
Oct. 30, 2016	07° Scorpio 43'
Nov. 29, 2016	07° Sagittarius 42'
Dec. 29, 2016	07° Capricorn 59'
Jan. 28, 2017	08° Aquarius 15'
Feb. 26, 2017	08° Pisces 12'
Mar. 28, 2017	07° Aries 37'
Apr. 26, 2017	06° Taurus 27'
May 25, 2017	04° Gemini 47'
June 24, 2017	02° Cancer 47'
July 23, 2017	00° Leo 44'
Aug. 21, 2017	28° Leo 52'
Sept. 20, 2017	27° Virgo 27'
Oct. 19, 2017	26° Libra 35'
Nov. 18, 2017	26° Scorpio 19'
Dec. 18, 2017	26° Sagittarius 31'

TABLE 3: NEW MOON TABLE, 2015–2025 (CONTINUED)
(Calculated for Greenwich Mean Time)

Jan. 17, 2018	26° Capricorn 54'
Feb. 15, 2018	27° Aquarius 07'
Mar. 17, 2018	26° Pisces 53'
Apr. 16, 2018	26° Aries 02'
May 15, 2018	24° Taurus 36'
June 13, 2018	22° Gemini 44'
July 13, 2018	20° Cancer 41'
Aug. 11, 2018	18° Leo 41'
Sept. 9, 2018	17° Virgo 00'
Oct. 9, 2018	15° Libra 48'
Nov. 7, 2018	15° Scorpio 11'
Dec. 7, 2018	15° Sagittarius 07'
Jan. 6, 2019	15° Capricorn 25'
Feb. 4, 2019	15° Aquarius 45'
Mar. 6, 2019	15° Pisces 47'
Apr. 5, 2019	15° Aries 17'
May 4, 2019	14° Taurus 10'
June 3, 2019	12° Gemini 33'
July 2, 2019	10° Cancer 37'
Aug. 1, 2019	08° Leo 36'
Aug. 30, 2019	06° Virgo 46'
Sept. 28, 2019	05° Libra 20'
Oct. 28, 2019	04° Scorpio 25'
Nov. 26, 2019	04° Sagittarius 03'
Dec. 26, 2019	04° Capricorn 06'
Jan. 24, 2020	04° Aquarius 21'
Feb. 23, 2020	04° Pisces 28'
Mar. 24, 2020	04° Aries 12'
Apr. 23, 2020	03° Taurus 24'
May 22, 2020	02° Gemini 04'
June 21, 2020	00° Cancer 21'
July 20, 2020	28° Cancer 26'
Aug. 19, 2020	26° Leo 35'
Sept. 17, 2020	25° Virgo 00'
Oct. 16, 2020	23° Libra 53'
Nov. 15, 2020	23° Scorpio 17'
Dec. 14, 2020	23° Sagittarius 08'

TABLE 3: NEW MOON TABLE, 2015–2025 (CONTINUED)
(Calculated for Greenwich Mean Time)

Jan. 13, 2021	23° Capricorn 13'
Feb. 11, 2021	23° Aquarius 16'
Mar. 13, 2021	23° Pisces 03'
Apr. 12, 2021	22° Aries 24'
May 11, 2021	21° Taurus 17'
June 10, 2021	19° Gemini 47'
July 10, 2021	18° Cancer 01'
Aug. 8, 2021	16° Leo 14'
Sept. 7, 2021	14° Virgo 38'
Oct. 6, 2021	13° Libra 24'
Nov. 4, 2021	12° Scorpio 40'
Dec. 4, 2021	12° Sagittarius 22'
Jan. 2, 2022	12° Capricorn 20'
Feb. 1, 2022	12° Aquarius 19'
Mar. 2, 2022	12° Pisces 06'
Apr. 1, 2022	11° Aries 30'
Apr. 30, 2022	10° Taurus 28'
May 30, 2022	09° Gemini 03'
June 29, 2022	07° Cancer 22'
July 28, 2022	05° Leo 38'
Aug. 27, 2022	04° Virgo 03'
Sept. 25, 2022	02° Libra 48'
Oct. 25, 2022	02° Scorpio 00'
Nov. 23, 2022	01° Sagittarius 37'
Dec. 23, 2022	01° Capricorn 32'
Jan. 21, 2023	01° Aquarius 32'
Feb. 20, 2023	01° Pisces 22'
Mar. 21, 2023	00° Aries 49'
Apr. 20, 2023	29° Aries 50'
May 19, 2023	28° Taurus 25'
June 18, 2023	26° Gemini 43'
July 17, 2023	24° Cancer 56'
Aug. 16, 2023	23° Leo 17'
Sept. 15, 2023	21° Virgo 58'
Oct. 14, 2023	21° Libra 07'
Nov. 13, 2023	20° Scorpio 43'
Dec. 12, 2023	20°Sagittarius 40'

Jan. 11, 2024	20° Capricorn 44'
Feb. 9, 2024	20° Aquarius 40'
Mar. 10, 2024	20° Pisces 16'
Apr. 8, 2024	19° Aries 24'
May 8, 2024	18° Taurus 02'
June 6, 2024	16° Gemini 17'
July 5, 2024	14° Cancer 23'
Aug. 4, 2024	12° Leo 34'
Sept. 3, 2024	11° Virgo 04'
Oct. 2, 2024	10° Libra 03'
Nov. 1, 2024	09° Scorpio 35'
Dec. 1, 2024	09° Sagittarius 32'
Dec. 30, 2024	09° Capricorn 43'
Jan. 29, 2025	09° Aquarius 51'
Feb. 28, 2025	09° Pisces 40'
Mar. 29, 2025	09° Aries 00'
Apr. 27, 2025	07° Taurus 46'
May 27, 2025	06° Gemini 05'
June 25, 2025	04° Cancer 07'
July 24, 2025	02° Leo 08'
Aug. 23, 2025	00° Virgo 23'
Sept. 21, 2025	29° Virgo 05'
Oct. 21, 2025	28° Libra 21'
Nov. 20, 2025	28° Scorpio 11'
Dec. 20, 2025	28° Sagittarius 24'

TABLE 4: ECLIPSES TABLE, 2015–2025
(Calculated for Greenwich Mean Time)

Mar. 20, 2015	Solar	29° Pisces 27'
Apr. 4, 2015	Lunar	14° Libra 24'
Sept. 13, 2015	Solar	20° Virgo 10'
Sept. 28, 2015	Lunar	04° Aries 38'
Mar. 9, 2016	Solar	18° Pisces 55'
Mar. 23, 2016	Lunar	03° Aries 10'
Aug. 18, 2016	Lunar	26° Aquarius 00'
Sept. 1, 2016	Solar	09° Virgo 21'
Sept. 16, 2016	Lunar	24° Pisces 13'
Feb. 11, 2017	Lunar	22° Leo 34'
Feb. 26, 2017	Solar	08° Pisces 11'
Aug. 7, 2017	Lunar	15° Aquarius 30'
Aug. 21, 2017	Solar	28° Leo 52'
Jan. 31, 2018	Lunar	11° Leo 39'
Feb. 15, 2018	Solar	27° Aquarius 07'
July 13, 2018	Solar	20° Cancer 41'
July 27, 2018	Lunar	4° Aquarius 45'
Aug. 11, 2018	Solar	18° Leo 41'
Jan. 6, 2019	Solar	15° Capricorn 25'
Jan. 21, 2019	Lunar	00° Leo 49'
July 2, 2019	Solar	10° Cancer 37'
July 16, 2019	Lunar	24° Capricorn 00'
Dec. 26, 2019	Solar	04° Capricorn 07'
Jan. 10, 2020	Lunar	19° Cancer 53'
June 21, 2020	Solar	00° Cancer 21'
July 5, 2020	Lunar	13° Capricorn 29'
Nov. 30, 2020	Lunar	08° Gemini 44'
Dec. 14, 2020	Solar	23° Sagittarius 08'
May 26, 2021	Lunar	05° Sagittarius 25'
June 10, 2021	Solar	19° Gemini 47'
Nov. 19, 2021	Lunar	27 °Taurus 14'
Dec. 4, 2021	Solar	12° Sagittarius 22'
Apr. 30, 2022	Solar	10° Taurus 28'
May 16, 2022	Lunar	25° Scorpio 17'
Oct. 25, 2022	Solar	02° Scorpio 00'
Nov. 8, 2022	Lunar	16° Taurus 00'

Apr. 20, 2023	Solar	29° Aries 50'
May 5, 2023	Lunar	14° Scorpio 58'
Oct. 14, 2023	Solar	21° Libra 07'
Oct. 28, 2023	Lunar	05° Taurus 09'
Mar. 25, 2024	Lunar	05° Libra 07'
Apr. 8, 2024	Solar	19° Aries 24'
Sept. 18, 2024	Lunar	25° Pisces 40'
Oct. 2, 2024	Solar	10° Libra 03'
Mar. 14, 2025	Lunar	23° Virgo 56'
Mar. 29, 2025	Solar	09° Aries 00'
Sept. 7, 2025	Lunar	15° Pisces 22'
Sept. 21, 2025	Solar	29° Virgo 05'

WORKSHEET: PRIORITIZING YOUR TRANSITS

Are you within one of these critical age groups? If so, you're reaching one or more critical milestones that you share in common with others your age:

14—Pressure to plan ahead

21—Rebellion

28–29—Coming to grips with maturity and mortality

35–42—Midlife crisis: the second big rebellion

55–60—Menopause, preparing for retirement

Is transiting Uranus, Neptune, or Pluto within a few degrees of a conjunction with your Ascendant, IC, Descendant, or Midheaven? Are they in a conjunction or opposition to your natal Sun or Moon?

Uranus: a personal declaration of independence, a breakthrough in your career

Neptune: sadness, yearning, losing something, succeeding in enchanting the world, possibly a big move

Pluto: being faced with raw, unadulterated reality

Is transiting Saturn within a few degrees of a conjunction with your Ascendant, IC, Descendant, or Midheaven? Is it in a conjunction, opposition, or square to your natal Sun or Moon? You're reassessing whether something in your life is worth the difficulty of keeping it.

Are you having a Jupiter return (Jupiter returning to its natal position)? You're beginning a new twelve-year cycle of success and prosperity.

Is transiting Jupiter conjunct your Ascendant, IC, Descendant, or Midheaven? You are coming into your own. Some kind of reward is on its way.

Are you having a Mars return (Mars returning to its natal position)? Fight hard for what you think you want.

This year's eclipses will make aspects to roughly the same points in your chart as nine to ten years ago. What was happening in your life then? If faced with situations that awaken the same feelings, how will you handle them?

Are Saturn, Uranus, Neptune, or Pluto conjunct, opposed, or square to your natal Moon, Venus, or Mars? Read the sections on Saturn and Pluto for more insights.

Is it your birthday? You're having a Solar Return! Calculate your Solar Return chart and have a look. The house the Sun is in is where you will shine this year. The house with Leo on the cusp catches some of the sunbeams. Planets close to the angles represent the forces that propel you forward this year.

WORKSHEET: MAPPING YOUR YEAR

THIS YEAR'S PLANETARY RETROGRADE PERIODS *(SEE TABLE 2.)*

See chapter 1 for tips about best practices for retrograde planets. Mercury will turn retrograde three times. Venus and Mars may not be retrograde in a given year. The Sun and Moon are never retrograde.

	RX	DIRECT	RX	DIRECT	RX	DIRECT
Mercury						
Venus						
Mars						
Jupiter						
Saturn						
Uranus						
Neptune						
Pluto						

THIS YEAR'S NEW MOONS *(SEE TABLE 3.)*

Where does each of the year's New Moons fall in your birth chart? See part III for the meaning of the Moon in each house; a New Moon is more powerful but affects the same areas of your life.

DATE	DEGREE AND SIGN	HOUSE OF YOUR CHART	WISHES AND INTENTIONS

TRANSITS OF THE SUN

See chapter 9 to read about the transiting Sun in your chart.

When is your Solar Return? _____

When will the Sun cross your . . .

    Ascendant _____

    IC _____

    Descendant _____

    Midheaven _____

THIS YEAR'S ECLIPSES *(SEE TABLE 4.)*

Eclipses indicate where things need to change in your life. See chapter 9 for more about eclipses.

DATE	SOLAR/LUNAR	DEGREE/SIGN	HOUSE OF YOUR CHART	ASPECTS TO NATAL PLANETS

YOUR PLANETARY RETURNS

Are you having a Mars, Jupiter, Saturn, or Uranus return this year? Planetary returns mark the beginning of important planetary cycles—see chapters 3 to 8 for more.

Mars return (about every 2 years) _____

Jupiter return (every 12 years)   _____

Saturn return (every 29 years)   _____

Uranus return (age 84)   _____

OTHER MAJOR TRANSITS

Are any of the transiting outer planets making a conjunction, square, or opposition to your natal Sun, Moon, Mercury, Venus, Mars, Ascendant, or Midheaven this year?

	SUN	MOON	MERCURY	VENUS	MARS	ASC	MC
Tr. Jupiter							
Tr. Saturn							
Tr. Uranus							
Tr. Neptune							
Tr. Pluto							

RESOURCES

BOOKS

Kent, April Elliott. *The Essential Guide to Practical Astrology* (Alpha/Penguin, 2011). If you're very new to astrology and finding that some of the material in this book is a tad over your head, never fear! I cover everything from the signs of the zodiac to houses, planets, and aspects in this cheerful primer.

Forrest, Steven. *The Changing Sky* (Seven Paws Press, 2008). Steven Forrest is one of my favorite astrologers, favorite writers, favorite people. This book gives a very good overview of transits, as well as progressions and how the two systems work together. Highly recommended.

Hand, Robert. *Planets in Transit: Life Cycles for Living* (Whitford Press, 2002). This has been astrology's go-to transit book since the 1970s, and deservedly so. It's huge and comprehensive, and it breaks down each planet/planet transit by aspect. As of mid-2014, Hand has announced he'll be publishing an updated version of the book sometime in 2015.

Pottenger, Rique. *The American Ephemeris for the 20th Century, 1900–2000 at Midnight* (Starcrafts Publishing, 2008) and *The New American Ephemeris for the 21st Century, 2000–2100 at Midnight* (Starcrafts Publishing, 2006). This pair of books covers two centuries' worth of planetary tables. I always like to joke that these hefty volumes could, in fact, serve as tables themselves in a pinch.

   At midnight means that the tables show planetary positions as calculated for midnight at Greenwich, England, home of the prime meridian. Unless you live in the same time zone as Greenwich, you will have to do additional and complex calculations to adjust the planetary positions to your time zone and location. But the positions given for Greenwich at midnight will at least get you into the ballpark, since apart from the Moon, nothing moves all that quickly over the course of a day.

   Occasionally you'll find ephemerides that are calculated for noon at Greenwich. I used to prefer these, because living on the West Coast, eight time zones from Greenwich, I found the noon positions at Greenwich were a little closer to their positions on the West Coast of the United States at the beginning of each day.

CALCULATING YOUR TRANSITS ONLINE

For chart calculation and personalized reports, visit Astrodienst at www.astro.com.

SOFTWARE

The charts and tables in this book were generated using Win*Star professional software from Matrix Software, www.astrologysoftware.com.

ACKNOWLEDGMENTS

If ever there were evidence of Jupiter's benevolence, it's the opportunity to write this book during his transit of my ninth house. So thanks to Jupiter, as well as non-planets Marilyn Allen, my agent, and Jill Alexander, the editor who launched this ship and kindly invited me aboard. I'm indebted to the Fair Winds Press production team, particularly John Gettings, Leah Tracosas Jenness, and Kathy Dvorsky, for ironing out the rough edges and making it all look so classy.

No one has come right out and said it, but I know I'm not easy to live with when I'm writing a book. So I'm particularly grateful for my tolerant and encouraging friends (especially Tim Tormey, Doug Adair, Frank Gualco, Jeannel King, Natori Moore, Simone Butler, Lori Rodefer, Dana Gerhardt, Jessica Shepherd, Matthew Currie, everyone at the San Diego Astrological Society) and family (Drew Elliott and Heather Galluzzi, the Strouds, Kathy McLaughlin), who endured my crankiness, tears, and unavailability for the duration.

Respectful bows to Robert Hand and Steven Forrest, esteemed astro-yodas whose previous work with transits inspired me to the point of crippling self-doubt, and to Diane Ronngren, my first teacher and forever friend.

Most of all, my thanks to Jonny Kent, the most patient man I've ever known. The transits that brought you to me were the very luckiest of my life.

ABOUT THE AUTHOR

April Elliott Kent is the author of *The Essential Guide to Practical Astrology* (Alpha/Penguin, 2011) and *Star Guide to Weddings* (Llewellyn, 2008). A professional astrologer since 1990, April has written for *The Mountain Astrologer* and *Dell Horoscope* magazines and contributed to Llewellyn's annual *Moon Sign* and *Sun Sign* books. She has won praise for her warm writing style and ability to make complex astrological concepts accessible.

April's website, BigSkyAstrology.com is extremely popular, as are her lectures for astrology groups. She served on the faculty of the 2012 United Astrological Conference and belongs to the International Society for Astrological Research (ISAR). She lives in San Diego, California, with her husband and two surly cats.

INDEX

DON'T MISS THESE OTHER BOOKS!

**What Your Birthday
Reveals about You**
Phyllis Vega
ISBN: 978-1-59233-170-3

The Ultimate Guide to Tarot
Liz Dean
ISBN: 978-1-59233-657-9

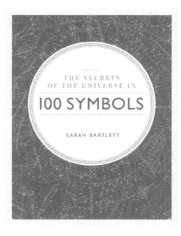

**Secrets of the Universe
in 100 Symbols**
Sarah Bartlett
ISBN: 978-1-59233-676-0

Spellcraft for a Magical Year
Sarah Bartlett
ISBN: 978-1-59233-680-7

**The Complete Illustrated
Encyclopedia of Magical
Plants, Revised**
Susan Gregg
ISBN: 978-1-59233-583-1

**Encyclopedia of Crystals,
Revised and Expanded**
Judy Hall
ISBN: 978-1-59233-582-4

CPSIA information can be obtained
at www.ICGtesting.com
Printed in the USA
LVHW070203180723
752758LV00022B/475

9 781592 336838